CW00970754

VIKINGS

Also by Paul Cavill:

Anglo-Saxon Christianity

VIKINGS

FEAR AND FAITH
IN ANGLO-SAXON ENGLAND

PAUL CAVILL

HarperCollins*Publishers*

HarperCollins*Publishers*
77–85 Fulham Palace Road, London W6 8JB
www.**fire**and**water**.com

First published in Great Britain in 2001
by HarperCollins*Publishers*

1 3 5 7 9 10 8 6 4 2

A catalogue record for this book is available
from the British Library

ISBN 0 00 710401 4

Printed and bound in Great Britain by
Creative Print and Design (Wales), Ebbw Vale

To my father
And in memory of my mother

CONTENTS

ACKNOWLEDGEMENTS

It is a pleasure to acknowledge the kindness of many people expressed to me during the writing of this book. My greatest thanks must go to my family for all the obvious reasons: putting up with me when my frustration with trying to get the wording right made me irritable, doing without me on Saturdays, and so on. My sincere thanks go, too, to my colleague Judith Jesch, who read the manuscript as a Viking scholar at an early stage and with an acute eye for detail. I thank David Pugh for sharing his research on the topic with me. And there are many others, not least the editors at HarperCollins, who deserve thanks. All errors of fact or interpretation remain my responsibility.

I was allowed study leave from my work at the English Place-Name Survey and in the School of English at the University of Nottingham to do the research and writing for this book, and I am pleased to acknowledge the kindness of Victor Watts, Honorary Director of the Survey, and Thorlac Turville-Petre, Head of the School of English in this respect.

PAUL CAVILL

October 2000

INTRODUCTION

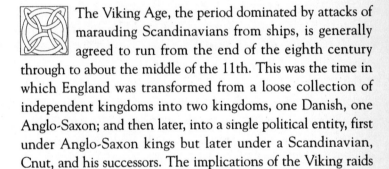The Viking Age, the period dominated by attacks of marauding Scandinavians from ships, is generally agreed to run from the end of the eighth century through to about the middle of the 11th. This was the time in which England was transformed from a loose collection of independent kingdoms into two kingdoms, one Danish, one Anglo-Saxon; and then later, into a single political entity, first under Anglo-Saxon kings but later under a Scandinavian, Cnut, and his successors. The implications of the Viking raids are immediately apparent. They changed the political face of England for ever. In the process they changed much else.

Not only the political face of England, either. Scandinavian armed traders established bases along major river routes into the Near East through eastern Europe. The typically Russian name Igor derives from the Scandinavian name Ingvar, and the name Russia itself derives from the Arabic name for the Scandinavians, *rus*. Some Scandinavians became familiar with the Mediterranean, some served the Byzantine emperors in their personal bodyguard, some raided the Islamic North Africans. Expeditions went to the Faroes, the Orkneys, Ireland, Iceland and Greenland, and from there into what is now Canada and North America. Dublin became a recognizable city because the Vikings made it their trading base. Any river became a thoroughfare for the Scandinavians: the Volga, the Rhine, the Seine, the Loire, the Thames, the Trent. They got everywhere with an inch or so of clinker-built ship-planking between them and the most dangerous of the elements, the sea.

The Anglo-Saxons were warlike people and came from the same ethnic stock as the Vikings. The summer activity of high-born men was, early on, fighting the Celtic peoples on the edges of the Anglo-Saxon kingdoms. When the Celts were suppressed or conquered, the Anglo-Saxon kingdoms turned on each other. There was a consistent jockeying for overlordship, a desire for supremacy. It gave colour and activity and a sense of adventure to what could be a pretty dreary life. It gave the poets material for their verse. Campaigning went on even after the conversion to Christianity, and religion gave an illusion of high-mindedness to those other activities. Kings could put pressure on others to convert, and if these other kings did not see the cogency of the new faith, a few army exercises, a few towns ravaged could always persuade them. The end justified the means.

If all this mayhem went on among the Anglo-Saxons in Christian times, why were the Viking attacks on England beginning in the latter years of the eighth century greeted with such fear? Surely rape and pillage were much the same experiences whether the perpetrators were fellow Anglo-Saxons or Vikings? The cynic might say that the only thing that was new about these attacks was that they were initially directed against the people who have left written records, namely the monks. It was a new experience for monasteries to bear the brunt of violence: they were now tasting what life was like for the ordinary people.

But this explanation hardly fits the evidence from Anglo-Saxon England. The monastic sources are remarkably restrained, and much concerned with the larger picture as well as the details directly affecting the monasteries. Almost in passing we see that the Viking attacks were sudden and unpredictable, and left behind any of the 'rules' of engagement that the Anglo-Saxons had developed in their years of infighting. Atrocities were committed against anybody, king or commoner. King Edmund of East Anglia was used as a target for arrows and spears and King Ælla of Northumbria possibly had his lungs ripped out of his chest. When in 1012 Archbishop Ælfheah refused to let ransom be paid for him, he was pelted to death with animal heads and bones. Though these were people who were made an example of, it seems unlikely that ordinary folk were treated with much more restraint.

The Anglo-Saxon poem on the battle of Maldon in 991, between the men of Essex and an army of Vikings, describes and names the Englishmen in detail. The Vikings are left as an anonymous mass, a killing machine devoted to gaining wealth. Here, perhaps, is another indicator of what made the Vikings so terrifying. What the English had to face in the Vikings was an enemy that had developed the technology of fighting to its highest degree, but that lacked any regard for civilization. Viking attacks on the monasteries showed utter contempt for things the Anglo-Saxons held sacred. But the Vikings were not only heathen and contemptuous of Christianity. Silver and gold was what they wanted, and it came by weight, whether it was from chalices, book-mounts, personal ornaments, sword-hilts, coinage or ingots. Sentimental, religious, or any civilized values were simply not rated by the Vikings. In the words of Oscar Wilde, they knew the cost of everything and the value of nothing.

Monastic chronicles from all over civilized Europe record plaintively, and with varying degrees of detail, the cruelty, ruthlessness and rapacity of the Vikings. It is hardly surprising that there is a marked difference between the Vikings' own records and stories about their adventures, and the records of those they visited – in perspective if not in informational content. Viking poetry in praise of Scandinavian kings and warlords focuses on courage and carnage. The prose sagas of Iceland, telling stories of the Viking days, tend to romp, bringing in stories of intrigue, magic, feud and later, love too, in addition to courage and carnage. Vikings are heroes doing what men have to do, but often having a poetic, sometimes tragic side. These Scandinavian sources give a very different perspective on what was going on in the Viking Age, but the picture of devastation is one that largely agrees with the monastic sources.

The Vikings showed the Christian Anglo-Saxons how fragile their civilization was, how thin the veneer of their culture, and how the delicate treasure of faith and learning needed feats of doggedness and courage in its defence. Yet the Vikings also showed how strong and compelling Christian faith and culture was in its local expression. The raiding and settlement of the Viking Age exposed the Scandinavians to Christianity, and the Viking Age was followed in almost the entire Scandinavian world by conversion. Normandy was settled by Vikings who became Christian. The English Danelaw was settled by Vikings who became Christian. And the former Viking homelands, Norway, Sweden and Denmark became Christian. The civilizing effects of Christianity were soon apparent at the level of everyday life, as the church came to dominate the rites of passage and patterns of living of the people.

How, then, did these savage and materialistic people come to be church-builders, missionaries, monks, bishops, educators and statesmen in the later years of Anglo-Saxon England? The story is a complex one, intimately connected with

Christian conversion, but also involving the civilizing influences of settlement and intermarriage. The sources from
Anglo-Saxon England dealing with this story in detail are
sparse. But it is clear that however their understanding of
Christianity changed, the Anglo-Saxons preserved their faith
despite the Vikings. And however the Anglo-Saxons presented Christianity to the new settlers, in a relatively short
time the Scandinavians in the Danelaw, the area of England
north and east of the ancient Roman road, Watling Street,
were themselves expressing faith of some sort.

The grand gestures which we like to think of as decisive
appear in the story. King Alfred appears to have put implicit
faith in the word of the Vikings given to him on oath, that
they would keep the peace, or leave his land, or otherwise not
do all those things they were in the habit of doing. It is never
recorded that Alfred broke his word, of course. The resolute
faithfulness of martyrs such as King Edmund and Archbishop
Ælfheah in the face of torment and horrible death is
recorded. But though these gestures were significant and
strikingly Christian, they are only seen to be significant in
retrospect. Not even the writers of the lives of the saints, for
whom stories of miracles and transformations on a grand scale
were the stock-in-trade, see these gestures as decisive in the
conversion of the Vikings.

There was good reason to fear the Vikings. Reactions to
them in the Anglo-Saxon sources vary, from despair and
anger, to the occasional scornfully dismissive poem like
The Battle of Brunanburh, the occasional remark in the
Anglo-Saxon Chronicle which suggests that the Vikings were
less of a problem than an epidemic of illness which was
going the rounds. The deeper effects of the Vikings on
English Christianity, and the effects *on* the Vikings of English
Christianity need rather more unpacking. Fear is expressed at

the threat from outside; faith develops, changes, grows and spreads from the inside. Fear is relatively easy to document because it deals with reactions to numbers, actions, movements; faith is much harder to pin down, even in sources which are fundamentally Christian, because it is concerned with the way people understand their world.

This book is the story of the clash of two quite similar peoples. The process of clashing was a long one, covering more than 200 years from the end of the eighth century to the 11th century and beyond. But in the process, both peoples were changed. The Vikings were assimilated and converted; the English were united and dominated. Tactics, leaders, responses, attitudes, regions, patterns of life and much else, change constantly throughout the story. It is not a simple story, and there is no clear pattern or straightforward explanation of events. But there is one thread that runs through the complex web of the times: the thread of faith. Sometimes that faith expresses fierce denunciation of the Vikings, but more often it focuses on the failure of Christians to live up to its own ideals.

Faith expressed itself in different ways. But in Anglo-Saxon England we find a civilization which kept faith. There have been many accounts of the Viking raids; King Alfred has attracted biographers and historians alike; the policies and reputation of King Æthelred have been discussed frequently. But less attention has been given to the role of ideas, the way people understood what was happening to them and their nation in the light of their faith in God. This faith appears not only in sermons and saints' lives, where we might expect it. It also appears in the apparently secular poems of battles, the prose of chronicles, in the expressions of the imagination and devotion of art and stonework. It appears in the ideals and fantasies of the people whose thought-world was conditioned by Christianity, and who felt the shock and offence and fear of the Viking attacks. Fear of the Vikings and the faith of Christianity shape the literature and the monuments of the time, and it is that distinctive shape that we will try to discern in this book.

The book explores characteristic themes in the sources, and while it does not leave non-literary sources out of consideration, it attempts to listen to the voices in the literature, by turns plaintive, courageous, aloof, fearful, defiant, serene. Sometimes this defers questions of precise historical interpretation, but it also reckons with the Anglo-Saxon response to the Vikings in a way that questions of, for example, the size of the Viking armies do not.

As part of this 'listening', texts are quoted within the chapters where possible, but longer excerpts and complete texts are given at the end of the book, with a reference in the chapter. This is to enable the reader to see the text as a whole rather than as just an illustration for a particular point I would like to make. Suggestions of further reading are also given, so that the reader can find more information, and follow up academic debates and particular interests in works written on the subject.

1

FROM VIKING RAIDS
TO KING CNUT

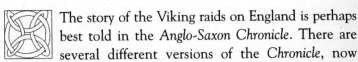 The story of the Viking raids on England is perhaps best told in the *Anglo-Saxon Chronicle*. There are several different versions of the *Chronicle*, now known by the places they were kept – Winchester, Peterborough, Abingdon and so on. They are unique in being written in the vernacular, the Anglo-Saxon language, rather than Latin, by people contemporary or nearly contemporary with the events they record. Most importantly, several of them cover the entire period of Viking attacks. There are some gaps and biases, different traditions and additions from various sources. For most of the Viking Age, there is a central core of information, while the different versions have their own local additions. Some parts of the tradition show the influence of a kind of royal public relations office, other parts blame the king. But whatever the flaws and unevenness of the *Chronicle*, it seems to tell a broadly reliable story.

Much of the detail we would like to know about, the kind of detail that catches our attention, is lacking in the *Chronicle*. The entries are frustratingly spare. We can supplement the information from poems and letters, saints' lives and later histories, from archaeology and place-names. It has to be admitted that not all the information we might glean from these sources is quite reliable. Even with this material we often have what amounts to a series of cinematic stills rather than a proper feature film, but there is enough material to give colour and life to the picture. We have an incomplete, but gripping story. It is to that story of the Vikings in England that we turn now.

BEGINNINGS

In many ways the Vikings were doing what the Germanic peoples had done for centuries. Tacitus, a Roman historian in the first century, saw that the Germanic tribes preferred to raid each other rather than do the hard graft of farming for themselves. Their code of honour was born out of, and sustained by, constant raiding. Saxon raiders annoyed the Romans in Britain. The Anglo-Saxon conquest of Britain is not dissimilar from the Viking conquest of the northern and eastern parts of England, the Danelaw. The Anglo-Saxon kings maintained this predatory warfare against the Celts and each other. So what was new about the Vikings?

The *Anglo-Saxon Chronicle* towards the end of the eighth century shows that while warfare was not unusual, the main preoccupations of those in power in England by this time were to do with the church and power politics. There was a fight for the crown of Wessex in which 85 men died in 786, and some nasty feuding in Northumbria. But for many of the years, versions of the *Chronicle* read like 'clergy movements' and obituaries pages from a modern religious newspaper: 'Archbishop Æthelberht died', 'Eanbald was consecrated archbishop', 'Abbot Botwine died', and so on. And to continue the analogy, the entry for 787 is a banner headline, shocking and unprecedented: 'Contentious synod at Chelsea'! Struggles for power were going on, but they were internal and domestic.

The chroniclers are absolutely clear that something new was happening when the Vikings arrived:

> 789. [In the days of King Beorhtric] three ships came for the first time. The reeve rode over to them and wanted to force them to go to the king's residence, because he did not know what they were. He was killed. Those were the first ships of Danish men that came to the land of the English.

This chronicler misses out some of the details we would like to know in the process of emphasizing the novelty of the attack and the nature of the men. Several versions of the *Chronicle* give further detail, principally that the 'Danes' were Northmen 'of Heretha lande', that is from Hordaland, the area around Bergen in Norway. Since it was the Danes and not the Norwegians who were the main attackers later in England, the use of the word 'Danes' to identify Vikings must come from a later time when it was the Danes who were attacking England. The *Annals of St Neot's*, a Latin chronicle, adds that the three ships arrived at Portland, near Dorchester. Another chronicler, Æthelweard, writing towards the end of the 10th century, and possibly using a lost version of the *Anglo-Saxon Chronicle*, tells the story in his florid Latin. He does not provide much more information, but elaborates the suddenness of the attack, gives the reeve's name and mentions that his men were killed along with him:

> When the very pious King Beorhtric was ruling over the domains of the West Saxons, the people spread over their fields were then making furrows in the grimy earth in serene tranquillity, and the burden-bearing frames ... of the oxen placed their

necks under the yoke in nearest love. Suddenly a
not very large fleet of the Danes arrived, speedy
vessels to the number of three: that was their first
arrival. At the report the king's reeve, who was
then in the town called Dorchester, leapt on his
horse, sped to the harbour with a few men (for he
thought they were merchants rather than marauders), and admonishing them in an authoritative
manner, gave orders that they should be driven to
the royal town. And he and his companions were
killed by them on the spot. The name of the reeve
was Beaduheard.

All the writers who tell this event stress that this was the first
time that the Scandinavians came, implying that it was similar to the way they came later. It was a kind of portent of what
was to come. They emphasize that the over-conscientious
steward failed to understand the sort of people he was dealing
with. There was a clear distinction in their minds between
merchants and marauders.

But although this was undoubtedly a significant event, the
continuities with later raids are noticeable for their absence.
The 'Danes' were Norwegians. In the Chronicle they killed
only the reeve, though Æthelweard might have had access to
a more detailed tradition in which it was recorded that they
also killed Beaduheard's men. There is no mention of robbery.
Moreover, unless the statement that the Scandinavians came
from Hordaland is a guess, which seems unlikely, some kind of
conversation must have been entered into, possibly as a prelude to trade. According to all the sources, these men were
provoked. So it looks as if it was only by hindsight that the
merchant-marauder distinction was clear, and these 'Danes'
may not initially have been marauders in intention at all.

Hindsight gave the key for the interpretation of this ambiguous event.

Scandinavian narrative sources for the attacks on England are sparse and often far distant from the time of the events they record. But the famous Icelander Egil Skallagrimsson spent time in the country in the tenth century. In his youth, he and his brother Thorolf got up a ship for Viking activities. The account in *Egils saga* (a 13th-century Icelandic source) shows how even at the mid-point of the Viking Age, the merchant-marauder ambiguity remained, at least in the Vikings' understanding of themselves:

> In the spring Egil and Thorolf got a longship ready and men for it, and went to the Baltic for the summer. They raided and seized property and had many battles. They also sailed as far as Latvia and stayed offshore for half a month's peace and trading. When this time was over, they started raiding again and they called in at various places.

The raiding-trading activities of young Scandinavian men in the Viking Age gave them wealth, adventures, and opportunities to prove themselves. The object was to get money and reputation, and they would raid if opportunity offered, trade if there was no easier way of obtaining what they wanted. It all rather depended on the local conditions. The novelty of the Vikings perhaps lay in the distances the raiders now covered, and the uncertainty they bred as to their intentions.

DAWNING REALIZATION

If initially there was ambiguity about the nature and intentions of the ships and their crews, this did not remain for long in England. A northern version of the *Anglo-Saxon Chronicle* saw the advent of the Vikings as apocalyptic:

> 793. In this year terrible omens appeared over the land of the Northumbrians and miserably distressed the people: these were immense lightning-flashes, and fiery dragons were seen flying in the sky. A great famine immediately followed these portents, and a short while later in the same year, on the 8th of [June], the ravaging of heathen men miserably destroyed God's church in Lindisfarne through plundering and slaughter.

The end of the world, in the teaching of Jesus in the gospels, would be preceded by signs in the heavens and famine, wars and disruption in human relations. The fact that the attacks by these heathens were directed at the monasteries and holy sites helped to confirm the view that there was something unusually sinister about the Vikings.

Alcuin certainly thought so. He had been brought up in Northumbria, a monk of the great monastery at York. In his maturity he had been recruited by Charles the Great, or Charlemagne, to re-establish learning within the Frankish empire which now comprised most of north-west Europe. He maintained a lively correspondence with kings and churchmen in England, and seems to have missed little of the news and gossip which circulated. From the court of Charlemagne Alcuin wrote to King Æthelred of Northumbria and his noblemen after the sack of Lindisfarne by Vikings in June 793:

> It is now nearly 350 years that we and our fathers have been in this beautiful land, and never before

has such terror been seen in Britain as we have suffered from heathen people. Nor indeed was such a voyage thought possible. The church of St Cuthbert is sprinkled with the blood of the priests of God, and all the utensils have been plundered; a place more sacred than any in Britain has been given over to the plundering of heathen people. And where the Christian religion first began in our nation after the departure of St Paulinus from York, there distress and disaster have started. Who is not afraid at this? Who does not lament at this as if his own home had been captured? The chosen vineyard [of God] has been plundered by foxes, the inheritance of the Lord has been given to a people not his own. And where there was the Lord's praise, there is now the jesting of heathens; holy celebration is turned to mourning.

The rhetoric of the letter is powerful, particularly in the contrasts Alcuin draws between what has happened in the Viking attack and everything that is right, proper and expected. He expects the recipients of the letter to know all about Jewish sacrifices in the Old Testament. The Jewish priests sprinkled the blood of sacrificial animals around the Temple and on the people as part of the purification process in worship. In the New Testament, in the first epistle of St Peter, 1:2, the Christians to whom the apostle writes are 'sprinkled with the blood of Christ', and so pure and chosen. Alcuin points up a horrific contrast between this picture of holiness and consecration and the heathen desecration made by the Vikings, who had sprinkled the priests' blood all over St Cuthbert's sanctuary.

So what does Alcuin mean when he states that no such voyage of depredation was thought possible? Simply that it

was inconceivable that anyone could do such a thing. Alcuin
shows us the incredulous horror with which the Viking
attacks were greeted, and moreover, the sense of affront that
Christians felt when their God was defied, his priests and
monks murdered, articles hallowed by generations of worship
were snatched from them, their civilization and social order
disrupted. He wrote further letters to the communities at
Wearmouth and Jarrow, warning them that as they too were
near the sea, they too were vulnerable to attack unless they
mended their ways: 'Let the punishment of others be a warning to you, and let the suffering of the few be the salvation of
many. You live by the sea from which this plague first came.'
Alcuin did not expect the first attack, and evidently did not
see it as the start of a continuing trend. He urged his corre-
spondents not to trust in weapons for defence, but to look to
the saints and turn to God. Whether or not they mended
their ways, Alcuin's words proved prophetic and Jarrow was
attacked in the following year, 794.

The *Chronicle* continues:

> 794. ... The heathens ravaged in Northumbria, and
> they raided Ecgferth's monastery at Jarrow. One of
> their leaders was killed there, and in addition some
> of their ships were smashed in the bad weather and
> many of the men drowned there. Some came
> ashore alive at the mouth of the river, and were
> immediately killed.

The treatment these Vikings received in Northumbria was
apparently sufficient to dissuade raiders for over 40 years.
But the interesting thing about the *Chronicle* account of
these Northumbrian raids and Alcuin's letters, is that the
merchant-marauder ambiguity has disappeared. The focus of

these attacks was on the monasteries. These were deliberate raids, not misunderstood trading voyages. And this was not really unexpected, since the monasteries were repositories of wealth and hardly designed to be impregnable even if there were armed men present.

More detail is given to confirm the nature of the raids by Symeon of Durham, a 12th-century historian with access to local sources. He writes of the omens mentioned by the *Chronicle*, and continues:

> Heathens from northern regions came with a naval army to Britain like stinging hornets. Like savage wolves, they overran the country in all directions, plundering, rending and killing not only sheep and cattle, but also priests and deacons and congregations of monks and nuns. They came ... to the church of Lindisfarne and devastated everything with dreadful looting, trod the holy things with sacrilegious feet, dug up the altars and carried off all the treasures of the holy church. They killed some of the brothers, they took some away in bonds, they loaded many with insults and threw them out naked, and some they drowned in the sea.

Symeon saw the shipwrecks and slaying of the survivors of the following year as St Cuthbert's vengeance for these things. The great saint of Lindisfarne would not let the insult to his shrine and injury to his followers go unpunished. The similarities between Symeon's version and the earlier ones are clear – there is the same focus on the church and religious people. The detail of what the Vikings did also rings true: carrying men off for future sale as slaves was one of the customs of the Scandinavians. The digging up of the altars might seem bizarre, but the saints and their relics were buried under the altars, and this suggests the heathen Vikings had learned where to find the best church plunder. They did not get St Cuthbert's rich relics nor the Lindisfarne gospel-book, which shows that members of the community had enough time to hide, or run with, the most treasured pieces. Perhaps this was one of the reasons why the others were treated so badly.

But though there were no significant raids recorded for another 40 years, these early attacks are ominous: there were merciless raiders about who knew where to find what they wanted, and they were waiting to pounce.

AN EMERGING PATTERN

Pounce they did. The next phase of attacks made a transition between the isolated raids of the eighth century and the more or less permanent presence of Scandinavian armies in England in the second half of the ninth century.

In 835 the Isle of Sheppey in Kent was attacked and devastated. From then on the raids increase, and the numbers of Vikings grow. Plainly the word got round that there were rich pickings to be had in England, and men all around Scandinavia wanted to have their share. Their targets were the coastal trading towns, particularly in the south of England. For shallow-draught vessels such as the Viking ships were, rivers were navigable for very considerable distances: Canterbury and London, both a long way inland but on rivers, were just as vulnerable as the coastal towns. Both were raided by a huge force of Vikings in 851. The reported number of ships was 'four hundred less fifty'. This number is unprecedented, and along with other improbably large figures has fallen under suspicion of exaggeration. That anyone would be counting the ships in before the mayhem started is less than probable, so the chroniclers most likely recorded the larger and more impressive figures with a view to projecting an image of numberless hordes of attackers.

An armada of 350 ships represents possibly a Viking army of 7,000 men, if we reckon 20 men to a ship. With this we have to compare the guidelines for assessing dangerous groups of men issued by King Ine of Wessex in his laws: 'Up to seven men are thieves; from seven to 35 men are a band; over that, it is an army.' Even allowing for exaggeration in the number of Viking ships and men involved, the situation was becoming very serious indeed.

The Vikings were taking on local levies, the men called out by the shire governors, the ealdormen, or the king, to fight. Every town or small group of farms had to provide men to fight if summoned and they were provided with arms by the overlord. In the early years of the ninth century, some of them may have become a little unused to the life-or-death combat they now faced, but those who survived would have had plenty of opportunity to get their hand in. This 15-year spate of Viking activity shows that considerable armies were involved. There was a threat to the church, and several shire governors or ealdormen were killed. The Vikings were not just groups of ruffians, they were organized bands of well-equipped and purposeful men.

But whatever the real numbers of ships and men, a shift in strategy was taking place. The early raids were hit-and-run, and the objective was clearly the maximum return for the minimum risk. The higher numbers of ships allowed the Vikings to fight pitched battles for richer prizes. But in 850–1 a fleet stayed over the winter on Thanet, in Kent, and another overwintered on Sheppey in 855. These were defensible sites for a seagoing army, being 'islands' in the sense that they are wholly or partially surrounded by water. Staying over the winter suggests that the men were no longer summer adventurers, who would leave at the end of the season. The stage was set for a longer, harder and more dangerous battle against a persistent enemy.

THE GREAT ARMY

In 865 a 'great army' of Vikings based itself in East Anglia and sufficiently overawed the populace for them to negotiate peace and provide the army with horses. The army – and it is constantly referred to from this point on in the *Chronicle* simply as 'the army' – was now as mobile on land as it was by sea, and, exploiting internal dissensions among the Northumbrians, it moved north and stormed York, gaining control of the city and the kingdom in 867:

> 867. In this year the army travelled from East Anglia over the Humber estuary to York in Northumbria. The people there were at loggerheads with each other: they had deposed their king Osberht and had taken Ælla, a man not of the royal family. They only resolved their differences sufficiently to fight the army late in the year. But they gathered a large force and attacked the army at York. They broke into the city. Some got inside. There was an immense slaughter of the Northumbrians, some inside the city, some outside; both the kings were killed, and the remainder made peace with the army.

The ancient, powerful kingdom of Northumbria was now in the hands of the Vikings. Within two years, they defeated and killed King Edmund of East Anglia and overran his kingdom. After a further two years, in 871, King Æthelred I of Wessex had died, and Alfred his brother was defeated in battle and went into hiding.

The *Anglo-Saxon Chronicle* for these years is mostly concerned with the affairs and fate of the kingdom of Wessex, and particularly King Alfred. The overcoming of the kingdoms of Northumbria and East Anglia are given a couple of lines each, though more attention is given to Mercia because it was closer to home. But there are other sources which tell of the fate of Kings Ælla and Edmund. A poem in praise of Cnut, composed by a skald or court poet in Cnut's reign, sometime about 1030, hints that Ælla's fate was not a pleasant one. Skaldic verse is extremely complex in metre and style, so it is difficult always to be sure precisely what it means. But part of a verse in Sighvat Thordarson's *Knutsdrápa* seems to refer to Ælla being subjected to a torture known as the 'blood eagle':

> Ivarr, who ruled at York, had
> an eagle cut on the back of Ælla.

In this practice, as a sacrifice to Odin the victim's ribs were cut away from the spine and the lungs were pulled out like wings. In the various versions of the martyrdom of King Edmund of East Anglia, the king was used as a target, and with the ribs gaping from the wounds, the result of this was rather similar to the cutting of the blood eagle. So it is possible that both kings fell victim to Odin.

In the years succeeding the fall of East Anglia and Northumbria, the Viking army moved from base to base, principally in Mercia: Reading, London, Torksey, Repton, Cambridge. From Repton, the Viking army took over Mercia in 874, expelling King Burgred and giving the kingdom to Ceolwulf, 'a foolish king's thane, who gave hostages and

swore oaths to them that whenever they wanted it, the kingdom would be ready for them, and he himself and all those
who followed him would be ready if the army had need'.
Repton was a Mercian royal estate, and making a camp there
was also making a statement and a claim to some kind of royal
authority.

Archaeologists have found Scandinavian artefacts in
graves from this time at Repton and at Heath Wood, Ingleby,
nearby. The most interesting remains are those of around 250
people, mostly young and male, whose bones were stacked in
the Mercian royal burial chamber near the church which
functioned as part of the palisade of the Viking camp. It is
difficult to interpret this evidence, and the bones are not
necessarily all those of Scandinavians. The men might have
died in battle or from disease. But it strikingly suggests that
the army, which remained 'great' in the terms of the *Anglo-
Saxon Chronicle* even after it divided in the following year,
was genuinely large.

So within a relatively few years from their first over-
wintering in England, the campaigns of the Vikings had
brought them within grasp of the whole country. They had
made a bloody example of two kings and defeated and subdued two others. They had taken over effective control of
three kingdoms, Northumbria, East Anglia and Mercia. The
army's next moves seem to indicate that they wanted to dominate the whole of the island, including Wessex and the Celtic
kingdoms in the west and north. But one factor they had not
taken into account was King Alfred.

KING ALFRED'S RESISTANCE

With Ceolwulf's puppet kingdom of Mercia as an 'insurance',
something to fall back on or possibly even retire to, the

Viking army split up in 875. Some under Halfdan went north
to raid the Celts on the northern and western borders of
Northumbria, the others under Guthrum, Oscytel and Anund
moved south to Cambridge. Heading south and west towards
Wessex, Guthrum's army was opposed by King Alfred, who
used every means of resistance, by land and sea, tribute and
treaty, siege and pursuit, guerilla warfare and pitched battle.

The Alfred we see throughout his reign, 871–99, and in
his battles against the Vikings, has two qualities which are
rarely found together. He is utterly, restlessly, opposed to the
marauders and utterly committed to defending his people.
And he is generous and noble to the point of gullibility to his
enemies when he has reached an agreement with them. Even
in the cut and thrust, the bloodiness and implacability of these
years of warfare, the Christian stature of the king stands out.

The chronicler is quick to point out that the Vikings took
advantage of King Alfred's nobility.

> 876. In this year the Viking army stole away from
> the West Saxon levies into Wareham. King Alfred
> made peace with them, and to him they swore
> oaths on the holy ring, such as they never would to
> any other people, that they would quickly leave his
> kingdom. And under cover of this, the army,
> mounted on horses, stole away from the levies and
> into Exeter.

This willingness to accept oaths (and we are not told what
oaths King Alfred swore, nor whether he kept them) left the
king vulnerable at times. But he backed his bargain-making
with military resolution.

The battle of Edington in 878 was a turning-point in this
phase of Viking activity. King Alfred's small company met

the levies of Somerset, Wiltshire and part of Hampshire
in the early summer, marched to Edington, and there defeated
the Viking army. The Viking king, Guthrum, gave Alfred
hostages and agreed to leave Wessex. He and 30 of his men
also received baptism under the king's sponsorship and
enjoyed King Alfred's hospitality and gifts for 12 days. The
generosity and evident military strength of the king, as well as
what might perhaps have been a genuine change of heart on
the part of Guthrum, brought about an effective truce between
the two in the Treaty of Wedmore agreed soon after (Text 1).

When a new force of Vikings in two parties came in 892,
250 ships from the continent and 80 ships under the Viking
leader Hæsten from somewhere else, Alfred was faced with
potential chaos. He took station between the two parties
camped at Milton and Appledore in Kent to prevent them
joining forces. Then in 893 he made approaches to Hæsten,
who agreed to be baptized, and was, along with his sons. But
Hæsten later moved to Benfleet in Essex and used it as a base
for raiding. In the pursuit which followed, it is clear that if
Hæsten would not accept the king's friendship, he would
have to endure the king's enmity. Alfred shadowed Viking
armies from Benfleet, to Farnham in Essex, to Exeter, back
to Benfleet, over the West Country and up to Chester.
He deprived the Vikings of food by siege, deprived them of
transport by damming the river, deprived them of spoils by
recapture, deprived them of rest by his implacability. The
English did not win every encounter, but they were not going
to let the Vikings alone. In the end Hæsten left the country.

Alfred left no possibility of resistance and opposition
unexplored. His armies outmanoeuvred the Vikings, his ships
outperformed the Danish ships. The sheer inventiveness and
persistence of his tactics must have worn the Vikings down.
And in the last years of Alfred's life it is clear that the tide has

turned: Alfred was the one who threatened the Vikings, many of whom were killed in battles or besieged or pursued, and who even lost the booty they had taken.

Alfred died in 899. The chronicler records very simply,

> In this year Alfred the son of Æthelwulf died, six nights before All Saints Day. He was king over all the English people except that part which was under the power of the Danes. He had ruled the kingdom for one and a half years short of 30. And his son Edward succeeded to the kingdom.

The division of English lands between the king of Wessex and the settled Danes in the Danelaw was the price of Alfred's success. The total victory of the Vikings was entirely conceivable when Alfred came to the throne, but Alfred had carved an English kingdom out of the chaos. The years of his reign had seen the final demise of the old order where the Anglo-Saxon kings fought with each other for overlordship while broadly respecting boundaries. An interim order, where two powers contended for supremacy, replaced it. The new order to come is almost foreseen: one English kingdom united under a single king.

CONSOLIDATION

The history of the years after Alfred's death is one of attempts by his successors to consolidate their boundaries and gradually to bring the lands of the Danelaw back under their authority. Æthelwold, Alfred's nephew, made an early attempt to take control of the whole country by making alliance with the Danes of the Danelaw; this came to nothing when King Edward 'the Elder', Alfred's son, defeated Æthelwold in a bloody battle. Thereafter Edward and his son Æthelstan began working energetically towards the unity of the kingdom.

By Alfred's treaty with Guthrum, the land was divided along a line roughly from London to Chester with the land to the north and east being the Danelaw, the land to the south and west being Wessex and English Mercia; the north-south divide we hear so much of these days goes at least as far back as Anglo-Saxon times. The Danelaw boundary ran through the middle of the old kingdom of Mercia, which had covered most of central England. Staffordshire, Warwickshire, Northamptonshire, Bedfordshire, Hertfordshire and Middlesex were all cut in two. Edward and the rulers of English Mercia initially concentrated on strengthening their presence in this divided region, and in due course Edward took submission from many of the rulers along his borders.

The Danelaw was not only under the control of Viking chieftains from whom Edward took submission. There is evidence (discussed in chapter 8) that the Vikings were being integrated and assimilated into a society that was neither wholly English nor wholly Scandinavian, but Anglo-Scandinavian. The English language of the Danelaw adopted Scandinavian words, people and places were given Scandinavian names, and the Christian culture of the area adopted Scandinavian styles. There were tensions between the different ethnic groups, but the Viking annexation of the Danelaw seems to have been a genuine settling down of warriors. Some of these men found the opportunity offered by continuing raids and skirmishes too tempting to resist. But they now had lands, families and responsibilities, and long campaigns seem to have lost some of their appeal. Certainly Edward was a very determined opponent, who like his father spent most of his life fighting: the Viking veterans probably would prefer to let him be king as long as he left them in peace.

After Edward's death, Æthelstan extended his influence into Northumbria, taking overlordship of the surrounding kings, both Celts and Vikings, as Edward had done. When those kings reneged on their oaths, he fought them, winning a great victory at the battle of *Brunanburh* in 937. The poem on this event inserted in the *Anglo-Saxon Chronicle* (Text 2) is discussed in detail in chapter 4 below. Æthelstan's successors in turn continued campaigning, sometimes ruthlessly, against the settled Danes until in 954, Erik Bloodaxe, the last Norse king, was driven out of Northumbria; with this act the integration of the Danes into a united England was all but complete.

By the middle of the 10th century, people in England must have begun to think that they were finally free of the fear of attack. The ship-borne raids of Vikings had practically ceased, and the English kings ruled not only the English, but also the Anglo-Scandinavian population. Peace brought renewed prosperity. Normality resumed, and the reign of Eadwig, who came to the throne in 955, was notable mainly for domestic incidents such as the exile of the future archbishop and saint, Dunstan, for questioning the morals of the king (see below, chapter 5). Edgar, his successor, ruled over a country in which faith was restored. Religious faith, certainly, was revived. But there was also a more pervasive belief in civilization and education and law than there had been for a century. It seemed possible that the golden age might return. Edgar was a strong king and a religious one, as the poetic prose entered in the *Chronicle* observes:

> 959. In his days things improved much, and God granted to him that he lived in peace as long as he lived. And he did the work that was necessary for him to achieve this. He lifted up the praise of God

far and wide, and loved God's law, and improved
the peace of the people more than any of the kings
who preceded him as far as people could remember.
And God also strengthened him so that kings and
noblemen readily submitted to him, and became
subject to his wishes. Without fighting he had his
will and wish in everything. He was widely honoured throughout the lands because he greatly
honoured God's name, and often meditated on
God's law, and lifted up God's praise far and wide,
and wisely guided all his people on every occasion
in matters secular and religious.

As will be seen in chapter 5, learning and religion flourished
in these years. Edgar's reign was seen as an interlude of peace
and tranquillity and also a time of spiritual regeneration,
based firmly in a revival of monasticism. The writers of the
Chronicle made a connection between the peace and the way
Edgar honoured God. But even in the same entry, a note of
foreboding and doubt is struck about Edgar, an intimation
that all was not well with the spiritual state of the kingdom:

Yet he did one wrong thing too much: he loved
wicked foreign practices, and established heathen
customs in this land all too firmly, and drew
foreigners here and attracted dangerous people to
this country. But may God grant to him that his
good deeds outweigh his misdeeds, that his soul
may be protected on its long journey.

Quite what these heathen customs were is the subject of
continuing debate and speculation. But already after the
accession of his son, Edward, it seemed that things were

beginning to go seriously awry once more with the spiritual state of England:

> 975. In his days because of his youth, God's adver-
> saries broke God's law: Ealdorman Ælfhere and
> many others. They obstructed the monastic rule
> and dispersed monasteries, they drove out monks
> and put to flight God's servants, whom King Edgar
> had commanded the holy Bishop Æthelwold to
> establish. And they plundered widows again and
> again. Many injustices and evil lawless deeds rose up
> afterwards, and always after that it grew much worse.

Of course, these pieces were written in hindsight by monks who naturally connected the worsening conditions following Edgar's death with the 'anti-monastic reaction'. But before long, the terrible events of the eighth and ninth centuries seemed to be happening all over again. Fear was once again overtaking faith.

THE REIGN OF KING ÆTHELRED II

In 978 Edward was murdered. His murder was covered up, and there were rumours that the mother of Æthelred, Edward's half-brother, had arranged the horrid deed. Æthelred was nevertheless elected king to popular acclaim, and was then consecrated with a large showing of ecclesiastical support. But in the following year, Viking attacks began again: seven ships attacked Southampton, Thanet was ravaged, and a separate force ravaged Cheshire. Once more, the south initially bore the brunt of the Viking attacks, but this second wave of Vikings had no scruples about also raiding the Anglo-Scandinavian population of the former Danelaw. A great

force of 93 ships under Olaf Tryggvason attacked Folkestone,
Sandwich, Ipswich and Maldon in 991. A battle was fought at
Maldon, in which Byrhtnoth, an experienced elder statesman, a great military leader, and one of the most important
landowners, died.

Tribute was paid to the Vikings, thus setting a precedent
for ever-greater payment in the years that followed. History
was repeating itself, as greater and greater prizes fell into the
hands of the attackers and visions of conquest presented
themselves to the minds of the Viking leaders. Æthelred's
reign had been tainted from the very beginning, and once
under way it went from bad to worse.

One indication of how bad things were becoming is the
fact that the Winchester version of the *Anglo-Saxon Chronicle*
effectively stops at this point. Winchester being the West
Saxon capital, the version of the *Chronicle* written here naturally tended to be friendly towards Æthelred. It gives an
account of the fighting in 1001, but although other versions
continue at length and in detail to record the debacle of
English resistance to the Viking forces, none of this appears in
the Winchester *Chronicle*. Although there might have been
many reasons for the drying up of the account, it is at least
conceivable that having nothing but bad news to record was
one of them.

Yet it is perhaps not surprising that Æthelred's reign
brought so much bad news when one considers the calibre of
the leaders on each side. The Viking leaders were forceful
men: Olaf Tryggvason, future king of Norway; Swein
Forkbeard, king of Denmark and briefly of England; and his
son Cnut, future king of England, Denmark and Norway. In
addition there was Thorkel the Tall, foster-father of Cnut and
a significant leader on both sides in the Viking wars before
Cnut's accession.

The contrast between the powerful and ruthless leaders of the Vikings and the English leaders, from the king himself down, could hardly have been more marked. All over the country the English leadership was frequently irresolute, sometimes completely feeble. Æthelred consistently backed the wrong men: two ealdormen, Ælfric and Eadric, are notable for their duplicity as leaders. It is possible that these two men may have been made scapegoats for the appalling conduct of the English armies. But as we shall see in the unfolding disasters of Æthelred's reign, if even only a little of what the chroniclers report of these two is true, they deserved their king and their king deserved them.

The peace bought by Æthelred after Maldon was not to last. In 994 Olaf and Swein attacked London, but meeting unexpected resistance from the people, they took up quarters at Southampton and accepted Æthelred's offer of 16,000 pounds in tribute, along with provisions. Æthelred did as his predecessors had done, and persuaded Olaf to convert properly to Christianity. Olaf was confirmed at Andover under the sponsorship of King Æthelred, was given gifts, and promised never to come back to England in hostility. In due course he left for Norway and became a keen Christian missionary. If we are to trust Icelandic sources, he remained a forceful man, not averse to chopping off the hands or feet of some who would not abandon heathenism. Olaf was dealt with relatively simply. But the others became a thorn in Æthelred's side, not least because of constant crises of English leadership.

The decade before the end of the first millennium provides a list of failures, in which, according to the *Chronicle*, the English seem constantly to snatch defeat from the jaws of victory. In 992 a force of ships was assembled at London and put under the command of Ealdorman Ælfric, who 'sent to warn the enemy army, and then on the night before the day

when they would have joined in battle, he fled in the dark
from the army'. It was not just Ælfric either: the leaders of the
English army fled when the Vikings attacked Bamburgh and
the north in 993. In the south, the English fled when Dorset
was attacked in 998, and a Kentish army fled in 999.

The warning Ælfric gave to the Vikings in 992 was just the
start of his miserable military career. The year after, Æthelred
had Ælfric's son blinded, presumably in retaliation for this
farce and the resulting escape of the enemy, and as an encouragement for him to do better. One of the *Chronicle* versions
adds that Ælfric was 'one of the people whom the king had
greatest trust in'. The king's lack of judgement was making
itself felt.

Then in 1003 Ælfric appears again, leading his Hampshire
men against the enemy army in Wiltshire:

> Ealdorman Ælfric had to lead the army, but he got
> up to his old tricks then. As soon as the armies
> were close enough to see each other, he pretended
> to be sick, and began to retch and vomit, and said
> that he was ill. And thus he betrayed the army that
> he should have led. As the saying goes, 'When the
> general weakens, then all the army will be greatly
> set back.'

Perhaps it is fitting that Ælfric died in the battle of Ashingdon
in 1016, the battle which gave Cnut the English crown. In a
curious way, the career of Ælfric, with its vacillation, pretence
and ultimate failure, mirrors that of Æthelred himself.

ST BRICE'S DAY
King Æthelred had his own decisive and unfortunate influence on events in the early years of the 11th century. More

than a hint of paranoia is evident in the main event of
the year 1002. What happened in the baldest of terms is as
the Chronicle records:

> in that year the king commanded all the Danish
> men in England to be killed on St Brice's Day,
> because the king had been told that they had been
> plotting and wanted to kill him, and afterwards his
> entire council, and have the kingdom thereafter.

The paranoia may have been the king's, though it could be
said that the Vikings had in some sense been plotting against
him for twenty years, trying to kill him and have the kingdom
for themselves. Perhaps the paranoia was more that of the
people, who were given an invitation to carry out what has
become known as ethnic cleansing, targeting especially the
innocent or vulnerable traders and temporary settlers whose
race could easily be ascertained, and whose army was some
distance away.

The planned massacre might have been a bold, if underhand, stroke on the part of King Æthelred. In the spring of
1002, Æthelred had married Emma (who was bizarrely
renamed Ælfgifu, the name of Æthelred's first wife). Emma
was a sister of Duke Richard II of Normandy, and Æthelred
thereby cemented a cross-Channel alliance against the
Vikings. This put Æthelred in a strong position, which might
have given him the confidence to try a new way of dealing
with the Viking threat. In the event it only made things worse.

There are several testimonies to the brutality of the massacre. A contemporary charter of St Frideswide's monastery in
Oxford mentions it, recording that some Danes fled to the
monastery, and refusing to come out, were burnt to death in
the building (Text 3). Henry of Huntingdon records that

people still talked of the massacre and the mutilations when he was a boy at the end of the 11th century. A later chronicler from Wallingford, one of the places that had to bear Swein's blood-soaked revenge, records that the Danes 'were destroyed most ruthlessly, from the least even to the greatest'. He goes on:

> They spared neither sex nor age, destroying together with them those women of their own nation who had consented to intermix with the Danes, and the children that had sprung from the foul adultery. Some women had their breasts cut off; others were buried alive in the ground; while the children were dashed to pieces against posts and stones.

It is small wonder that the *Chronicle* records little of the events for very shame, if this is true.

Pallig, brother-in-law of King Swein, and his family, were among those certainly killed in the massacre. Pallig was mentioned in the last Winchester annal in the *Chronicle* under the year 1001, as one who had deserted King Æthelred to aid the Danes in Dorset. The 12th-century historian William of Malmesbury describes the death of Gunnhild, Pallig's wife and Swein's sister:

> Gunnhild, a woman of beauty and breeding, had come to England with her powerful husband Earl Pallig. She had accepted Christianity and given herself as a hostage to make peace for the Danes. Eadric ordered her to be beheaded along with the other Danes in his ill-omened rage, though she declared openly that the letting of her blood would cost all England dear. She bore herself well in the face of

death ... though her husband had been killed before her eyes, and her son, a pleasant-natured child, had been pierced with four spears.

The slaughter of many Danes, and in this case Christians who had voluntarily made their lives surety for the good behaviour of their people, was a despicable trick, carried out with gross savagery by Ealdorman Eadric. The death of members of Swein's family was to have dire consequences. Gunnhild herself had predicted as much, and William informs us that 'Swein had a tendency towards blood-lust' and came hurrying in his ships 'with the main intention of avenging his sister Gunnhild'. The *Chronicle* accounts of the campaigns of the succeeding years several times add just one word to the normal descriptions of devastation by the Vikings: *eall(e)* 'completely'. In 1003 Exeter was 'completely destroyed', Norwich 'completely ravaged and burnt' in 1004, Wallingford 'completely burnt' in 1006. The chronicler even ventures into irony:

> The Viking army did as they usually did, they lit their beacons as they went. They went to Wallingford and completely burnt it, and then they went along Ashdown to Cuckhamsley Barrow, where they waited for what had been boastingly vowed, for it was often said, 'if they went to Cuckhamsley, they would never get back to the sea'. They then went home another way. Then the English army was assembled at Kennet, and they joined battle there, and the Vikings soon put the army to flight. Afterwards, they carried their spoils of war to the sea. There the people of Winchester could see the proud, valiant army as they went past their gate to the sea,

and brought food and treasures for themselves over
50 miles from the sea.

The 'beacons' are the burning towns left in the wake of the
Vikings. And in every movement recorded in this passage, the
Vikings are taunting the English, waiting for them to fulfil
their boasts and brazenly carrying their booty past the gates of
the West Saxon capital, Winchester. Very obvious insult is
being added to very deliberate injury, and the English can
only watch. From Shropshire, the king and his councillors
offered tribute and provisions once again.

THE BEGINNING OF THE END

Even in the depths of English despair, the so-called leaders
continued to pursue their own interests at the expense of the
kingdom. Notably there was Ealdorman Eadric, whose zeal in
pursuing the king's ill-considered policy on St Brice's Day is
noted by William of Malmesbury. He was not apparently a
coward as was Æthelred's other principal leader, Ealdorman
Ælfric, but an unscrupulous opportunist. He played a significant part in many of the events of the later part of Æthelred's
reign, and through it all he seems to have worked only for his
own advantage.

It was actually Brihtric, Eadric's brother, who was the
instigator of the trouble that led to the loss of practically
the entire English fleet in 1009, after the king had decided
to take the battle to the Vikings by sea. A new fleet had
been built with the proceeds of a harsh tax on the people. A
dispute originated by Brihtric led to 20 ships absconding
from the main English force to raid their own people along
the coast from Sandwich. Brihtric took 80 ships to capture
the renegades, but was caught in a storm, wrecked, and the
ships surviving the storm were burnt by the men whom they

were intended to capture. The remains of the fleet went with the king to London, giving another Scandinavian fleet under Thorkel the Tall the opportunity to take Sandwich, the very port where the English ships had been assembled.

Even after the disastrous loss of the English fleet, the English army nevertheless managed to cut off the Vikings from their ships. But now, prepared for a desperate battle, the army 'was hindered by Ealdorman Eadric, as it always was'. We are not told how he hindered the English, but his action was decisive; the Viking army was left in control of the lower Thames valley without opposition.

So the Scandinavians carried on systematically ravaging as much of the south of England as they could reach. In 1011 the chronicler summarizes lugubriously:

> 1011. In this year the king and his councillors sent to the Viking army asking for peace, and promising them tribute and provisions if they stopped their harrying. They had overrun at that time (i) East Anglia, (ii) Essex, (iii) Middlesex, (iv) Oxfordshire, (v) Cambridgeshire, (vi) Hertfordshire, (vii) Buckinghamshire, (viii) Bedfordshire, (ix) half of Huntingdonshire, (x) much of Northamptonshire, and south of the Thames, all of Kent, Sussex, Hastings, Surrey, Berkshire, Hampshire and much of Wiltshire.

Although the overrunning of these areas does not amount to being in control of them, it does echo the process by which the earlier Vikings gained control over the Danelaw. And the fact that about half of the area overrun was not in the original Danelaw would not have been missed. Æthelred's kingdom was in tatters. In the chronicler's summary there is a sense

of having repeated the same old formula, 'the king and his
councillors sent to the Viking army asking for peace', and
absolutely none of the jaunty bravado that characterized the
Alfredian chronicler's summary in 896, that 'the Viking army
had not too severely afflicted the English people'. The chronicler could only fear for the future, with no prospect of a
change in the fortunes of the English.

There were some, however, who gave an example of
courage that put the political leaders of England to shame.
Archbishop Wulfstan of York was preaching and teaching,
devising laws and working for the reform of society, and probably many others with him who never had much recognition.
But the events of 1011 show that some things were rotten in
Canterbury, the very heart of English Christianity, and in the
depths of fear the light of faith shone the more brightly.
Canterbury was captured by the treachery of one Ælfmær, an
archdeacon, and Archbishop Ælfheah was taken. The lurid
details of the capture of Canterbury provided by Osbern in his
Life of Ælfheah, and by John of Worcester, who borrows from
Osbern, serve to exalt the courage of the archbishop:

> Some were killed with cold steel, others burnt in
> the fire; many were thrown from the walls, a con-
> siderable number died from being hung up by their
> testicles; mothers, dragged through the streets of
> the town by their hair, were finally thrown into the
> flames and died in that way; little children,
> snatched from their mothers' breasts, were [thrown
> in the air and] caught on the points of spears, or
> crushed to pieces under cartwheels.

If there is even a shred of truth in Osbern's account, those who
died in the battle were the lucky ones. Tribute amounting to

48,000 pounds was paid, but Ælfheah refused to allow a ransom to be paid for him. In due course he was martyred by being pelted with animal bones, and was given the burial of a saint. Much was made of Ælfheah's stand, and there is more to be said about it in chapter 6. The attention given to the martyrdom of Archbishop Ælfheah in nearly all the sources might at first seem disproportionate. But when the leaders of the nation were saving themselves at the cost of ordinary people, and when the king was so ineffectual, the courage, self-sacrifice and decisiveness of the archbishop stood out in bold relief.

THE FINAL CHAPTER

By the following year, 1013, most of England had submitted to King Swein, and 'all the people regarded him as full king'. Perhaps the most symbolic act was the surrender of King Alfred's capital, Winchester. Even London, Æthelred's base and the focus of any remaining resistance, submitted in due course, Æthelred escaping by sea to the Isle of Wight and then to France. After Swein died early in 1014 – to the relief of the chronicler, who calls his death a 'fortunate event' – the Vikings elected Cnut as king. The English recalled Æthelred, on condition that the king would rule 'more justly than he had before'.

Æthelred's army marched against Cnut in Gainsborough, catching him unawares. But Cnut sailed away in his ships, leaving the people of Lindsey, who were loyal to him, to be killed and their land ravaged. A group of hostages who had been given to Swein were put ashore by Cnut at Sandwich, having had their noses, ears and hands cut off. And once again, Eadric's treachery manifested itself. For after Cnut left Gainsborough, Eadric had the chief thanes of the east Midlands, Sigeferth and Morcar, murdered. These were men

who, having originally supported Cnut, had submitted to
Æthelred after Cnut's departure.

The reason for the murder of these leaders can hardly
have been a high-minded, if violent, revenge for their shifting
allegiance, which was after all born of necessity. For in the
same year, 1015, Eadric himself changed sides and joined
Cnut with 40 English ships and an army. Eadric seems on the
contrary to have been keen to dispose of anyone who might
challenge his own personal position of leadership. In 1016 he
repeated the murderous trick: he arranged the deaths of
Uhtred and Thurcetel, the chief noblemen of Northumbria,
after they had submitted to Cnut.

By now Æthelred was dying, and Prince Edmund, his son,
took a prominent role in events. Edmund was briefly effective, and almost as ruthless as Cnut. In a series of battles
Edmund more than held his own against the Danes.

But the battle of Ashingdon in 1016 was decisive, and
Eadric played one final disastrous role by changing sides
again. Given command of part of the English forces, he instigated them to flee; the battle was lost, and Cnut had 'won for
himself all the English people'. In the settlement between
the two kings, Edmund took Wessex and Cnut took Mercia,
giving control of it to Ealdorman Eadric apparently as reward
for his helping hand in Cnut's victory. Then after Edmund
died in 1017, Cnut banished Æthelred's sons and married
Æthelred's widow, prudent courses of action for one determined to take the kingship. In 1018 tribute of 72,000 pounds
was paid by the English in a tax, some of which was used to
pay off the Danish ships and crews, who left for Denmark.
Cnut and the English then reached agreement at Oxford.
Thus Cnut became the first Danish king of all England.

And one of his first acts, which may well have endeared
him to his new subjects, was to dispose of Ealdorman Eadric.

Having rewarded Eadric with the province of Mercia for his betrayal of the English, Cnut had no wish to go the way of his predecessor; he had Ealdorman Eadric killed in London and his body thrown over the wall as carrion. Rather like both Ealdorman Ælfric and King Æthelred himself, Eadric's career, marked by constant intrigue, pointless violence and irresolution, ended in ultimate ignominy.

Later in his reign, Cnut succeeded to the throne of Denmark and also made good his claim to Norway. For all practical purposes, the activity known as 'Viking' was over in England.

LOSERS AND WINNERS

The English had emerged with pride intact after the first period of Viking activity. Although the Danes had taken over whole Anglo-Saxon kingdoms to make the Danelaw, they had met their match in King Alfred. His descendants contin-ued the work of unifying and controlling the land. But all the gains were lost under King Æthelred. The losers in the second Viking period were undoubtedly the English people, who had suffered the ravaging of various armies almost indis-criminately, along with oppressive taxation and execrable leadership. Æthelred, too, lost everything, including the confidence of his people and his reputation, in the desperate vicissitudes of his reign. Cnut gained England, but had to work hard to transform his image from that of a man who horrifically mutilated his hostages, to that of a man so holy he could try to command the waves.

Cnut had the power to impress his will on the people of England, and he would have had followers enough simply for being a strong king. But he had two particular helpers in the business of becoming a good king. In Ælfgifu Emma he had a shrewd wife, with powerful connections where Cnut had few, in Normandy. It was as her relatives that the succeeding kings came to the throne, including William of Normandy, and there is no question that she quietly manipulated the political events of four reigns, those of her husbands Æthelred and Cnut, and those of her son Harthacnut and her stepson Harold Harefoot. Ælfgifu also did a great deal to sanctify Cnut's reputation as we shall see in chapter 2. Ælfgifu and Cnut are shown together presenting a cross to New Minster at Winchester in a manuscript picture of the time, both acting as patrons of the church. And in Archbishop Wulfstan, Cnut had a tireless campaigner and administrator, with a gift for clear and compelling writing, who presented Cnut and his wish for godly order in the kingdom to the people. Wulfstan's hand is discernible in Cnut's early law-codes, and through Wulfstan, Cnut could write to the people of England in 1020, with the engaging first sentence after his greeting, 'I declare to you that I intend to be a gracious lord, faithfully upholding the rights of the church and just secular laws'. And so by all accounts he was and did.

2

QUESTIONS AND ANSWERS

 The *Anglo-Saxon Chronicle* gives a fairly dispassionate account of the Viking attacks. The various versions tell us the battles and movements, the policies and tactics, significant deaths and the amounts of money changing hands. Only rarely do we taste the bitterness as it must have been tasted by the English.

We have to imagine for ourselves the impact on the senses and emotions of the people attacked. Uncertainty as armed men approach, acting as traders. The attempt to make a deal as the strangers look inquisitively around. Things turning ugly, and more men coming from the ships, fully armed. Skirmishes as the people are rounded up, and their valuables or ornaments snatched. Casual cruelty, violence and mutilation as the Vikings try to persuade the people to give up more of their goods. Then the Vikings go through the houses and stores taking anything of value and burning the rest. They carry off their booty, the livelihood of the people. And as the night falls, the dying glow of the burning thatch, the acrid smell of the smoke and ashes, the moans of the injured, all linger in the summer air. Salvaging whatever can be salvaged in the morning, and the realization that without help, people will starve over the winter. Extreme anticipation, anger, alarm, horror, fear, despair, anxiety, all in the space of a few hours. And this might represent just a day in the life of an Anglo-Saxon during the early Viking period. Far more complex emotions must have forced themselves on the people when the Vikings stayed for days, weeks, years and ultimately for good.

For ordinary people, their way of life remained. They still had to scratch their living from the earth, graze the survivors of their cattle, build and repair houses, trade goods, serve in the army, pick up the pieces generally. These things did not change. Perhaps it was harder for the monks. Not only were they specific targets because of the wealth of the monasteries, but when the Viking attacks were repeated there ceased to be the economic foundation for monastic life. Monasteries needed large endowments to support those engaged in serving God, to provide the food, clothing and money necessary for the upkeep of substantial communities. When it became physically dangerous to be a monk, and economically impossible to keep the communities together, many monasteries simply folded. The monk lost his way of life.

THE FATE OF
THE LINDISFARNE COMMUNITY

Lindisfarne, the cradle of northern English Christianity, was attacked early and repeatedly. By 875, the community had dwindled and the monastery itself had become uninhabitable. One of the vows taken by monks was the vow of stability: they would not leave the monastery where they professed except for very good reason. The Vikings were very good reason, and with what must have been heavy hearts, Bishop Eardwulf and Abbot Eadred and the remainder of the monks took what was left of their treasures and wandered over the country trying to escape from marauding Vikings. Eventually they planned to move over to Ireland, where they thought they might be able to find a place to stay. They were prevented by bad weather, which they took as divine guidance that they should stay in England. In 883 they settled in Chester-le-Street, apparently supported by a grant of land in Northumbria from the Viking King Guthfrith. They remained there until 995.

It is impossible to tell how they did it, but the monks managed to keep in their possession St Cuthbert's relics and the Lindisfarne gospel-book. They carried St Cuthbert's coffin containing his richly dressed body and episcopal regalia on a cart, which they pulled themselves. The privations and discomforts of the life they entered upon are barely imaginable, or the desperation that led them to it. But if they had not retained their sense of community and their focus on their patron St Cuthbert, we would almost certainly have lost some of the most important material remains of early Anglo-Saxon Christianity: the Lindisfarne Gospels, most spectacular of manuscripts, St Cuthbert's pectoral cross, the fine silks of his vestments, the carved runes and Latin script of his wooden coffin. These few but significant tangible remains, now mostly kept in the British Museum and Library, were preserved through the centuries because of the devotion of a small number of harried and hounded men.

Symeon of Durham in the 12th century tells a story which shows how precarious the survival of community and treasures was. In the raging storm which prevented the planned move to Ireland, a gospel-book fell overboard. From the description given by Symeon, and the almost word-for-word translation he gives of the Anglo-Saxon note at the beginning of the book, the volume was certainly the Lindisfarne Gospels (Text 4). The loss of the book caused the monks

great grief, and their lament poignantly expresses the predica-
ment of the times:

> 'What shall we do?' they said. 'Where shall we go
> carrying the relics of the father? For seven years we
> have travelled across the entire province fleeing
> from the barbarians, and there is no place of refuge
> left in the whole country. By the obvious punish-
> ment of the scourge we have been prohibited from
> seeking rest as pilgrims elsewhere. In addition to
> all this we are weighed down by cruel hunger
> which forces us to seek relief for our lives, but the
> sword of the Danes ravaging everywhere will not
> allow us to travel with this treasure. But if we
> abandon it and look after ourselves, what shall
> we answer Cuthbert's people when they afterwards
> ask us where their pastor and patron is?'

In a vision St Cuthbert instructs the monks how to find
the horse that will pull the cart of his relics, and how to
find the book that was lost. Three miles out towards the
receded sea near Whithorn, they find the book in the sand,
undamaged. Indeed, apart from having lost its jewelled
covers, the book is undamaged today, with no water-stain evident upon it. St Cuthbert's community barely survived, most
others in the north of England disappeared.

The dilemma of the Lindisfarne monks was a real one:
stay a community and starve, or give up and live off the land.
It was the few portable relics of St Cuthbert that kept them
together, the last physical shreds of the dignity and order and
power of their monastic life. But the immediate and obvious
questions asked by the community of St Cuthbert were not
the only ones prompted by the coming of the Vikings. There

were many who naturally asked the much more profound question: 'Why?'

QUESTIONING

When we are faced with suffering or disaster, we often ask this question. We ask it on two levels. First, we want to know 'Why did this happen?', in the sense of 'who is to blame?' If the suffering could have been prevented, why was it not prevented? The Anglo-Saxons hardly questioned why the Vikings came, because it was obvious: in this sense they did not blame the Vikings for what they did. But they did question very earnestly why they were not always dealt with firmly and with courage. The writers of the period and later had very definite views as to who was to blame. But the question can be asked at another level. We still ask why the innocent suffer, what we or they have done to deserve suffering, though we usually prefer to leave it unanswered, as a rhetorical question. For the Anglo-Saxons, this question was fundamental and real: Why did God allow the Vikings to do what they did? What message or judgement from God might the Vikings unwittingly be bringing? A pressing issue for the Anglo-Saxons, Christians as they were, was quite literally why they should deserve such attacks from the heathen.

Actually these two levels of questions are very different. They both see events as *caused* and not random. The causes on the first level of questioning are human and natural. The focus here is on policies and tactics, and unpredictable and variable factors like the weather. The ultimate cause in the second level of questioning is the providence of God. The question was an attempt to see some sort of divine purpose in the events of history. These two levels of causation both fell within the Christian world-view of the Anglo-Saxons. But the answers they gave to the question 'Why?', and the solutions to the problems posed by the question, could be, and often were, quite different if not contradictory.

Some kind of reasoning, some process of understanding which helped them to cope with the reality of failure and defeat, was necessary for English Christians in the face of the Vikings. Failure was something of a novelty, on a national and international scale at least. The shocking thing was that western Europe's most sacred Christian places were attacked and pillaged: Lindisfarne, Canterbury, Tours, Paris. Hitherto, disputes had been mainly localized, between small kingdoms with recognizable strategic aims, or between factions within Christianity itself. Now here was a series of armies, as mobile by land as by sea, of indeterminate size, with no apparent strategic end in view, no fixed – and hence vulnerable in the long term – military base, and no scruples. They simply wanted portable wealth initially, and did not much care how they got it. How did they fit into God's plan for his people? How could they be contained and Christianity and its civilized way of life defended?

WHO IS TO BLAME?

Throughout the first wave of Viking attacks and settlement, the compiler of the *Anglo-Saxon Chronicle* at King Alfred's court recorded the events with something close to detachment. He wrote of the year 879:

> In this year the Viking army went to Cirencester from Chippenham and stayed there for a year. In this year a host of Vikings assembled and stayed at Fulham by the Thames; and the same year the sun was darkened for an hour of a day.

It is almost as if the Vikings were as mysterious, inevitable and unfortunate as the eclipse. These things happen, and they have to be dealt with in the best way possible. And according to the chronicler, King Alfred did deal with them in the best way possible. Both king and chronicler had a great confidence in the rightness and justice of the English cause at this particular time. Oppressed by the heathen they might be, but God was undoubtedly on their side. This is reflected in the way the chronicler keeps a stiff upper lip as he summarizes the recent Viking wars (896):

> The Viking army, through the mercy of God, had not entirely crushed the English people. They were much more severely afflicted by the plague of cattle and men during those three years, most especially by the fact that many of the best of the king's noblemen in the land died in those three years.

The sense that the English were in the right appears from time to time when the occasional morally loaded statement is allowed to pass the chronicler's pen: the Vikings broke their oaths in 876 (bad), and in 878 Guthrum and 30 of the 'most honourable' men in his army were baptized under the king's sponsorship (good).

There is a strong contrast between the Alfredian chronicler's view of things and that of the later chroniclers, writing about the reign of King Æthelred. Playing, perhaps, on King Æthelred's name, 'noble advice', he blames *unrædes*, 'bad advice', 'bad policy' for the desperate state of the English:

> All these misfortunes came upon us because of bad policy, in that tribute was not offered to the Vikings early enough. But as soon as they had done as much

damage as they could, then truce and peace was made with them. Truce and peace and tribute notwithstanding, they nevertheless went about like flocks of birds and harried and robbed and killed our wretched people.

Here in 1011 the chronicler seems to be desperately casting around for some explanation for the sufferings of the people, hinting at the king's vacillation, the failure of his advisers to confront the real problems, blaming the Vikings for not keeping to the terms belatedly offered. English military and moral nerve had collapsed, and in such circumstances damage limitation seemed to be the best that could be hoped for.

But the rot had set in much earlier. In 991 the English started paying tribute, in 992 Ealdorman Ælfric traitorously sprang the trap that would have caught an entire Danish fleet. In 993 the leaders of a powerful English army ran before the battle was properly joined. Tribute and provisions were given to the Vikings in 994. In 998 the chronicler comments,

Often forces were assembled against them, but as soon as they should have joined in battle, there was always some reason for starting the flight. The Vikings always won in the end.

And so it goes on. The chronicler is fairly discreet, but it is always the king who, with his councillors, decides to pay tribute. The very language puts the emphasis on the king, literally translated, 'the king decided, and his councillors', where the verb is singular. 'The king decided, and his councillors' to pay tribute in 1002 and 1006, and 'the king sent, and his councillors' to sue for peace in 1011. It is always the king's plans that come to nothing. And indeed nothing at all is said in the *Chronicle* about the effectiveness or otherwise of the St Brice's Day massacre in 1002. The plan is mentioned, but it is passed over in a loaded silence. And the Vikings go about and ravage as they please, and the people bear the brunt of the depredations and demands of the unrestrained enemy. The blame for the debacle of Æthelred's reign is laid squarely, if quietly, at the king's door, and at that of his chief councillors.

Later historians had more to say about Æthelred and his men. According to William of Malmesbury, Æthelred was idle, insolent, proud and perfidious. He had the habit of robbing his people of their property. And he would rather sleep with his whores than with his wife. William seems almost to have some sympathy for Ealdorman Ælfric, who was merely a coward, a 'base deserter', but that is all. But as for Ealdorman Eadric, the man King Æthelred trusted far too often, the page drips with acid:

> the dregs of humanity and the disgrace of the English; an utter profligate, a cunning rogue, provided with wealth by his noble birth, and having increased it by fluent and impudent speech. This skilful deceiver, able to carry off any pretence, sought out the king's plans as a faithful retainer and spread them around as a common traitor. Often when he was sent to make peace with the enemy, he inflamed them to war.

William had no doubts as to who was to blame, and points the finger at king and councillors. There were undoubtedly flaws in Æthelred's character that unfitted him to be the man to oppose the Vikings.

KINGS ALFRED AND ÆTHELRED

Comparing the reigns of the two kings most afflicted by Viking raids, it is hard to avoid the judgement of popular history that Æthelred (whose name means 'noble counsel') was indeed 'Unready' or ill-counselled. Alfred was a tactician, with great personal charisma. The *Anglo-Saxon Chronicle* mentions some of his tactics without giving them undue prominence: dividing his army so that they had tours of duty (893, where, the chronicler notes, the change of duty-roster allowed a strong Danish force to escape); a 'scorched earth' policy that prevented the Danish army living off the land (893); building fortresses on two sides of the River Lea, and damming the river to prevent the Viking ships from escaping (895); and building ships better than the Danish ones and manning them with the best sailors available, Frisians (896). Alfred knew when to force a pitched battle and when to avoid it. And he knew that he had the support of the men whose lives he did not risk without good reason and without risk to himself. In all of this he also had the approval of the compiler of the *Anglo-Saxon Chronicle*.

By contrast, the damning judgement of the later chroniclers was that under Æthelred the English army hardly ever forced a battle, but 'when the Viking army was in the east, the English army was kept in the west' (1010). In 1016, the English army was called out 'on pain of the full penalty', which in terms of Æthelred's laws was death and forfeiture of property if they failed to do as the king required, but to no avail. The only one of the fortresses in the land built and maintained by Æthelred's predecessors to resist the Vikings consistently and successfully was London. This was given over to the Vikings by Æthelred's son, Prince Edmund following the advice and intervention of Ealdorman Eadric. The debacle of the Sandwich fleet in 1009 is a kind of reverse image of

Alfred's naval operations: not only was the command uncertain, there were individuals out purely for their own glory, and few of them seem to have been experienced seamen. The chronicler was fully aware of these contrasts, having the manuscript of the earlier chronicle in front of him.

It is perhaps fair to say at this point that history, as told by the *Anglo-Saxon Chronicle*, is not totally unbiased. The earlier annals in the various versions of the *Chronicle* were compiled around the year 892 at the court of King Alfred in Winchester. A small number of copies were despatched to various parts of the kingdom, where they were annotated and continued. Although it was not written directly under the king's eye, the *Chronicle* was undoubtedly a document with royal sanction. Later additions were sent out for the years 894–924 and 925–75 and though these show independence of judgement as we have seen in the previous chapter, they are still sympathetic to the English crown.

For the years 983–1018, covering the majority of Æthelred's reign from 978 to 1017, however, the fullest account is provided by *Chronicle* versions which originated in Mercia or Northumbria, possibly in London or York. Furthermore, the fact that this material was compiled after 1018 means that it was written in the time of Cnut. And although Cnut probably had no more to do with the compilation than Alfred had with the first composition of the *Chronicle*, the attitudes of the writers were clearly affected by the political circumstances of the time. By 1018, the events of Æthelred's reign had brought Cnut to power, and this continuation of the *Chronicle* was written in the full knowledge of English defeat. In short, the accounts of the first Viking attacks were written from a pro-Wessex perspective, indeed so much so that the *Chronicle* from this time has been called Alfredian propaganda. But the accounts of the renewal of the Viking attacks in the reign of

King Æthelred were written with one eye on the approval of a
Scandinavian king, Cnut, and in an area much affected by
Viking activity. The versions preserved outside Winchester are
deeply critical of Æthelred's policies. And the one kept in
Winchester has no records at all for most of the second half of
Æthelred's reign. So our picture of these later events is filtered
through the bitterness of defeated and demoralized people.

Some of the contrasts between the two kings, Alfred
and Æthelred, are the making of the writers of the *Chronicle*.
But plainly not all of them. When all proper allowances
have been made, the fact remains that Alfred preserved
half of Anglo-Saxon England for his successors whereas
Æthelred lost it all to Cnut. And Æthelred was in some
sense to blame.

WHY DOES GOD ALLOW IT?

Back in the golden days before the Vikings, in 731 when Bede
was writing his *Ecclesiastical History*, he could look around and
see progress in civilization and peace and culture. Life was settled enough for him to be able to communicate with the entire
Christian world. Remote as the monastery of Wearmouth-
Jarrow might have been, its intellectual culture was as
advanced as any in Europe. Some things needed reform, certainly, and in faraway places Bede knew of Moors attacking
Christian territories. Some details of polity and the relations of
king and church still had to be worked out. But Bede could be
satisfied that the Kingdom of God was advancing, and that the
English were central to God's plan for the world. Churches
were being built, monasteries established, libraries expanded;
saints were becoming more numerous, the Celts were becoming orthodox, missions to the heathen on the Continent were
bearing fruit. In Bede's day, in Europe, civilization and
Christianity were more or less synonymous.

Bede took a fairly balanced view of all this, but there can be no doubt that he was cautiously optimistic. He, or any of his contemporaries, could never have imagined that about 150 years after he was writing, the fate of English Christianity would hang by a thread, that monasticism and libraries and missions would be the memories of the distant past, and the new saints would mainly be martyrs, and often royal ones at that. The Vikings devastated more than just buildings, communities and kingdoms. They shattered the illusion of the smooth, divinely ordained progress of Christianity.

When Alcuin in Frankia heard of the Viking raids on Northumbria, he wrote letters to comfort the king and his people, deploring the atrocities. In the same letter in which he imagines the blood-spattered sanctuary at Lindisfarne, sacked by Vikings in June 793, he continues,

> Think carefully and investigate thoroughly whether this unprecedented and unheard-of evil has not been merited because of some unheard-of evil practice.

He wrote in similar fashion to the bishop and monks of Lindisfarne,

> In what is the confidence of the churches of Britain if St Cuthbert and so great a number of saints do not defend their people? Either this is the beginning of greater trouble or else the sins of those living there have brought it upon them. To be sure, it has not happened by chance, but is the evidence of some great guilt.

This might not seem the most sensitive of comments to make. But it shows one of the characteristic answers the Anglo-Saxons

gave to the question of why the Vikings came. It was as a punishment for, and a corrective to, the sins of the people. Alcuin
goes on to suggest that showiness of dress, drunkenness and
other indulgences among the monks might be the sort of things
that were being punished. But for his justification he turns to
the Bible and history: he quotes Hebrews 12:6, 'God chastises
every son whom he receives', and talks about the Babylonian
destruction of Jerusalem, the sack of Rome, and then the more
recent ravaging of Europe by the heathens as examples of that
chastisement.

When they thought about what purpose the Vikings might
have in the greater scheme of things, the Anglo-Saxons
showed a degree of ambivalence. The shock and horror were
natural responses to the attacks, but those responses included
a deep unease that God, St Cuthbert and all the saints were
not protecting everything that the Christian Anglo-Saxons
held to be good and right. Perhaps making a virtue of necessity, they chose to see the attacks as punishment for sin
within God's providence. In this way the Vikings became
God's scourge, after the pattern of scripture and history, to
purify his people, but also to confirm them as his people. Thus
even the savagery of the Vikings curiously reinforced one
important aspect of the Christian world-view of the Anglo-
Saxons, their sense of being the people of God, their growing
sense of Christian nationhood.

NATIONHOOD

It was to history and Christianity that the Anglo-Saxons
owed their sense of nationhood. Before they were ever united
as one nation under one king, the Anglo-Saxons had a sense
of who they were as a nation which derived from their past
and their faith. It was an idea before it was a practical reality

in political terms. The idea was that they were the chosen people of God even before they were Christians, and hence all that happened, past, present and future, was part of God's plan for them. Ultimately the idea came from the Bible, where the tribes of Israel conquered a land, became a united kingdom, then divided and were oppressed and conquered by savage nations, but always kept a hope that their nation would be restored. The historical and prophetic books of the Old Testament constantly make a connection between Israel's obedience to God and the good or bad characters of the kings, and the fortunes of the nation in war and peace. The pattern was one which impressed itself upon the Anglo-Saxon Christians as relevant to their situation. But one event in their own past was particularly important in forming this identification of themselves as the people of God. That was the conquest of Britain.

When the Roman legions left Britain to defend Rome at the beginning of the fifth century, they left behind a civilized, partially Christianized country. The country was threaded by good roads and dotted with rich villas, orderly estates and bustling towns. The remains of this great culture are still impressive. The many inscriptions, sculptures, buildings and roads testify to a wealthy and refined society. Agriculture and trade supported an élite not unlike that of Rome itself, and from Rome came the most important influences on the local culture.

The legions had used the roads to deploy against attackers, often the Picts and Scots in the west and north. With no legions, sub-Roman Britain lay open to armies using the same roads, and the Picts and Scots took full advantage. They mercilessly devastated the country, and about the middle of the fifth century King Vortigern hired some Germanic mercenaries from the Continent to help defend his domains

against the Pictish threat. The Romans had used mercenaries
for centuries, and they had quite frequently been Germanic,
so there was nothing unusual in this. The fact that Rome
needed the legions she recalled because she was being
attacked by Germanic warriors might have alerted some of
the more thoughtful, but Britain had to be defended.
According to Gildas, a sixth-century British monk who tells
the story, the mercenaries came in three ships and were based
initially in Kent. Soon the mercenaries and their hosts fell
out, and more Germanic warriors were invited to these shores
by their relatives to fight for themselves, to take land and to
settle and establish their own way of life.

Like wolves the Angles and Saxons fell upon Roman
Britain, destroying, burning and killing. A society which
employed an army to support and protect its way of life was
confronted by a society which *was* an army, and whose
essential lifestyle was warlike. Roman Britain was engulfed.
And though the Anglo-Saxons were happy to have British
workers on their estates, happy enough for a few Britons to
retain land in marginal areas, the infrastructure of Roman
Britain disappeared. The invading Anglo-Saxons had little
regard for religion, culture or civilization. Shreds of these
remained, as indicated by the evidence of place-names:
Eccles- place-names such as Eccles, Ecclesfield, Eccleshall and
Eccleston refer to places with Celtic churches; Flore and
Fawler refer most likely to Roman mosaic floors; and
Wal- names like Walton, Walcot and Walden, where the
Anglo-Saxon word *wealh* means 'a Briton' and sometimes 'a
serf', refer to places inhabited at some stage by Celtic Britons,
the names given by Anglo-Saxons and reflecting the low
status of the occupants.

Within 150 years, the Germanic Angles and Saxons had
conquered most of what is now England, and it was divided

into various Anglo-Saxon kingdoms: Kent, Wessex and Essex in the south; East Anglia, Mercia and the kingdom of the Middle Angles across the middle of England; and Northumbria in the north. Throughout the Anglo-Saxon period, fighting against the Celtic peoples and kingdoms in the west and north of the country remained one of the perennial occupations of Anglo-Saxon kings. This remained constant despite the conversion to Christianity and later unification of England under one king.

Reflecting on what was to him an unmitigated disaster, Gildas saw these Germanic incursions as the judgement of God on the sins of the British. His book is called *The Destruction of Britain*, and the title reflects both the tone and the content of the work. After a brief and affectionate description of the land, Gildas launches into his diatribe:

> This island, stiff-necked and stubborn-minded, from the time of its being first inhabited, ungratefully rebels, sometimes against God, sometimes against her own citizens, and frequently, also, against foreign kings and their subjects. For what can there be, or be committed, more disgraceful or more unrighteous in human affairs, than to refuse to show fear to God or affection to one's own countrymen, and (without detriment to one's faith) to refuse due honour to those of higher dignity, to cast off all regard to reason, human and divine, and, in contempt of heaven and earth, to be guided by one's own sensual inventions?

Gildas reports a current saying that Britain is fertile in tyrants, he deplores habitual civil wars, he denounces the corruption of the clergy. He uses fanciful animal images and

insistently biblical language to refer to people and their
unpleasant habits. But throughout it all, he is convinced that
the sufferings endured by the British are God's correction and
purgation. The account of the attacks of the Picts that
prompted Vortigern to employ Germanic mercenaries is
introduced by 'God wished to purify his family ...' Though the
British had squandered their opportunities as Christians, they
were still God's people.

GILDAS AND BEDE ON THE ANGLO-SAXON CONQUEST

Bede the Anglo-Saxon copied from Gildas the Briton when
he wrote about the Anglo-Saxon conquest in his *History*. But
Bede changed the emphasis rather subtly. Gildas wrote of the
Germanic scourge,

> the fire of vengeance, justly kindled by former
> crimes, spread from sea to sea, fed by the hands of
> our foes in the east, and did not cease, until,
> destroying the neighbouring towns and lands, it
> reached the other side of the island, and dipped its
> red and savage tongue in the western ocean.

Bede clarified both Gildas's language and his meaning:

> the fire kindled by the hands of the heathen exe-
> cuted the just vengeance of God on the nation for
> its crimes ... Here in Britain the just Judge ordained
> that the fire of their brutal conquerors should
> ravage all the neighbouring cities and countryside
> from the east to the western sea and burn on with
> no one to hinder it, until it covered almost the
> whole face of the doomed island.

Gildas in his role as prophet had no intention of disguising the sins and follies of the Britons which brought God's judgement on them. Bede did not disguise the heathenism and brutality of the Anglo-Saxons. But Bede made explicit Gildas's notion that the Anglo-Saxons were God's instrument, bringing divine vengeance on the sinful Britons.

Bede followed Gildas and his account of the fate of the Britons: sometimes they were successful and faithful and heresy was put down and the Anglo-Saxons defeated. But by the time Gildas's account runs out, so does Bede's patience. An interlude of peace brings a recrudescence of former sins, and Bede makes his mind up about the Britons:

> a generation grew up which knew nothing of all these troubles, familiar only with the present state of peace. Then all restraints of truth and justice were so completely destroyed and abandoned that not only was there no trace of them surviving, but only a very few people could even remember them existing. To other unspeakable crimes which their historian Gildas describes in mournful words, they added this, that they never preached the faith to the Angles and Saxons who lived with them in Britain. Nevertheless, God in his goodness did not give up the people he foreknew, but he had appointed much worthier heralds of the truth to bring this people to the faith.

Bede has changed Gildas's idea of the nature of the Britons fundamentally. No longer are the Anglo-Saxons merely God's instrument to chastise the Britons. Bede has the Anglo-Saxons *replace* the Britons as God's chosen people, 'the people he foreknew'. The Britons abandoned God's ways, but God did not abandon his purposes for the Anglo-Saxons. The focus has shifted from the Britons and what God expected of them, to the Anglo-Saxons and what God intends for them. The next chapter of Bede's *History* introduces the account of the conversion of Anglo-Saxon England by the mission sent from Rome by Gregory the Great in 596. God's immediate purpose for them is fulfilled as they receive the faith.

IMPLICATIONS OF THE ANGLO-SAXON CONQUEST

The conquest was the defining period of Anglo-Saxon nationhood. It was remembered and talked about for generations. For the pre-Christian and secular Anglo-Saxons, nurtured in the ethos of the warband, might was generally right. Victories were deserved, and numbers could be offset by greater courage and strength. From this perspective, the conquest of the Britons clearly showed the superiority of the Anglo-Saxons. The poem on the Anglo-Saxon victory at the battle of *Brunanburh* in 937 against a mixed force of Celts and Vikings, looks back to the conquest of the Britons as simply a landmark in bloodshed, the gaining of a prize which required no justification:

> There was never
> a greater number of the dead, those killed in the army
> by the edges of the sword, on this island
> before this up to the present, of which books, ancient
>   witnesses,
> tell us, since the Angles and Saxons
> came up from the east here
> over the spacious sea to find Britain;
> proud craftsmen of battle, warriors eager for battle,
> they conquered the Welsh and gained a homeland.

Might was right here, and no further explanation of the victory was needed. The battle of *Brunanburh* was a kind of re-enactment of the earlier victory: the old enemy, the Celts, had been joined by the new enemy, the Vikings, but both had been overcome and the carnage was witness to Anglo-Saxon power.

But when might is clearly wrong from a Christian perspective, greater subtlety and discrimination are called for. Disaster has to be set in some context where the greater good is served. The understanding of his people's history adopted by Gildas, in which they were being punished by God, was not an easy one for him, though as a latter-day prophet it gave him occasion to use all his eloquence. For Bede the notion that the Anglo-Saxons were God's scourge went some way towards excusing or explaining their savagery as they carried out their conquest. But if, as Bede believed, the Anglo-Saxons had replaced the Britons as God's chosen people, and if the Anglo-Saxons themselves were the subject of savage attack, just as the Britons had been, then the situation had some very uncomfortable implications. The main implication of Bede's high view of the calling and destiny of the Anglo-Saxons must be that the English were under the judgement of God.

The Vikings very nearly re-enacted the Anglo-Saxon conquest of Britain. They were savage, they were heathen, and they were comparatively small in number, but disproportionately successful. But in addition, they fell upon the monasteries and milked the religious institutions of the country unmercifully. This gave an edge to the argument that they were divine punishment on sin. Archbishop Wulfstan the homilist early in the 11th century saw around him the devastation inflicted by the Vikings. He also saw the follies and gross sins of the English. In the third and longest edition of his famous *Sermo ad Anglos*, his 'Address to the English' (Text 5), he describes at length the lawlessness and breakdown of civilization in England around the year 1014. He specifically draws attention to Gildas, and echoes Gildas's warnings to his people:

> In the time of the Britons there was a learned man called Gildas, who wrote about their sins, how they so very greatly angered God by their sins that he at last had the army of the English conquer their land and destroy the power of the British altogether. That happened, according to Gildas, because of robbery on the part of the powerful, coveting of ill-gotten gains, because of injustice on the part of the people and unjust judgements, because of sloth on the part of bishops, and because of the base cowardice of God's messengers who kept silent about the truth more often than not, and mumbled into their beards when they should have shouted. Through disgusting luxury and gluttony and numerous other sins, they forfeited their land and perished themselves.
>
> Let us do what is necessary for us: let us take warning of such things. It is true what I say: we know of worse doings among the English than we ever heard of among the British. So it is a priority for us that we examine ourselves and earnestly intercede with God himself. Let us do what is necessary for us, namely, return to justice and abandon injustice as far as possible, and fully compensate where we formerly transgressed.

Wulfstan does not deny the implications of the long Christian tradition which interpreted the English as God's scourge and then God's chosen people. If they were, then they, too, were being scourged by God just as the British had been earlier. Again and again in this sermon he sees the English as subject to the wrath of God, and he points out that only urgent action could save them from utter ruin because they had failed to live up to their high calling.

Major Christian writers applied to their own times and their own experience this uncomfortable doctrine that God disciplines his people through events. It was not merely a way of understanding the past, it was also a key to the present and future benefit of themselves and the nation. Wulfstan was decisively instrumental in the moral, social and political reformation of England in the last years of Æthelred and the early years of King Cnut. He at least practised what he preached. And as the nation assimilated and Christianized the Vikings, order, and with it presumably morality, were restored and the doctrine justified itself. Reform combined with the decline of attacks made it clear that the heat of the punishment of God on the nation was cooling.

REMEDIES

So, two very different answers were given to the question 'Why?' when it was asked of the cause and progress of the Viking attacks. On the one hand, there were those who found scapegoats for English defeat in King Æthelred and his leaders. Æthelred was as unlike King Alfred as it was possible to be, and his bad decisions and poor leadership were to blame. On the other hand, there were those who saw the root cause for the Viking scourge as God's judgement on the people for their sins. Both church and state were implicated in this judgement.

Now writers making these two responses could, and did, advocate contradictory remedies. The compiler of the north-ern *Anglo-Saxon Chronicle* in Æthelred's reign obviously thought that with a bit of determination, a lot of courage, a strategic aim, and an effective leader or two, the English could have successfully opposed the Vikings. The remedy obviously lay in military strength properly directed. But Alcuin, among others who saw the problem as spiritual, also saw the remedy as spiritual. He insistently advised the Northumbrian monks who had fallen victim to the Vikings to avoid the temptation to trust in military strength: 'the intercession of the saints who rest among you is a stronger defence than the amassing of arrows, and amendment of life than the gathering of weapons', 'do not put your hope in weapons, but in God', 'trust in the protection of God', he wrote in various letters.

These differences of opinion as to how to deal with the Vikings had different effects on different kings. King Alfred not only trusted in God but also, metaphorically speaking, kept his powder dry. Yet the problem was one which appealed to him intellectually, and he devised a division of spiritual, military and economic responsibilities which went some way towards resolving the issue, as we shall see in chapter 5. Early in his long reign, in 986, King Æthelred ravaged the diocese of Rochester, showing no respect for the church. But in later years, when the Viking threat increased, Æthelred tried to keep the church on his side by favours and donations of land, some of which was confiscated from his nobles. He apparently failed in both military and spiritual areas (not to mention in the area of tactful common sense), and tried to make up for his deficiencies in the first by efforts in the second.

Other kings tried both remedies and succeeded in one. King Burgred of Mercia played his traditional part in the fighting of the third quarter of the ninth century, but from the beginning he seems to have adopted a slightly more conciliatory stance. He entered into an alliance with the West Saxons in 853 to fight against the Welsh and married King Alfred's sister. In 868 the great Viking army captured Nottingham, and Burgred revived the pact with Wessex in a vain attempt to drive the Vikings out of the city with a combined force of West Saxons and Mercians. When the siege failed, he made peace with them. In the space of three more years, the Vikings had martyred King Edmund of East Anglia and had driven King Alfred of Wessex into hiding. In 873 the Mercians made peace again with the Vikings, and the following year Burgred himself was driven out of Mercia after 22 years of rule, to end his days in Rome. Burgred's kingdom was given to 'a foolish king's thane', Ceolwulf, to be held in readiness for the Vikings to take possession of it whenever they wished.

There were limits to what military power, alliances and peace-making could do, and Burgred's choice to travel to Rome, passed over without comment by the chronicler, was regarded by both Asser, the biographer of King Alfred, and Æthelweard as a positive Christian response. Asser notes,

> Burgred did not live long after he arrived in Rome, but died there, and was buried honourably in the church of St Mary in the Saxon School, where he awaits the return of the Lord and the first resurrection of the just.

Giving similar details, Æthelweard observed simply that Burgred 'did not lose hope in Christ'. Burgred might well have wished to avoid the fates of the Northumbrian Kings Osbert (killed) and Ælla (blood-eagled), the East Anglian King Edmund (used for target-practice and beheaded), and indeed of King Alfred of Wessex, holed up in a swamp. But he might

genuinely have seen his part in the brief time before his death as
one of spiritual battle. Some were called to fight, some to glorious martyrdom, some to honourable and prayerful resistance
against the forces of evil. Having failed in the military struggle,
Burgred turned to prayer to play his part in the spiritual struggle.

SPIRITUAL AND SECULAR

The Vikings thus brought to the fore another question that
had occupied the Anglo-Saxons since the conversion to
Christianity in the seventh century: how should the spiritual
and royal powers relate to each other? A number of cases of
dispute are recorded before the Vikings came which show
that, in general, while the church expected to have royal
patronage, it held itself to have independence of royal control, but also had the right to correct the king if he strayed
from the straight and narrow.

Bede tells many stories which reflect this view, and he
probably wrote them with the purpose of reinforcing the
principles. A key figure was Bishop Wilfrid. As a young man,
Wilfrid had ably argued the Roman cause at the council
of Whitby in 664. Differences in practice between the Irish-
influenced Christians of Northumbria and the Roman-
influenced Christians elsewhere in England, had led to King
Oswiu celebrating Easter a week before his queen. At the
council, Wilfrid convinced the king of the rightness of
the Roman practice, and from Bede's account, the king had
the decisive say in the matter. Soon after, Wilfrid was elected
bishop, but according to his pious biographer, Eddius
Stephanus, he feared consecration by those tainted with the
heresy he had argued against. So with the king's permission,
he went to Gaul to be consecrated. Because he was away for
above two years, Oswiu had another bishop, Chad, consecrated to the see, and when Wilfrid returned he had to retire

to Ripon for a time. No doubt he thought the king unnecessarily prompt at replacing him. But in due course this matter was resolved.

Wilfrid made an enemy of Oswiu's successor, Ecgfrith, by supporting his wife Æthelthryth in her determination not to consummate the marriage for religious reasons. Ecgfrith therefore supported Archbishop Theodore when he decided to split Wilfrid's Northumbrian bishopric in three for the more effective government of the church. Wilfrid was implacably opposed to the plan and went to Rome to appeal to the Pope, who supported Wilfrid. Wilfrid returned to England in 680, only to be imprisoned by Ecgfrith.

After the death of Ecgfrith, Archbishop Theodore was reconciled with Wilfrid and King Aldfrith restored him to the see of York in 686 or 687. Five years later disputes again erupted over land and the enforcement of Theodore's decrees, and Aldfrith expelled Wilfrid, who again appealed to Rome. Once again, the Pope vindicated Wilfrid, but King Aldfrith refused to accept the Pope's decision. Aldfrith's successor, Osred, reinstated him, however, and for the last four years of his life he was again bishop in Northumbria. He died in 709 at the age of 75.

The root of the disagreements between Wilfrid and the Northumbrian kings was partially personal and partially political. Wilfrid was of noble birth and was a man of considerable strength of character. Eddius writes at length of his humility, but that clearly coexisted with a high view of his own responsibility and dignity as a bishop. Wilfrid's see was practically the whole kingdom of Northumbria, and the independent lands of the church were considerable. Wilfrid lived in a style befitting a magnate, too: when he was returning from Gaul after his consecration his retinue, according to Eddius, consisted of 120 'well-armed, brave men', able to beat off an army of heathen warriors in Sussex. No king would wish for such an alternative to himself in power and prestige, and no king would willingly endure the questioning of his decisions by appeal to the Pope. Wilfrid won the battle against three kings (not counting Oswiu) partly by outliving the opposition. And although his see was divided, the principle of appeal to the Pope in cases of dispute in religious matters was to remain until the Reformation. Bede, writing the story, did not particularly like Wilfrid's style, but approved of the principle.

Another, much sweeter, story in Bede tells of the rebuke of King Oswine by the saintly Irish missionary bishop, Aidan. Oswine had given Aidan a fine horse for travelling about the kingdom, though Aidan normally preferred to walk. On one occasion, when he was accosted by a beggar for charity, Aidan gave him the horse, apparently without a second thought. King Oswine was, unsurprisingly, a little put out, and asked why he had done such a thing: did Oswine not have many less valuable horses that the bishop could have given away? Aidan's response, brilliant in its simplicity, was, 'What are you saying, O king? Surely this son of a horse cannot be dearer to you than that son of God?' Having reflected on this rebuke, the king determined never again to interfere with the disposal of his gifts by the bishop.

Other kings were chided by churchmen, who saw this as a serious responsibility. In about 747 the powerful King Æthelbald of Mercia was rebuked in a letter by Boniface and his colleagues from the Anglo-Saxon mission in Germany (Text 6). Although he was generous to the church and an effective ruler, as Boniface was concerned to affirm, Æthelbald was not married and made free with women religious. This letter is a masterpiece of tact and firmness, and it is possible that Boniface felt he could be so direct because he was out of the king's immediate reach. Certainly, he wrote to

Herefrith, the priest who had to deliver the letter, in more nervous terms, and to Archbishop Ecgberht, asking for his support and approval. Perhaps the most remarkable aspect of this confrontation between the church and its secular ruler is that to all appearances Æthelbald backed down. At a later council he exempted churches from normal tax demands by way of repentance and restitution.

Thus the relationship of church and state in early Anglo-Saxon England, though uneasy at times, was predominantly one of co-operation and mutual influence, rather than separation or complete agreement. It was an arrangement which benefited both parties and led to social and religious stability. The Vikings disrupted this arrangement for a long time, not least by destroying the monasteries. The revival of monasticism under King Edgar brought about renewal of the arrangement with its associated stability, but also enhanced the role of the king as patron of the church. In the turmoil of Æthelred's reign, the king had lost much of the support of the people, but the church by contrast had not. When he conquered England, Cnut made a choice: he would have none of Æthelred's half-measures in relation to the church. Having gained secular power, Cnut quite deliberately wooed the spiritual powers.

CNUT'S CONQUEST

In 1017 Cnut came to the throne as a military conqueror. His Scandinavian court poets, Ottar the Black and Sighvat Thordarson, composed praise poems, which detailed his bloody conquests in England, listing the battles and the quantity of carrion he left behind him. But Cnut conquered the English in quite another way too. He seems to have realized the imperative necessity of establishing his reign in the spiritual realm as well as the military. Once a settlement had been reached, he did all the things Christian kings should do: he passed and reaffirmed Christian laws, he patronized the monasteries, he promoted the cults of English saints even to the extent of repeating Æthelred's law making the day of St Edward (Æthelred's murdered half-brother) a festival, he went on pilgrimage to Rome, he reformed the monastery at Bury St Edmunds. After his death in 1035, Queen Emma had his memory, and the memory of his 'happy reign', preserved in the *Encomium Emmae Reginae* – not quite hagiography, but nearly. On his death, the *Encomium* records, he was lamented by all, poor and rich, bishops and clerics, monks and nuns, and left his earthly kingdom to be crowned at the right hand of God.

The reign of Cnut resolved many difficulties. His power in Scandinavia, although it brought problems for his son Harthacnut, gave England relief for a while from the expansionist attentions of Scandinavians. As a war-leader such as Æthelred never was, he quickly gained the support of the Anglo-Saxon nobility. His commitment to the church and monasticism pacified and reconciled the ecclesiastical powers. He paid his Scandinavian men liberally from the geld, tribute paid as tax, and the liberality is recorded more than once on Swedish rune-stones (Text 7).

Thus Cnut gave an answer to the questions that had been asked about the Viking attacks. He had the secular and military authority to expose the weakness of Æthelred, both on the battlefield and in the historical record of the *Anglo-Saxon Chronicle*. He gave the English someone to blame, neatly deflecting attention from his own role as attacker. But he also established his spiritual authority, answering the spiritual questions about why this trouble came on the Anglo-Saxons by bringing it to an end. He confirmed the sense of Christian nationhood the Anglo-Saxons had inherited and developed in their history. They were God's chosen people, and Cnut made it clear that the Viking attacks were a temporary punishment for their sins. He then empowered the church in its reforms, fulfilling the conditions for future prosperity, and reinforcing this way of understanding the role of God's providence in history.

In the terms of Christian history, Cnut was successful because he honoured God and the church, a view no less valid than the more modern one that sees him as honouring God and the church because it gave him success. The Anglo-Saxons might not have understood the difference.

3

KING ALFRED

History has been kind to King Alfred, and not without reason. Some writers still attach the epithet 'the Great' to Cnut, but for most, the only king of England to merit it was Alfred. There are various reasons for this, not least among them being the sense that we know this king with some intimacy, from the stories related of him over the centuries and from his own writings. And what we know of the king makes us warm to him. For most other Anglo-Saxon kings we lack the intimate portrait, the admiring biography, the picturesque folklore, the accounts of personal struggle.

The Victorians were particularly fond of Alfred because they saw in his life and rule the ideals they had for Victorian colonial rule: firm, fair, paternalistic, expansionist, cultured. The negative side of Alfred's character, for example his brutality and his readiness to keep his wife at home and out of his will, was the negative side of the pervasive Victorian character too, and was consequently not dwelt upon. But even for our own age, Alfred has become an archetype, and his story is the story of the overcoming of adversity, good triumphing over evil, wisdom banishing ignorance, order replacing chaos.

When we put Alfred's achievement in its context we can see that his success was not without cost, but it was real

nevertheless. We can see that the underlying point and purpose of most of Alfred's work and that of his supporters was a
response to the Vikings. So his Christianity is at least in part
a response to the heathenism of the Vikings; his prowess in
battle more obviously so. His support for education and the
English translation of the Christian classics is a response to
the illiteracy and foreign language of the Vikings. His affirma-
tion of loyalty and honour is a response to the opportunism
bred by the decay of social order in the Viking attacks. His
concern for tradition and sense of the past is a response to the
loss of a whole tradition in the conquered English kingdoms
around him. The remarkable thing is that these aspects of his
achievement remain an undercurrent. Alfred did not merely
react to events, he was genuinely original and creative. This
chapter explores these two aspects of Alfred.

THE MYTH

But first the myth. An old joke pictures King Alfred in a shop
which sells his clock candles. The king asks the shopkeeper,
'Well, my man, how are my clock candles selling?' The man
replies enthusiastically, 'My lord, they are selling like hot ca ...
er, they are selling very well.' The joke makes reference to two
different stories which circulated about the king. Asser,
Alfred's friend and biographer, tells how one of the king's
priorities was to devote sufficient time to the service of God.
Because of the darkness and the English weather, he could
not tell what the time was, so he worked out how long it took
a specific type of candle to burn, and marked off the hours on
the candle. Thus he produced a simple clock. Finding that the
wind not only disrupted the time-keeping of the candles, but
also the effectiveness of the light, he also crafted a lantern out
of horn, and is thus credited with another invention. The

second story is from the late 10th-century *Life of St Neot*, and tells that when he was on the run in the forest, he burnt the cakes of the swineherd's wife who had set him to keep an eye on them. If there was any truth in this story, the king might well find references to hot cakes embarrassing.

Two other famous stories concern mistaken identity. In the early 11th century, the tale is told of King Alfred on the run. Ever generous, he shares what food he has with a stranger. The stranger is revealed in a dream as St Cuthbert, who promises him help against the Vikings, and tells him that he has been chosen by God as king of Britain. In the other story, told in the 12th century by William of Malmesbury, King Alfred disguises himself as a minstrel and performs for the Vikings, finding out their plan of battle in the process. He defeats them in the ensuing battle.

Many more stories are told as time goes on. Later tradition attributed wisdom to Alfred. The 12th-century English debate-poem *The Owl and the Nightingale* uses sayings attributed to Alfred in the cut and thrust of the argument. The early 13th-century medieval collections of versified sayings known as *The Proverbs of Alfred* have the repeated introduction, *thus qweth Alured*, 'thus says Alfred'. Alfred has been honoured as the founder of the English Navy, defender of English Christianity, patron of education. Most of these stories either have some basis in fact or freely extrapolate from aspects of his character. But it is not always easy to tell the difference between reality and fantasy, even in the sources which are closest to the king in time of composition.

ALFRED AND ASSER

Several of the best stories about King Alfred come from Asser's *Life of King Alfred*. Asser was a Welsh churchman, possibly bishop of St David's, who met the king in 885. He joined the king in his efforts to re-establish the church and learning in England, and wrote his *Life* of the king in 893, well before the latter's death. Although the relationship is never explicitly acknowledged, it is probable that the *Life* written by Asser was modelled on Einhard's *Life of Charlemagne*, an idealized portrait of the Christian Frankish emperor. Much of Asser's *Life* borrows from a version of the *Anglo-Saxon Chronicle*, but there is a good deal of detail which is not available from the *Chronicle*. Some of this is padding, but some of it is information of a personal kind which would not particularly gratify the king if it were made up.

The story of Alfred's mother and the book of Old English verse is one such story. In the chapter preceding this pleasant picture of the young prince's domestic life, Asser has railed against the 'shameful neglect of his parents and tutors' by which 'he remained ignorant of letters until he was twelve years old, or even longer'. But he listened to, and memorized, Anglo-Saxon poems. And it was these which gave him a way into book-learning.

Asser tells the story:

> So, one day when his mother was showing him and his brothers a certain book of Saxon poetry which she held in her hand, she said, 'Whichever of you can learn this book most quickly, I will give it to.' Alfred, stirred by these words, or rather by divine inspiration, and drawn by the beauty of the initial letter of the book, said (forestalling his brothers, his elders in years but not in grace) in reply to his mother, 'Will you really give this book to one of us, to the one who can most quickly understand and recite it to you?' Pleased and smiling, she assured

him, saying, 'I will give it to him.' Then taking the
book from her hand, he went straight to his
teacher and read it. Having read it, he took it back
to his mother and recited it.

It is unclear who does the reading in the last two sentences,
the teacher or the prince. But Asser tells us enough for us to
discern that the future king's powerful memory played a large
part in his education and reading. He learnt the Psalms,
prayers and daily services, as well as many Saxon poems. 'But
alas!' Asser goes on to say, 'what he most wished for, he could
not satisfy according to his wish, namely the liberal arts. For
as he used to say, there were no good scholars in the whole
kingdom of the West Saxons at that time.'

   In the next chapter, the writer emphasizes this still further:
it was a cause of distress to the king that 'during the time
when he was at the right age and had the leisure and aptitude
for learning, he did not have teachers; but when he was older,
he did have the teachers and writers to some degree, but was
not able to study'. The reasons for this were his persistent illness, his royal responsibilities at home and abroad, and the
invasions of the heathen Vikings. In several passages like
these, Asser echoes what Alfred himself wrote, and it seems
to be genuinely what the king thought.

ACTIVE AND CONTEMPLATIVE

But there is, too, a parallel with the saint's life. A saint, such
as St Cuthbert, often finds a tension between what he has to
do and what he wants to do. St Cuthbert longed for the soli-
tary life of the hermit, but was called to the demanding and
difficult role of bishop. Then there was the example of King
Edmund of East Anglia, Alfred's contemporary martyred by
the Vikings. Edmund, according to Abbo his hagiographer,

was 'not so much elected in due course of succession, as forced to rule over [the East Anglians] with the authority of the sceptre'. Alfred in his turn longed for the life of the scholar, but was called to the harder and more dangerous duty of king. The interplay here between hagiographic conventions and the circumstances of the king's life is important. It determines the way the king's activities are interpreted, and suggests there was something about the king that was saintly as well as warlike. Asser's *Life of Alfred* is biography not hagiography, but both Asser and the king could see the ideological value of presenting the king as holy. Saints and holy men had a significant part to play in the struggle against the Vikings as we shall see in chapter 6. They reassured people that God was on their side, overcoming some of the fear inspired by the Vikings. But there was also a part to be played by the men of action as Asser goes on to show.

Asser consistently refers to the Vikings as 'pagans' and the English as 'Christians', and it is equally consistently part of the king's strategy to pit Christianity against heathenism in the documentary records of his reign as well as in the physical arena of battle. This helps us to interpret the events surrounding the battle of Ashdown in 871 recorded by Asser. Alfred's brother, King Æthelred I, and Alfred himself, had defeated a Viking army at Reading. Four days later, the two armies came together again at Ashdown. According to the *Anglo-Saxon Chronicle*, the Vikings were in two parties:

> in one were the heathen kings Bagsecg and Healfdene, and in the other were the earls. King Æthelred fought against the troop of the kings, and King Bagsecg was killed. Alfred, Æthelred's brother, fought against the troop of the earls, and earls Sidroc the Old, Sidroc the Young, Osbearn,

Fræna and Harold were killed; and both Viking armies were put to flight and many thousands were killed; and the fighting went on until the night.

Asser adds some revealing details.

> Alfred and his men arrived at the place of battle more quickly and better prepared ... Indeed his brother, King Æthelred, was still in his tent in prayer, hearing Mass, and stating unequivocally that he would not leave alive until the priest had finished Mass, and that he would not abandon divine service for human. He did as he said. The faith of the Christian king was effective with the Lord, as will be more clearly seen in what follows.

The two sides array themselves as the *Chronicle* indicates. Æthelred lingers at prayer, and Alfred finds himself in a diffi-cult position, having either to engage the Vikings without his brother, or to run away.

> In the end, courageously, and like a wild boar [for ferocity], he deployed the Christian forces against the enemy army as had been previously arranged (except that the king had not yet arrived). And, confident in divine counsel and sustained by divine aid, when he had closed up the shield-wall in orderly fashion, he quickly advanced his troop against the enemy.

And in the end, by the judgement of God, the Christians won. Asser does not for a moment deplore the fact that Æthelred should be dutiful in prayer. But his absence is noted, and it is

Alfred who takes the laurels. Again there is the implied contrast between the active and contemplative lives, and Asser sees the need for more of the boar-like active than the contemplative at this juncture.

THE DECLINE OF LEARNING

When some level of stability had been restored in England, and the Vikings had been contained and settled in the Danelaw, Alfred was able to turn his attention to scholarship. He set out his plans for a new system of education in the dedicatory letter attached to his translation of Gregory the Great's *Pastoral Care* (Text 8). This letter is addressed to the various bishops to whom copies of the work were sent, and it reveals a good deal about Alfred's view of the decline of learning in England and how the king intended to rectify it. It echoes Asser's account of Alfred's lament for the business of rule preventing him attending to literature as he would like. It also reveals some of the preoccupations and perceptions of the king as to his own role and the role of his kingdom.

Alfred clearly links scholarship and Christian behaviour with success. This is not perhaps a philosophy so much as an observation on life and its patterns. 'Formerly,' the king writes, 'there were happy times among the English ... the kings who had rule over the people obeyed God and his ministers, and they maintained their peace, morality and authority at home, while they also extended their territory abroad ... they prospered both in war and wisdom.' But the nostalgic vision is soon dispersed by the recollection that when he became king, learning was so decayed that priests did not even understand the church services in English, and very few either side of the Humber could translate Latin. If this is true, then the great flowering of Northumbrian

learning that produced Bede and Alcuin took not much
above 70 years to decline to profound ignorance. And if it is
true, one can understand Alfred's deep sadness, and his desire
to follow the track of those who loved knowledge and filled
the churches with treasures and books. Having achieved a
measure of success in war, he felt the desire to pursue wisdom.

Alfred pursued wisdom in more ways than one. In
Boethius's *Consolation of Philosophy*, Boethius and Lady
Philosophy discuss the problems of suffering and justice,
human pain and divine providence. Alfred's translation
adapts the original dialogue, giving it more specific Christian
reference, but also adding the king's own understanding and
reflection. His addition on the nature of wisdom follows in a
great tradition from the wisdom literature of the Bible
through to Boethius himself:

> Each virtue has its special graces, and the graces
> and dignity that it has, it very readily grants to
> each of those that love it. In this way, wisdom is
> the highest virtue and it has within it four other
> virtues: firstly, caution; secondly, moderation;
> thirdly, courage; fourthly, justice. Wisdom makes
> those who love it wise and cautious and moderate
> and patient and just, and it fills the one who loves
> it with every good quality.

Alfred also adds several proverbs to the text, drawing on the
association of wisdom and proverbs: 'The old proverb that
used to be said is very true, that they need much who desire
much, and they need little who ask for no more than enough',
he writes; and later in the same chapter, he reports 'the old
proverb that used to be sung, that the naked traveller
fears nothing for himself'. The proverbs have close English

parallels especially from later in history. But they ultimately derive from Boethius (though not in the context of the passage with which the translation is dealing) and the Roman classical writer Juvenal. Once again the virtue of moderation is taught, and once again ancient wisdom is given an English inflection.

EDUCATION AND LEARNING

Alfred was never one to be satisfied with the merely cerebral. He was a keen huntsman, Asser tells us, and he pursued wisdom and learning as he tracked game, never purely for his own pleasure but for the general good. His learning was hard-won, but he did not intend for it to remain inaccessible. So in the dedicatory letter to the *Pastoral Care*, he sets out his plan: 'It seems better to me, if you agree, that we also [like the Greeks and the Romans who translated the Bible] should translate certain books, which are most necessary for all people to know, into the language that we can all understand.' He also suggests that young men who are not slaves should be set to learning until they can read and write English. The practical good sense and the strategy which served him so well in his warfare is now directed towards education: he provides encouragement for others to follow, and devises a policy for implementation.

The interesting thing here is that Alfred is teaching his teachers. The *Pastoral Care* is, as its title suggests, a guide for bishops and priests from the hand of Gregory the Great. It treats all kinds of pastoral issues, with a sustained focus on the character of the pastor himself. Alcuin suggested to Archbishop Eanbald II in 796 that he should have a copy with him at all times for instant reference. The fact that Alfred sends out this book, that had been for nearly three centuries the standard work for the training of priests, suggests that the bishops may not have had copies. And the fact that he sends it out in an English translation, suggests that Alfred has doubts about the Latinity at least of their schools. Whatever the strict accuracy of Alfred's comments on the decline of learning and religion, he acts as if they were true. And since Alfred also lamented the fact that churches used to be rich in treasures as well as books 'before it was all ravaged and burnt', he includes with each copy of the book 'an *æstel* worth 50 mancuses'. The *æstel* was probably the pointer used for keeping the reader's place, and the famous Alfred Jewel may be the beautiful socket into which the wand of one of these pointers was inserted. The Alfred Jewel is kept in the Ashmolean Museum in Oxford; its worked glass insert depicts a man, and in the gold setting are the words 'Alfred had me made'; it is obviously both beautiful and valuable. At any rate, the *æstel* was worth the equivalent of 300 sheep or 75 cows – wealth indeed. Book and *æstel* were a step towards the enrichment of the church.

BOOKS, BOOKS, BOOKS

Alfred translated, had copied, bound, and sent out a book for the use of the bishops, and in the covering letter, suggests that they follow his example. One at least did: Bishop Wærferth, the addressee of one of the copies of the *Pastoral Care*, translated the *Dialogues* of Pope Gregory the Great. Under Alfred's sponsorship numerous other books were written, copied, translated and distributed. Some of these Alfred was personally responsible for; others, such as the Old English translation of Bede's *Ecclesiastical History*, and the *Anglo-Saxon Chronicle* itself, cannot certainly be connected with him. Even so, the Bede was translated within a very few years of Alfred's death, and so came out of the context of Alfred's reforms.

The list of works is impressive. The *Anglo-Saxon Chronicle* was first compiled and distributed in around 892; Gregory the Great's *Dialogues*, some of the Psalms, and the *Histories Against the Pagans* of Paulus Orosius were translated; Alfred himself was involved in the translation of St Augustine's *Soliloquies* and *The Consolation of Philosophy* of Boethius, as well as Gregory's *Pastoral Care*. In addition, Alfred drafted a code of laws, left a detailed will, and issued charters and treaties. The range of works is extremely impressive: history, hagiography, scripture, Christian apologetics, speculative theology, philosophy and pastoral guidance, as well as legal treatises. What is more, most of these works are extant in more than one copy.

None of the works is just a translation, or just a treatise, or just a record of history. All kinds of additions and adaptations to the translations, and the very existence of the original vernacular documents, testify to the ambition of King Alfred and to the intellectual, religious, social and national conflicts in which he was engaged. He was always defending and promoting Christianity, trying to build up the church and establish its customs, and here he might seem conventional, if not dull. His tendency towards the lugubrious can often be found in his writing, no doubt exacerbated by Viking attacks and his well-documented ill-health. But his curiosity and a kind of quirkiness show up in several works and passages from this time. We can see from these how the literary productions he inspired were used to engage with the political and social problems arising from the Viking attacks and their aftermath.

There can be no doubt about Alfred's concern with education. He himself became very thoroughly educated and wished the young men of his kingdom to be similarly trained. But he was also aware that fear and faith were battling for the minds of his people, and that literature and learning could decrease the former and augment the latter. Moreover, he had no narrow view of education: stories, traditions and poems had played a part in his own growth in understanding and he obviously harnessed all these in the education of his people. The variety of texts used in the process, from a tale inserted in the *Chronicle*, a disreputable story about a queen leaked to Asser, biblical poetry, genealogy, law, geography and proverbial wisdom woman, illustrates the king's versatility and determination. As we look at these examples of Alfredian literature we can see not only the king's general concern with education, but also his particular concerns in relation to the pressures exerted by the Vikings.

A STORY IN THE ANGLO-SAXON CHRONICLE

The Winchester Chronicle is the closest copy we have of the archetype or original of the *Anglo-Saxon Chronicle* compiled under King Alfred. While the *Chronicle* was not necessarily a direct production of Alfred's court, it is unlikely that he had no interest in it, or control over the material on the one hand and its distribution on the other. For the years before the ninth century the annals are sparse and concern themselves with deaths, accessions, battles and significant events such as plagues, comets and severe winters. Into this pattern enters a remarkable story, told in the breathless conversational style of oral narrative. Under the year 757, the events leading to a bloodbath in 786 are told: how Cynewulf and the West Saxon councillors deprived Sigeberht of the kingdom, and how Sigeberht's brother Cyneheard tried to get it back 29 years later. Both style and detail in this story are interesting: linguistic and narrative patterns recur, most obviously the survival of a single warrior in the two main battles. And an understated but definite moral point of view is expressed (Text 9).

King Sigeberht is deposed legally by the Witan, the council of chief men, and Cynewulf, because of his illegal actions. (The story does not tell us what these actions were, but the fact that Sigeberht kills his friend later gives a hint that either Sigeberht had a very short fuse, or he was psychopathic.) Sigeberht goes into exile with his companion the ealdorman Cumbra, but then kills him in an act of extreme disloyalty. Sigeberht is himself killed in vengeance by a swineherd loyal to Cumbra. Cynewulf becomes king, and the scene is set for Sigeberht's brother Cyneheard to make a bid for the throne.

Some years later, following the attempt of the king to exile him, Cyneheard attacks King Cynewulf when he is visiting a woman at a place called *Merantun*. Cyneheard's men kill the king before his retainers realize what is going on. The prince offers this small band of men life and money in exchange for their loyalty; when they refuse they are killed all but one. Cynewulf's larger band of retainers under Osric and Wigfrith ride up and surround the stronghold occupied by Cyneheard's men. Cyneheard offers them whatever they wish if they will recognize his kingship, adding that members of their families are in his company behind him: if Cynewulf's men fight him, they will also be fighting their own kinsmen. The king's retainers say that they cannot follow the one responsible for the death of their lord, indeed their lord the king was dearer to them than their family. In their turn Osric and Wigfrith offer the members of their families in the stronghold the opportunity to escape; they refuse, remarking that the same offer had been made earlier to the king's men who were now dead. In the ensuing battle, all but one of Cyneheard's men are killed. In all, 84 men die with Cyneheard.

LORD AND KIN

Apart from the fact that this is a powerful and fast-moving
story, it is notable for the way in which it depicts two different
groups of men being offered the chance to escape from an
unwinnable battle by their kinsmen, but choosing instead to
die with or for their lord. Loyalty is demonstrated not only by
implementing vengeance but also by dying. The appeal of this
particular story to a king in Alfred's position, locked in con-
tinual battle against the Vikings, is very evident.

Both the treaty with Guthrum (Text 1) and Alfred's laws
attempt to make enduring loyalty to the lord a principle. It is
possible for a man to change allegiance to another lord within
the provinces of Wessex, providing that it is done with the
witness (and presumably consent) of the local ealdorman, but
fines have to be paid and full responsibility taken by the new
lord for the man's misdemeanours, if any. And unprincipled,
opportunistic changing of sides across the boundary of the
Danelaw is forbidden. In the prologue to Alfred's law-code,
betraying one's lord is a crime for which there is no mercy,
since (Alfred argues) Christ did not grant mercy to Judas, and
since Christ 'commanded everyone to love his lord as himself'. This last provision is a little difficult to locate precisely
in scripture.

Moreover, in the terms of the story of Cynewulf and
Cyneheard, loyalty to one's lord takes precedence over loyalty
to one's kin. There is some ambiguity about the relation of
the two principles of loyalty in Anglo-Saxon England. But
the story articulates precisely the attitude a king like Alfred
would wish to promote, especially in a context where it was
possible for West Saxons to be fighting against close kin from
the other Anglo-Saxon kingdoms now under Viking rule.
Indeed, another part of Alfred's law-code specifically outlined
how loyalty to one's lord was to take precedence:

We also declare that a man is allowed to fight for
his lord, if his lord is attacked, without being liable
to feud; likewise a lord can fight for the man.

In the same way, a man is allowed to fight for his
blood relative, if he is attacked wrongfully, but not
against his lord – that we do not allow.

The fact that Alfred legislated about this suggests that it was
becoming custom, but also that there might be some doubt
about the proper way of behaving in such difficult situations.

DYNASTIC CONCERNS

There is another reason why this story would have significance for King Alfred. The death of Cynewulf in 786 brought
Beorhtric to the throne. A note written into the Parker
manuscript of the chronicle under that year tells us that
Alfred's great-grandfather Ealhmund ruled in Kent at this
time. Beorhtric was the son-in-law of Offa of Mercia, who
exercised authority over the English kingdoms in the late
eighth century. Between them, Offa and Beorhtric exiled
Ealhmund's son and Alfred's grandfather, Ecgberht, for three
years. But in 802, on the death of Beorhtric, Ecgberht
succeeded to the kingdom of Wessex, and when he died
in 839, he was in control of the entire south of England. In
short, the reigns of Cynewulf and Beorhtric saw the end of
one royal line in Wessex, and the beginning of a new one.
The story marks a pivotal point in the claim of Alfred's family
to the throne of Wessex.

Moreover, Asser has a rather scandalous tale about
Beorhtric's wife, Eadburh, and he tells it from the account of
the king himself and presumably with his approval. Because of
Eadburh's 'great wickedness' and tyrannical disposition,
the title of 'queen', and the right to sit beside the king on the

throne, had been denied to her. Eadburh had apparently poisoned one of Beorhtric's favourites, among other perverse and unpleasant things. In the context of the bond of loyalty between a man and his lord, this action was deeply sinister. After Beorhtric was dead, Eadburh went to Charlemagne, who asked her to choose between marrying him or his son; she chose his son because he was younger, and consequently got to marry neither the son nor the father. It was the wrong choice, and shows either a disarming honesty or a headstrong and undiplomatic attitude. But Charlemagne gave her a nunnery, and she ruled that until she was caught in *flagrante* with an Englishman, whereupon she was ejected and died in poverty.

The occasion for Asser to relate this tale is that when King Æthelwulf, Alfred's father, came back from his pilgrimage to Rome, he brought with him a new and very young wife, Judith, daughter of Charles the Bald. Æthelwulf overturned the tradition of the West Saxons, who had denied the title of queen to the king's wife since Eadburh, and allowed Judith to sit beside him as queen for his lifetime. After Æthelwulf's death, Judith had a brief interlude as wife of his son and the future King Alfred's brother, Æthelbald, of which Asser strongly disapproved, before returning to the court of her father on the Continent. Soon after that, she ran off with, or was abducted by, Baldwin Count of Flanders, although Asser does not tell us this if he knew it. Perhaps the telling of what was already widely known about Judith in England was enough.

The point of Asser's telling these events seems to be firstly to discredit the alliance of Offa and Beorhtric against Ecgberht, King Alfred's grandfather. The alliance brought misery to Beorhtric and disgrace to the West Saxons through Eadburh's machinations and later dalliance. And secondly, the Eadburh story overshadows the disgraceful

conduct of Judith and Æthelbald. The latter story is given
only a line or two by Asser, as against the lengthy treatment
of Eadburh.

Asser and King Alfred both understood the value of stories in forming the opinions of the people and the attitudes
of the educated. Education is never purely objective and
value-free. No Anglo-Saxon king could afford to ignore the
process of making his dynasty legitimate in every way and
setting his own priorities within a tradition which gave them
validity. The *Chronicle* story of Cynewulf and Cyneheard
encourages loyalty to the death to one's lord, an observable
preoccupation of Alfred's. Asser's stories of Eadburh discredit
the Mercian influence in Wessex and the alliance against
Alfred's predecessor, and moreover distract attention
from the indiscretions of Alfred's stepmother, Æthelwulf's
Frankish wife.

LOYALTY AND REBELLION

Because of the decline of learning in England, King Alfred
had to import scholars. One of Alfred's helpers in his educa-
tional enterprise was John the Old Saxon, that is, a man from
the area of Saxony on the Continent. It is impossible to be
sure if John had anything to do with the appearance of a
lengthy Old Saxon-derived passage, *Genesis B* as it is known,
in the Old English verse paraphrase of Genesis. But the language of the Old Saxon-derived part locates it in or around
the time of Alfred's reign. Much of the content is an engaging
version of the extra-biblical story of the rebellion of Satan
and his angels. Once again, it is the topic of loyalty which is
treated, and the Christian 'spin' put upon it shows how
important was the lesson being taught.

In pride, Satan thinks he is as good as God:

'Why should I struggle?' he said. 'I do not need
one bit to have a lord. I can do just as many
    miracles
with my hands. I have great power,
and can prepare a better throne,
higher in heaven. Why must I serve to gain his
    favour,
grovel to him with allegiance like that? I can be
    God just as well as he.
Strong retainers will stand by me, who will not fail
    me in the battle,
brave-hearted heroes. They, brave warriors, have
    chosen me
as their lord. With such as these one can devise
    strategy
and undertake it, with such companions in war:
    they are my ready friends
loyal in their hearts. I can be their lord,
I can rule in this kingdom. So it does not seem
    right to me
that I should have to flatter God at all in return
for anything good: I do not want any longer to be
    his servant.'

Satan is an opportunist, weighing up the odds. His words per-
vert the heroic notion of loyalty to one's lord into grovelling
and flattery, against which he artificially contrasts the bravery
and strategy of rebellion. He has a gracious lord, to whom he
is especially dear. Yet he relies on the loyalty of his angels and
his own power to foment rebellion. His punishment is exile in
hell and the enmity of his lord:

When the Almighty heard all this,
that his angel with great pride had
begun insurrection against his lord and had spoken
    proud words
foolishly against his ruler, he had to pay the
    penalty for that deed
and share the suffering for that action, and he had
    to have as his torment
the greatest of all punishments.

As the poet goes on to say, the punishment is hell. But in one of
a number of fascinating asides, he generalizes for his audience:

So does each one among men
who starts to fight against his Ruler,
fight wickedly against the glorious Lord.

The terms for 'Ruler' and 'Lord' here can be used equally well
for earthly and divine lords.

The focus of Satan's activity after he has fallen from
heaven is the temptation of Adam and Eve. Having failed in
his first attempt to persuade Adam to take the forbidden fruit,
the tempter persuades Eve. When he succeeds, he pretends to
be generous and kind, and promises Eve that he will forgive
the hard things that Adam had said to him earlier. In another
aside, noticeably misplaced, the poet remarks,

In this way her children have to live thereafter:
when they do something hateful, they have to do
    something praiseworthy
to compensate for insult to their lord, and have his
    favour thenceforth.

The urgency of making the point about sin and forgiveness, or rebellion and restitution, apparently overcame the original poet's sense of the poetic context. Plainly the poet would not wish people to be polite and submissive to demons: one of the conventions of the saint's life is the slanging match between the saint and a demon attempting to deceive him or her, and often the language is vivid and forceful. But the pattern of shifting loyalties, and the need for there to be some way of reconciliation, is one which was equally present in ninth-century Saxony and late ninth-century England. And neither the poet nor the translator felt it was inappropriate to include this generalization. The listener could hardly avoid the thrust of the poem: that opportunism and disloyalty to a gracious lord are devilish, but for those who have made mistakes, misled by circumstances and evil rhetoric, there is a way of reconciliation. The theological pattern of the fall of humanity from grace is echoed in the political circumstances of Alfred's reign and after.

GENEALOGY AND THEOLOGY

Genesis B is politically astute as well as theologically creative. There is something of both of these characteristics in the genealogy of King Alfred's father, King Æthelwulf, as it appears in the *Anglo-Saxon Chronicle* for the year 857. Genealogies were very important because they identified people as belonging to a certain class or to a clan or a noble family. There are several genealogies in the Winchester man-uscript of the *Anglo-Saxon Chronicle*: the very first paragraph of the *Chronicle* is the genealogy of Cerdic, the founder of the West Saxon royal house; under the year 597, Ceolwulf's genealogy is traced (and a different hand has added the details of Augustine's mission); and under the year 626, King Penda of Mercia's genealogy is given. All these genealogies go back to Woden, and it is probable that the idea of the 'divine right of kings' in England derives as much from this tradition as any other. But the genealogy of King Æthelwulf goes back through Cerdic, through Woden, back yet further:

> Æthelwulf was the son of Ecgberht, the son of Eahlmund, the son of Eafa, the son of Eoppa, the son of Ingild; Ingild was the brother of Ine the West Saxon king, who went to St Peter [Rome] and there afterwards died; they were the sons of Cenred, the son of Ceolwald, the son of Cutha, the son of Cuthwine, the son of Ceawlin, the son of Cynric, the son of Cerdic, the son of Elesa, the son of Esla, the son of Giwis, the son of Wig, the son of Freawine, the son of Frithogar, the son of Brond, the son of Bældæg, the son of Woden, the son of Frithuwald, the son of Freawine, the son of Frithuwulf, the son of Finn, the son of Godwulf, the son of Geata, the son of Tætwa, the son of Beaw, the son of Sceldwa, the son of Heremod, the son of Itermon, the son of Hrathra who was born in the Ark; Noah, Lamech, Methuselah, Enoch, Jared, Mahalaleel, Cainan, Enos, Seth, Adam. The first man and our Father is Christ, Amen.

There are numerous variations on this list in Asser, the various manuscripts of the *Anglo-Saxon Chronicle* and other sources. It may seem absurd to have a Celtic name, Cerdic, a number of legendary heroes, the name of a Germanic god, Woden, and several biblical characters appearing in the genealogy of a great English king. But these names not only record some of the real ancestors of the West Saxon kings, they also record their aspirations.

The names back to Cerdic place Æthelwulf and Alfred in a tradition of great warriors. Cerdic was one of the original invaders of Britain whose exploits are recorded in the *Chronicle*. This descent validates their right to rule, their exercise of power, and their warlike attributes. There seems little doubt that Cerdic was a genuine historical person, though it has been argued that he was invented on the basis of place-names.

The Giwisse, from the name Giwis, is a tribal name used by the Welsh annals for the West Saxons and Alfred as their king. Finn (and the scribe of the Winchester Chronicle has garbled and misplaced the name of his father, Frealaf) is known from a leaf of poetry now lost called the *Finn Fragment* and from *Beowulf*, as are Beaw and Sceldwa (Scyld, father of the Danish dynasty in *Beowulf*), Heremod and Scyld's father, Sceaf. The very word *cyning*, 'king', in Old English means 'a descendant of the [royal] family'. The point not to be missed here is that the genealogy of the West Saxon royal house goes back to Germanic ancestors shared by the Viking Danes. So King Æthelwulf and his descendants have a proven right to be considered for the royal office by the Danes as much as by the Anglo-Saxons, because they descend from the ancient Germanic kings. In fact many of these legendary names in the Germanic part of the genealogy are found as much in Anglo-Saxon literature as they are in early Scandinavian literature.

But Woden was a heathen god, and while it might be appropriate for a heathen like King Penda of Mercia to have his genealogy go back to Woden, this might cause some difficulty for a devout Christian like Æthelwulf. Woden and all he stands for is tamed somewhat by the process of taking the genealogy further back. The legendary heroes before and after him contribute to the process of 'euhemerization', the debunking of gods and myths by interpreting them as human beings and legendary stories. But the stroke of Christian genius about this genealogy is to link it with the genealogy of Jesus and the biblical patriarchs by means of an extra son born in the Ark. Beyond Hrathra or Hathra, who was born to Noah in the Ark, the names are biblical, derived from St Luke's genealogy of Jesus in his gospel, 3:36–7.

In the biblical narrative, Noah had three sons who went with him into the Ark. This addition of a son born in the Ark is apparently an English pseudo-biblical invention, with the only known early parallel in a Syriac source. And so Woden became a mere cipher, a name giving dignity to his descendants, reinforcing their divine descent and godlike battle prowess, but by no means as important as those who preceded or followed him. Woden comes between the biblical Noah, Adam and Christ himself, and the Christian Æthelwulf who gave a tithe of his lands to the church for the glory of God, and who went on pilgrimage to Rome. Woden, insofar as he represents anything heathen, represents a mere interval of heathenism, a temporary loss of the knowledge of the true God. This genealogy is a satisfactory and theologically creative response to several problems in the history of the West Saxon kingdom, but also a manifesto for a kingdom which includes the Danes in a Christian dynasty.

LAW AND CHRISTIAN TRADITION

This wish to be in the right and Christian tradition can further be seen in Alfred's laws. The laws make very sensible provisions for all kinds of practical matters, including stealing, adultery, oaths, compensation for injury and insult, national holidays and so on. It is perhaps in the prologue to the laws that we best see King Alfred's good sense and also the pressures he was under. The prologue is an edited version of Exodus chapters 20 to 23, containing the Ten Commandments and various other laws, and missing out obviously irrelevant ones. The simplest changes made are to replace 'Hebrew' with 'Christian', in, for example, 'If anyone buys a Christian slave, he shall serve for six years' (compare Exodus 21:2). But there are other changes.

Though the version of the Ten Commandments in the code is thought to be derived from an Irish text, it nevertheless reveals Alfred's clarity of thought and economy of expression. The first and second commandments, 'you shall have no other gods before me' and 'you shall not make for yourself an idol', are essentially similar, and the law-code omits the second altogether, though the provision of Exodus 21:23 forbidding gods of silver and gold is given later. Alfred's version of Exodus 23:9, 'Do not oppress the alien', shows the king's conciliatory stance towards the many foreigners who entered, settled and passed through England in his time: 'Do not behave in an unfriendly manner towards foreigners and people from abroad, and do not oppress them in any unjust fashion.' But perhaps most interesting of all is Alfred's version of Exodus 22:28, in the Vulgate (which is followed in the Latin *Quadripartitus* version of the collected Anglo-Saxon laws except for an added plural, 'rulers'), 'do not speak ill of the gods, and do not curse the ruler of your people'. Well aware of the ambiguity of earthly and heavenly 'lords' and 'rulers', Alfred makes this 'do not speak ill of your lord, and do not curse the ruler of the people'.

All this is reinforced by the summary at the end of the prologue:

These are the laws that the Almighty God himself kept speaking to Moses and which he commanded him to maintain. And when the only-begotten Son of the Lord, our God, that is the Saviour

> Christ, came to earth he said that he did not come
> to break or forbid these commands at all, but
> rather to extend them with all good things. And
> he taught mercy and humility.

The saying imputed to Christ seems to derive from Matthew
5:17, 'Do not think I have come to abolish the Law and the
Prophets; I have not come to abolish them but to fulfil them.'
The king's version is not a direct contradiction of the biblical
words, as he goes on to show. He relates the letter of the
Christian apostles from the Acts of the Apostles chapter 15,
commanding the new Christian converts of the ancient world
to keep only the necessary laws, namely to avoid idol-worship
(food offered to idols in the Bible), eating blood and strangled
animals, and fornication. And then Alfred goes on to say that
he has also selected from the laws of his predecessors Ine, Offa
of Mercia and Æthelberht of Kent and discussed the matter
with his council.

In this way Alfred sets himself within the Christian tradition of law-making, starting with Moses, endorsed in Alfred's
version by Christ, and filtering through the apostles, to
Christian Anglo-Saxon kings, down to himself. While he
does not claim that his laws will always meet with the
approval of his successors, he does claim the authority of God
and the church for the process and for some of the laws themselves. Throughout this prologue, the minor changes that
Alfred makes to the sacred text show his theological creativity, his desire for precedent and tradition, and his concern to
establish his authority.

HISTORY, GEOGRAPHY AND ANTHROPOLOGY

That conciliatory attitude to foreigners noted above in the
laws is displayed in two accounts of foreign parts included in

the Alfredian version of Orosius's *Histories Against the Pagans*. Orosius wrote under the encouragement of St Augustine to refute the notion that the disasters suffered by Rome and her empire in the fourth and fifth centuries were the revenge of the pagan gods, angered by people turning away from pagan worship. In a brief synopsis of ancient history, Orosius frequently turns on its head this notion of the revenge of the gods, by pointing out that disasters occurred as God's judgement for the persecution of Christians. Taken with Alfred's insistent condemnation of all kinds of heathen practice, the book might encourage those who read it or heard its message to see the difficulties of Alfred's times not as the revenge of the heathen gods, but as most contemporary Christians did, the judgement of God on sin.

In the section dealing with the geography of north-west Europe, the Old English Orosius has inserted into it a first-hand account of a voyage in the region of what is now northern Norway and Finland into the White Sea, by a man called Ohthere (Text 10). Following this is an account by the English sailor Wulfstan of his journey along the European coast of the Baltic to what is now Lithuania (Text 11). Some of the details in these accounts are so minutely accurate that they can be plotted on a map with confidence. But the anthropological detail is at least as interesting, partly because it contrasts with the bare tribal geography of Orosius, partly because it shows the kind of things King Alfred was interested in.

Ohthere claimed to live furthest north of all Norwegians. He had a little plough land, but made his wealth collecting tribute of feathers, whalebone, whale- and seal-skin ropes and other animal pelts from the Finns, and farming reindeer. He tells the king that the people living to the eastern side of the Gulf of Bothnia would raid those to the west and vice versa. As well as sailing north, Ohthere also sails south to Kaupang,

the great Viking-Age market town near Oslo, and to Hedeby
on the River Schlei in Jutland, another international market,
presumably to trade the skins and other goods. Ohthere made
King Alfred a gift of walrus-ivory. Many articles of whalebone
survive from Anglo-Saxon England, including the richly
worked Franks Casket now in the British Museum, to indicate
the value of the whalebone and walrus-ivory trade.

Wulfstan observed the customs of the tribe called the Este
around the estuary of the River Vistula. The eastern European
rivers, the Vistula, the Dvina and the Volga, gave the Vikings
access to trading centres like Kiev and the entire area surrounding the Black Sea and the Caspian: a market for slaves
and furs in return for Islamic silver. They could sail up
the rivers, then carry their vessels overland and sail down the
other side to the Black Sea. Wulfstan does not venture that
far, but Scandinavian traders had gone before him and would
follow. He notices the social structures and customs of the
people, particularly the way they divide up a dead man's
wealth. The people preserved the bodies of the dead, spent
much of the wealth on drinking, then divided the remainder
into portions gained by the men with the fastest horses in a
staged race.

With the benefit of scientific hindsight, we can see that
Wulfstan was fooled by a little trick. 'There is a tribe among
the Este who can make cold,' Wulfstan relates, 'which is why
the dead men lie so long without decaying, because they
make the cold on the man. And if someone puts in two containers [one] full of water and [the other] beer, they can make
it so that one of them is frozen over whether it is summer or
winter.' The 'refrigerators' in the tribe are generally thought
to be the people who looked after ice-pits, which, with
thatching, would keep a sub-zero temperature all year round.
Their knowledge of the technology would allow them to

observe the difference in freezing-point of an alcoholic liquid and a non-alcoholic one. Wulfstan is amazed at this magical ability to freeze one liquid but not the other.

There is sufficient about these two passages to indicate that they were practically dictated. The seamen's directions would make little sense to someone who had no acquaintance with the sea, and the account of Wulfstan uses the first-person 'we'. Ohthere's story does not use this, and it seems likely that an interpreter was necessary for the Norwegian. This means that the king took care to have their words recorded, which gives them importance beyond that of the tales of many seafarers. Moreover, the king apparently welcomed a Norwegian to his court, and was given gifts by him, at a time when Scandinavians would not normally have expected kindly treatment. The insertion of these passages is testimony to the king's curiosity and breadth of interest. His eagerness for knowledge even overcomes the polemic intention of the book, since the people described were heathen, and probably Ohthere himself was too.

WISDOM

Alfred's use of proverbs has already been noted. Later tradition also attributed wisdom to him. We have mentioned *The Owl and the Nightingale* and the collections of versified sayings known as *The Proverbs of Alfred*. But few of these later sayings can actually be attributed to Alfred with any certainty, at least in his extant works. One at least is of Norse origin, found in *Egil's saga* and elsewhere: 'cold is the counsel of women'; this saying is repeated by Chaucer. While it would not be implausible to see Alfred learning something from his Scandinavian neighbours, the sentiment does not seem characteristically Alfredian, not least because Alfred does not appear to have sought the counsel of women much. Indeed, in his translation of Boethius, the original Lady Philosophy (obviously a woman) becomes Wisdom, a man – this might be an accident of grammar, but it might also reflect the king's attitude. These sayings, then, are simply attributed to a man famous for wisdom, just as the proverb-collections in the Bible are often attributed to Solomon.

But from the Bible, Alfred knew that 'the fear of the Lord is the beginning of wisdom', and his piety was genuine, the mainspring of his action and thought. For the Anglo-Saxons, wisdom was a combination of sagacity, knowledge, practicality, curiosity and discernment. All we know of King Alfred shows these characteristics strongly. He prospered equally in warfare and wisdom, partly because he did not keep the two separate. He was a man whose wisdom often meant laborious calculation and attention to detail. This kind of wisdom showed itself in almost everything he did, from memorizing the church services, working out a shift system for his army, allocating rates for maintaining the defence-system in the *Burghal Hidage*, dividing his time accurately between the concerns of his kingdom and the service of God, right through to learning the Latin vocabulary for his translations.

In the light of this, we might believe Asser's story that Alfred invented, or had some part in improving, the candle-clock and the lantern. We might believe the story that he dressed up as a minstrel to spy on the Danes. But the story that when he was on the run in the forest, he burnt the woman's cakes, still seems frankly improbable.

Wise King Alfred certainly was, then, if not quite in the terms in which tradition portrays him. He was blessed with creativity and persistence, as well as a friendly biographer and chronicler of his reign. His achievement was that he not only responded effectively to his circumstances, developing strategies against the Vikings and trying to rebuild what was valuable from the past, he also transcended those circumstances, preserving for the future the language and literature, the faith and ideals of his time.

4

TWO BATTLES,
TWO TURNING-POINTS

From the *Anglo-Saxon Chronicle* accounts of King Alfred's reign, we can see that the battles of Ashdown in 871 and Edington in 878 were significant as the low and high points of Alfred's fortunes in the wars against the Danes. After Alfred's death, the *Chronicle* reverts to the earlier 'clergy movements' style of record. Although there are some longer and more detailed annals about wars and skirmishes with the Danes, the concerns of the chroniclers are principally the internal affairs of Wessex and the battles and exploits of the West Saxon kings.

This tends to obscure the fact that important things were happening in other areas. Sometimes we have to look much further afield to fill in the details of these events. For one very important battle, the battle of *Brunanburh* in 937, we have so little detail relating to the background that we cannot be absolutely certain where it took place. There is, however, a poem about it in the *Anglo-Saxon Chronicle* (Text 2). Another battle, the battle of Maldon in 991, is briefly mentioned in the *Anglo-Saxon Chronicle*, but a much fuller and more interesting account of the battle was recorded in a poem (Text 12). The manuscript of this poem was missing its beginning and ending when it was bound into a book and later copied by a scholar, and then it was destroyed in the library fire of 1731 which damaged so many Anglo-Saxon manuscripts.

These chances of history can sometimes be frustrating. But they also give us the opportunity to piece together the evidence which enables us to find *Brunanburh* and see the significance of Maldon. And while not even this detective work can tell us all we want to know about the two battles, the fact that the main sources are poems opens up new areas of information about the battles. In prose we get bald accounts of who did what, in verse we get a much richer picture. So first we explore the background of a great English victory at *Brunanburh*.

MERCIA IN THE EARLY 10TH CENTURY

Under King Alfred England was divided along Watling Street: between the Danelaw, subject to the Danes in the north and east, and English Wessex in the south and west. Alfred's son, Edward the Elder, succeeded to the throne on the death of his father in 899, and with it inherited the long-term struggle for supremacy in England. Edward's brother Ealdorman Æthelred, and Æthelred's wife Æthelflæd, 'the Lady of the Mercians', had responsibility for Mercia. Formerly this had been a large and powerful kingdom covering most of central England, but in the early years of the 10th century it was divided, with the Danes in control of the eastern parts, and Æthelred and Æthelflæd ruling the west. This was an unenviable role for an English nobleman or noblewoman. They were surrounded on all sides but the south by potential enemies: the Welsh in the west, a separate Celtic kingdom of Strathclyde in the north-west, Scandinavian-controlled Northumbria to the north, Norwegian influence further west in Ireland, Danish power to the east.

It might be supposed from the *Anglo-Saxon Chronicle* that western Mercia was politically stable and unimportant, because very little about the area is recorded. But the political situation in Mercia was delicately balanced. We learn from obscure Irish and Welsh chronicles that in the first years of the 10th century, Norwegian adventurers were expelled from Dublin, raided around Wales, and finally negotiated for land with Æthelflæd. The same sources tell us that Ealdorman Æthelred was ill and was playing little part in the everyday business of government. Æthelflæd gave these Norse Vikings land in the Wirral peninsula, and the evidence of place-names shows that they were independent and self-governing: their part of the land had boundaries, with Raby ('boundary settlement') on the Norse side; and they had their local council, which met at Thingwall ('place of the council-meeting'). These place-names are duplicated in the Norse settlement north of the Mersey, where we find Roby and another Thingwall.

In due course, these Vikings attacked Chester, but were repulsed. Æthelflæd began to encroach on the north-western parts of Danish and Norse territory, winning back the allegiance of the people south of the Mersey and west of the Pennines. She built fortifications and garrisoned towns throughout the West Midlands and as far north as Runcorn. In 918 Æthelflæd died, and the relative independence of Mercia came to an end when King Edward took over where she had left off. The western parts had always been English Mercia, but now English Mercia became part of the West Saxon dominions.

KING EDWARD THE ELDER
Edward seems to have spent his entire life campaigning, fortifying towns, and taking allegiance from his enemies. In 921

the *Anglo-Saxon Chronicle* records that he marched his army to Stamford and built a fortress there, then in midsummer he went to Tamworth to take the submission of the Mercians and the Welsh kings; then he marched on Nottingham, occupied it and garrisoned it, and all of Mercia submitted to him. The next year he garrisoned Thelwall and took Manchester in Northumbria. The year after that he built a fortress at Nottingham and another at Bakewell, and took submission from the Scots, the Danish king of Northumbria, the English and Norse inhabitants of Northumbria, and the Celtic king of Strathclyde. But the following year he died. And since loyalty to the king was loyalty to a person not to a dynasty, when Æthelstan came to the throne in 925, he had to go through the whole process again.

It is worth looking for a moment or two at what had been achieved in those years. Ealdorman Æthelred, Æthelflæd, and Edward had secured control of most of Mercia. The capturing and garrisoning of places like Nottingham, Stamford and Derby gave control of the essential power centres in eastern Mercia and the communications routes of the northern Midlands. Though the northern areas were less secure, Tamworth, Runcorn and Manchester gave control of the centres of western Mercia. Northumbria was still politically independent, as were the Strathclyde Celts in the north-west, the Danish in the east, and the Welsh in the west. But the kings of all these were nominally tributary to the crown of Wessex. It was precisely these kings that were to rise up against Æthelstan in 937.

KING ÆTHELSTAN

King Æthelstan made an agreement with Sihtric, the Irish-Norse king of Northumbria, in 926 and married his sister to him. The same year Æthelstan made a long-lasting peace with

Hywel Dda, the very powerful king of south Wales. He also made peace with Owein king of the Celtic Cumbrians or Strathclyde Welsh, and with the Scottish king Constantine, but these pacts did not last. In 927 Sihtric died and his brother Guthfrith, king of Dublin, tried to take over York and the Northumbrian kingdom. For unknown but perfectly guessable reasons – he had made no agreement with Guthfrith, for example, and could not be sure of Guthfrith's intentions – Æthelstan did not like this idea and expelled him, establishing an Englishman, Ealdwulf, as puppet ruler of Northumbria. Guthfrith died in 934, the same year as Æthelstan made a dev-astating raid on Scotland. Clearly Æthelstan was cementing his gains of territory and influence in the north by marriage, patronage and intimidation. The raid on Scotland signalled to the Northumbrians and the Strathclyde Welsh that Æthelstan was mobile, aggressive and meant to have his way.

Olaf Guthfrithsson raised a force of Irish-Norse Vikings in 937. He was joined by a Norwegian contingent from Northumbria, the Strathclyde Welsh under Owein, and the Scots under Constantine. All these forces had good reason to hate Æthelstan, and good reason to want to take their spleen out on the English. The most obvious place for the forces to assemble was somewhere in the north-west of England, where an army could plunder and intimidate the local people with-out being a drain on the resources of allies, and where there were easy escape-routes by land and sea. Olaf and his forces were raiding in Mercian territory before Æthelstan and his army were able to confront them.

In August 937 Æthelstan and his army were campaigning on the south coast. The king marched north with his Wessex men, gathering Mercian support as he went. Somewhere in the north-west of England, he confronted the enemy coalition forces, attacked and routed them. After an encounter lasting an entire day, the coalition forces broke and ran, and the English forces followed, hacking them down and eventually leaving great swathes of corpses for the carrion-eating birds and beasts. Olaf fled to Dublin by sea. Constantine went back to Scotland, and nothing more is heard of Owein.

After the death of Æthelstan in 939 Olaf Guthfrithsson succeeded, at least for a while, in getting his hands back on Mercia as well as Northumbria. But by the time of the death of Edmund in 946 all England, including Strathclyde, was in submission to the English crown. On the death of Erik Bloodaxe in 954, the remaining Scandinavian hold on York and Northumbria was broken. This battle of *Brunanburh* was a major step forward in the unification of England, a turning-point in which political supremacy was gained by the kings of Wessex over the ethnically different people within the country. We can now begin to piece together the evidence which may lead us to the exact location of that battle.

THE BATTLE OF BRUNANBURH

There are various accounts of this climactic battle. The most important and earliest is the heroic poem found in four different manuscripts of the *Anglo-Saxon Chronicle*. Like much heroic poetry, *The Battle of Brunanburh* seems to rely on an audience which knows the basic story line. Apart from the name of the site, we are not told where the battle took place.

Later chronicles sometimes illuminate, sometimes obscure the story. Æthelweard, writing his Latin *Chronicle* towards the end of the 10th century, records only Æthelstan's accession, this battle, and his death. Using a version of the *Anglo-Saxon Chronicle* as his source, he tells us that

a fierce battle was fought against the barbarians at
Brunandune, wherefore that fight is called great
even to the present day: then the barbarian tribes
are defeated and domineer no longer; they are
driven beyond the ocean; the Scots and Picts bow
the neck; the lands of Britain are consolidated
together, on all sides is peace and plenty, nor ever
did a fleet again come to this land except in friendship with the English.

There is more than a touch of irony about this passage: it was
not so long since the Welsh and Britons were calling the
Anglo-Saxons 'barbarians'; nor would it be more than a few
years – less than a decade in fact – from the time of writing
before many fleets came again in enmity on England. The
passage hints at the unpreparedness and sense of superiority
prevalent in Anglo-Saxon England prior to the renewal of
Viking attacks in the 980s.

John of Worcester's chronicle written in the early 12th
century adds certain details to the poem's account. John tells
us that Constantine, the Scottish king, was Olaf's father-in-
law, so that alliance between the Scots and the Norse Vikings
was cemented by marriage. Moreover, John, alone of all
the chroniclers, records that the coalition fleet entered the
Humber. He records the place of the battle as *Brunanburh*,
and some scholars have suggested that the battle might have
taken place at Brumby in Lincolnshire. At any rate there are
independent traditions in John's chronicle, possibly wrong
but interesting for all that. Symeon of Durham, also writing in
the early 12th century, records the following:

King Æthelstan fought at *Wendune* and put to
flight King Olaf with 615 ships: also Constantine

king of the Scots and the king of the Cumbrians
with all their host.

Elsewhere Symeon writes of the battle taking place at
Brunanburh, so this different name looks like a mistake.
Symeon gives us an improbable number of ships, a not untypi-
cal 'improvement' which enhances the significance of the
battle and the greatness of the victory. William of Malmesbury,
also in the 12th century, records a lengthy version of the battle
in verse, though there is not much new about it. In a prose
addition, there is quite a bit of legendary material, but the
basic details are as they are in the poem. New information
includes the fact that Ælwine and Æthelwine, Æthelstan's
cousins, died in the battle, and were buried at Malmesbury.

One final source, from the 13th century, is *Egils saga*, an
Icelandic prose text. There are problems with the chronology
of the saga in relation to events in England, but the broad
outlines of the battle are clearly there. The Icelanders Egil
and his brother Thorolf, whom we have met before as raiders
and traders, fight on the side of King Æthelstan in a battle at
Vinheith, near a wood and a fort. The fight is preceded by a
whole week of preparations and parleying of all kinds, including Æthelstan making generous offers of payment to
the Scots, Irish and Welsh if they will withdraw. In the battle
the coalition forces break first and run, they are pursued by
Æthelstan and his men, and since they had refused the offer
of peace before the battle, no quarter is given to those fleeing.
Like all the sources, the saga summarizes, 'King Æthelstan
won a very great victory there.' Thorolf dies in the battle, and
at the feast afterwards, Egil plays murderously with his sword
and takes no part in the festivities until he is personally com-
pensated by the king for his brother's death.

WHERE WAS THE BATTLE?

Each of these sources has its difficulties and novelties. One of the persistent problems is the location of the battle. We are given several varying locations: Æthelweard locates it at *Brunandune*, Symeon at *Wendune*. The Old English poem refers to the place of the battle as *Brunanburh*, and the water by which the fleeing forces escaped as *Dingesmere*. John of Worcester asserts that the coalition forces came via the Humber. *Egils saga* refers to the place as *Vinheith*. But we can find a way through these confusing accounts by taking them as complementary rather than contradictory, as each giving us a clue to the whole picture. We see that the names *Brunandune* and *Wendune* end in *-dune*, a word which in some of its senses overlaps with the Norse *-heith* in *Vinheith*: 'open, uncultivated land'. The first part of the English forms, *Brunan-*, looks like a personal name, Bruna. Putting these together, we have 'Bruna's open land', which may be the name of the land on which the battle was fought. Now *Egils saga* mentions a fort being near the battle site. It is therefore perfectly explicable that the poem refers to the battle by the name of the nearest settlement, 'Bruna's fort', or *Brunanburh*.

The evidence suggests that the battle took place in the north-west of England, in Mercia. There are three place-names in this region that probably derive from the personal name Bruna with various other elements attached: Bromborough, Brimstage and the now-lost Brimston on the Wirral. And although *Brunanburh* is not found as an exact early form of the name Bromborough, the forms which are found (such as *Brunburg*, early 12th century), are those which would be expected to develop from the proposed original. Moreover, the same scholar whose research gave us this information, convincingly argued that *Dingesmere* may well mean 'expanse of water associated with the River Dee', possibly the

Dee estuary. Although we do not know exactly what happened, it is therefore possible, discounting John of Worcester's tradition, to propose Bromborough on the Wirral as the site of the battle. We can imagine that Æthelstan trapped the enemy coalition forces on the English side of the Mersey and shadowed them to Bromborough, where he attacked and routed them. The battle can thus with some certainty be located in that politically sensitive area of northern and western Mercia, surrounded on all sides by potential enemies before the battle, by cowed and demoralized tributaries after it.

THE POEM

The poem (Text 2) is unusual in that it was inserted into the prose historical texts, copied from an original which was circulated to the different centres where the *Chronicle* versions were compiled. It is the first of a series of poems in the *Chronicle* manuscripts: there is another poem, *The Capture of the Five Boroughs*, concerning Edmund's victories in the east Midlands, inserted under 942, a poem on Edgar's coronation in 973, another on his death two years later. It is evident that the *Brunanburh* poem was circulated by Æthelstan's 'press office', as other bulletins were, following King Alfred's establishment of something like a central information office around 891 – and it was adopted almost verbatim by the chroniclers. The main manuscripts of the *Anglo-Saxon Chronicle* have no further information about the events of this year. And of course the poem is very much about a victory, with the particular heroic spin that victories have in Old English poetry, rather than the prosaic accounts that we find elsewhere.

Brunanburh has the preoccupations of most heroic poetry. Heroic poetry originated in the ethos of the warband in

the early years AD. This was the Migration Age, when the
Germanic tribes moved into new territories, including most
of the Roman Empire and England itself. The major concerns of
heroic poetry are battle and glory, loyalty and personal honour
among warriors. Curiously, the two poems at the core of this
chapter are, apart from the *Battle of Finnsburh* or *Finn Fragment*
and the parallel episode in *Beowulf*, the two clearest examples of
heroic poetry in Old English – curiously, because they are both
from Christian times, when the warband ethic and its expression had been modified to some degree if not by Christian
principle, then at least by the establishment of a church which
had control over the survival of literature. While they have a
similar informing heroic spirit, the poems on the battles of
Brunanburh and Maldon are radically different. Of course the
first is about an overwhelming victory, while the second concerns a crushing defeat. But in addition, the first revels in fierce
joy, with the only apparent Christian references being such as to
reinforce the magnificence of the victory, whereas the second,
The Battle of Maldon, calls into play all kinds of Christian and
religious ideas in order to cope with the defeat.

There are just the slightest echoes of biblical images in
Brunanburh.

> The plain darkened
> with the blood of warriors after the sun,
> glorious heavenly body, bright candle of God,
> the eternal Lord, rose up in the morning,
> glided over the vast expanse, until the noble creation
> sank to its setting-place. There lay many a warrior
> destroyed by spears, Northern men
> shot over their shields, likewise also Scotsmen,
> weary, had had their fill of battle. The West Saxons
> advanced in troops for the entire day,

pursued in their tracks the hateful peoples,
fiercely hacked those fleeing from the battle from behind
with milled-edged swords. The Mercians did not withhold
hard battle-play from anyone among the warriors
– those who had come to the land with Olaf
in the ship's bosom over the heaving water,
doomed to death in battle. Five young kings
lay dead on the battlefield,
snuffed out by swords, likewise also
seven chiefs of Olaf's, and innumerable warriors,
both Vikings and Scots.

All this is expressed in conventional heroic terms. But there is a curious parallel between the poem and a story in the Old Testament book of Joshua, chapter 10. Here a coalition of five Amorite kings attack the forces of Israel under Joshua. Catching the enemy by surprise, Joshua puts them to flight. He prays that the sun might stand still so that he can finish his enemies off, pursuing them from the rear. It does so, and after the battle he executes the five kings. The monastic readers of the poem in the manuscripts of the *Anglo-Saxon Chronicle* might well recognize an echo of Joshua's exploits, and God's support and help for him, in this heroic poem.

The image of the sun's rising and setting works even without this parallel. The Old English word for 'noble' and its derivatives is *æthel*. The sun is a 'noble creation' and this nobility links it with Æthelstan (literally 'noble stone') and Edmund, the prince or *ætheling*, who do what comes naturally to noble men (*geæthele*, line 7) in battle. So as the noble sun progresses from its rising to its setting, Æthelstan and Edmund, the nobles, are in the ascendant. The poet tells us towards the end that their ancestors came from the east, the place of the sunrise. The Scots and the Norsemen who came from the north and the west, sink like the sun as it goes down. The image of the sun is a simple device, but it is fully exploited in the rhetoric of the poem.

The poem is highly rhetorical and this gives it a very sharp focus. It is a panegyric, a song of praise and victory, and in its delight at the outcome of the battle, it may seem to lack subtlety. But that may be because it uses subtlety in the service of a very obvious message. The Old English device of understatement is here, with slightly ironic vocabulary: the Mercians did not withhold sword-play from the Vikings. But most particularly this device is used in the form of *litotes*, the denial of a proposition for emphasis, to pour scorn on the defeated. Constantine had no reason to delight in the battle; he had no reason to boast; and Olaf and the tatters of his army had no reason to laugh about the battle. Implied in each denial is of course the utter discomfiture of Constantine, Olaf and their men, and perhaps at the same time, good cause for exultation, boasting and laughing among the English.

There is a hint or two of humour here too. In line 19 we are told the Scots were 'shot over their shields'. The pronunciation of *Scot* and *shot* were the same in Old English, and the grim pun would not have been missed by the audience. The poet refers to Constantine as a grey-haired and experienced warrior, terms of respect in normal circumstances; but then as he warms to his theme, he modifies this by calling Constantine a 'wily old devil' in line 46. The word used here, *inwidda*, is used in other places for Satan and demons. And the picture of Olaf, a great Viking king, at the prow of his ship (and the poet mercilessly borrows the Old Norse word for a ship, *cnear*, for this) is rather punctured by the fact that he is at the prow not to wave regally, but to push it out so that he can flee – a rough equivalent would be a Prime Minister push-starting his Daimler to escape from the Leader of the Opposition.

The rhetorical pinpointing of the differences between the two sides is taken further as the poem goes on, when implication gives way to explicit contrast. From line 53, we see the miserable, shamed Norsemen go back to Ireland; the rejoicing brothers go back to the land of the West Saxons exultant. Then the poet tells us that they left the unholy trinity of battle to enjoy the feast: the raven, the eagle and the wolf remain to clean up the biggest slaughter that was ever known since the days when the Anglo-Saxons conquered the Britons many years ago and gained the land for themselves. By contrast, Constantine left behind him his own son dead on the battlefield, having gained nothing in the clash.

Brunanburh is a very skilful poem. What it lacks in nuance it definitely gains in rhetorical power. What it omits in the way of historical detail, it makes up for in its perception of the historical significance of the event. *Brunanburh* uses the inherited resources of the old tradition in much the same way as heroic poetry of earlier ages. Its metre is regular, as befits an official production, and the other poems inserted in the *Anglo-Saxon Chronicle* suffer by comparison. It perfectly expresses the Anglo-Saxon pride in the victory which concentrated power in the hands of the West Saxon kings. This was a turning-point in Anglo-Saxon history, and it seems appropriate that the *Chronicle* should break into song.

The 'hero' of the poem is the English people. Æthelstan and his brother are the noble leaders of the army, who returned from the battle in triumph. But it is not particularly Æthelstan who stands out: more space is given to the sun, the defeated leaders Constantine and Olaf, and indeed the beasts of carrion which clean up at the end. This shows us a king who is confident that his people's glory is his glory, his people's victory is his own, and their heroic spirit is his also. Æthelstan was content to let the traditional art of poetry tell the story for posterity.

THE BATTLE OF MALDON (TEXT 12)

Half a century later and things have changed. In 980 seven ships of Vikings attacked Southampton; in 982 three ships attacked Portland in Dorset; in 988 there was an attack on Watchet in Somerset. There were several attacks on Wales that are not noted in the Anglo-Saxon sources. These attacks were small in scale, probably the kind of summer vacation activity that is depicted in the Icelandic sagas. Certainly there was no cause for general alarm. But the fleet of 991 was different. It was certainly much larger, though persistent records of more than 90 ships may be doubted. And the leader of this fleet is named: it was Olaf Tryggvason, along with his uncle Josteinn, and someone called Guthmund, son of Steita. This was still a roving force apparently in search of plunder, which years of peace and plenty had given in abundance to England at this time. Before landing on the island of Northey near Maldon, the fleet had sacked Ipswich and Sandwich. The attraction of Maldon was undoubtedly the mint there: a source of ready money. There is no record of an actual sacking of Maldon, but they got 10,000 pounds weight of silver, the tribute they were looking for.

The following year, the Viking fleet sailed around East Anglia; in 993 the fleet moved north and sacked Bamburgh; the year after London was attacked but repelled the fleet, which then harried on the south coast. King Æthelred made a treaty in 994 with Olaf Tryggvason, Josteinn and Guthmund, in which he promised to give them winter quarters and food, and tribute as long as they stopped the harrying. The amount of tribute rises steadily: from 10,000 pounds in 991, it was 72,000 in 1016, and though we might doubt the precise figures, there are plenty of rune-stones in Sweden recording the fact that Vikings from there took geld in England, in the raiding and under Cnut as king of England (Text 7).

On 9 August 991, the fleet landed at Northey in the tidal estuary of the Blackwater near Maldon in Essex. Northey is an island at high tide, but connected to the mainland at low tide by a causeway. The island itself is roughly one and a half kilometres square, and the causeway is about 200 metres long. Geologists calculate that it would have been shorter in 991, perhaps 130 metres or so, and therefore it would be possible to shout over it or to shoot arrows over it, as men do in the poem about the battle. However, at either end of the causeway are saltings of muddy land and scrub grass which add perhaps another 100 metres to the effective distance between the two areas of firm land on the island and on the mainland.

Byrhtnoth was the leader of the English forces. He was a pious man and benefactor of monasteries, but also a warrior from the old heroic mould, and something of an elder statesman in the country. His lands were considerable, and he was ealdorman, or governor, of Essex. Hearing that the Vikings were encamped on Northey, he called out the Essex militia, men from the local estates who were responsible for fighting when necessary. Each estate of five hides had to provide one man for armed service, and if the response was quick Byrhtnoth should have had available around 4,000 men. If the figure of 93 or 94 ships of Vikings is correct, the Vikings may have numbered around 3,000, possibly more, although we cannot be precise: the numbers may have grown in the telling, and all the vessels may well not have been warships.

In tactical terms, Byrhtnoth had the advantage initially because he stood between the Vikings and the money at

Maldon. His forces were drawn up along the mainland side of the causeway. But the Viking force was more mobile, and impregnable on the island without a large English fleet – which was not in existence at the time. According to the poem, the Vikings offered Byrhtnoth a choice: pay up or suffer the consequences. Byrhtnoth was not a man to take threats quietly, and ensured that any Viking attempting to cross the causeway did not get very far. But having prevented the Vikings crossing the narrow causeway, he must have realized he was in no position to take the island by storm. And while his forces were probably growing by the hour, as the Vikings were cut off from the mainland by high tide, the accumulation of men at Maldon necessarily meant that other areas would be vulnerable. Byrhtnoth might not wish, therefore, to turn down the offer of a pitched battle, even if he could. Implicit in the Vikings' offer to sail away and keep the peace if they got the money, was the threat that they would sail away and wreak havoc if they did not. Byrhtnoth accordingly allowed the Vikings to cross the causeway, was killed, and his death precipitated a mass desertion. A few men remained, fighting to the death, and encouraging one another in the heroic duty of attempting to avenge their lord in the battle.

SOURCES
The Battle of Maldon is different from Brunanburh in many ways. The only known manuscript was fragmentary when it was bound into a book with others concerned with the Vikings. It was copied out and printed before the manuscript was burned in the disastrous fire of 1731 which decimated the library of Sir Robert Cotton. The poem gives us rather more information than any of the other sources, especially about the site and details of the progress of the battle. While the story as given in the poem is inevitably literary rather than

documentary, there are certain details in the other sources which might suggest either that the poem was quite widely known, or that traditions about the battle circulated independently. There are brief accounts of events in the *Anglo-Saxon Chronicle*, in Byrhtferth of Ramsey's *Life of St Oswald* from around the year 1000, and several mentions in 12th-century histories and monastic records.

There are two slightly different accounts in versions of the *Anglo-Saxon Chronicle*. Both accounts mention the death of Byrhtnoth and the victory of the Vikings; the Peterborough Chronicle mentions the beginning of the policy of paying tribute. In Byrhtferth of Ramsey's *Life of St Oswald* there are certain parallels with the poem. Both sources talk about Byrhtnoth's grey hair, his bravery, his prayers and good deeds, his having a personal retinue, his encouragement to all the others to fight to the death. Byrhtnoth's size is a feature of sources outside the poem, and analysis of his bones has confirmed that he was probably a big man. The *Life of St Oswald* additionally depicts Byrhtnoth as a protector of the church, mentioning that in the turmoil after the death of Edgar, he was among those defending the monasteries in a council at which a man was killed. The *Life* also gives a detail found nowhere else, stating that the Viking army was so depleted after the battle that they could hardly man their ships.

The account in the *Liber Eliensis*, or *Book of Ely*, is most interesting. According to this source there were two battles, four years apart. In preparation for the second battle, Byrhtnoth was marching south and was not given hospitality by Wulfsige, abbot of Ramsey, but was welcomed by Ælfsige, abbot of Ely. This information was repeated in the *Ramsey Chronicle*, and explains why Byrhtnoth's donations to Ely, known from various sources, were greater than those to Ramsey. Overall there is quite a bit of overlap between the poem and this account: the defence of the causeway is mentioned, a second message from the Vikings, which caused Byrhtnoth to let them across the water to the mainland, details of Byrhtnoth generally. There is a problem in that Wulfsige is not known to have been abbot of Ramsey before 1006. But overall, it is reasonable to conclude that traditions about Byrhtnoth and the battle at Maldon circulated around East Anglia and developed especially at Ely because of Byrhtnoth's generosity to the monastery there.

HEROIC CONVENTIONS

The poem is deeply imbued with the heroic spirit. All the positive heroic clichés are used of the English: time and again we have the stress on not fleeing a foot's space, not caring for life, fighting as long as they could wield weapons, fulfilling boasts, repaying gifts, being loyal to one's lord, having courage and focused intention, avenging and obeying Byrhtnoth, using broad and bright-edged swords, applying proverbs which summarize their duties and loyalties, even down to the use of a dignified verb (*mathelian*) for their speeches, with which we might wish to contrast the uncouth 'errand' that the messenger sends to Byrhtnoth.

The interchange between Byrhtnoth and the Viking messenger is a brilliant set-piece, a 'flyting' or formal swapping of demands and insults. The messenger makes his insulting offer that the Vikings will leave for the cheap, simple and very prudent payment of tribute that they demand, with all the assumptions of superiority it implies. Byrhtnoth replies saying that the English will give rich heirlooms to the Vikings, but that these will be weapons and the Vikings will not find them useful in the way they want. Byrhtnoth states his heroic loyalty to his lord, King Æthelred, and his determination to defend the land, and when the battle is joined and Byrhtnoth is killed, the theme of loyalty is elaborated over and over again.

The second half of the poem follows roughly the same repeated pattern: an Englishman steps forward, makes a speech declaring his lineage, his intention to avenge his lord, and encouraging his companions to do the same, before he fulfils that intention and dies in the battle. Many of these men say something about what they are doing and why they are doing it: Ælfwine remembers the promises they had made at the banquet, and recalls that Byrhtnoth was both his lord and his kinsman, so he has a double responsibility to avenge him; Offa curses the sons of Odda for running away, and urges each one of those who remain to encourage the others; Leofsunu vows to avenge his lord and not to suffer the ignominy of lordlessness; Dunnere simply expresses in a proverb the duty of striving to avenge one's lord. And so it goes on. But the thing to notice about these passages, in direct speech and in the course of the narrative, is that these are people with fathers and grandfathers, a lord, brothers and kinsmen, people who know the kind of gossip that circulates in Sturmer village. They have relationships and obligations, a sense of companionship and a noble aim.

Many of the names given to characters and their relations in the poem can be reasonably traced to actual people who owned land locally, attended the king's meetings and signed charters which still exist. Sturmer, for example, is a hamlet on the River Stour near Haverhill in Essex. But more than that, it was clearly the poet's intention to individualize as wide a range of men as possible: we have the powerful and wealthy Offa and Leofsunu, and the simple farmer Dunnere; we have old Byrhtwold and young Wulfmær; we have the Mercian Ælfwine and the Northumbrian hostage Æscferth, who fights on the English side; we have the pure-blood English Wulfstan alongside the man of Scandinavian descent Maccus. Wistan, one of the loyal English, also has a father with a Scandinavian name, Thurstan. But the loyalty these men have to Byrhtnoth overcomes any temptation they might feel to side with the Vikings.

This elaborate detail about the English is in marked contrast to the depiction of the Vikings, not one of whom is named in the poem, and whose only motivation seems to be to despoil the English. As Byrhtnoth falls wounded, a Viking tries to strip his body of its valuable trappings even before Byrhtnoth is dead. While many of the words used for the Vikings in the poem are the normal words for warriors, and they are used indifferently of men on either side, the poet chooses to emphasize this rapacious, scavenging side of the Vikings. In the lines dealing with Byrhtnoth's concession of land, the slyness of the Vikings is emphasized: they 'began to use cunning' by asking Byrhtnoth for a free passage over the causeway. And here the poet twice uses the word 'hateful'. Then in line 96, the poet refers to the Vikings as 'wolves of slaughter'. In lines 106–7 we see the carrion eaters anticipating the battle and the feast ahead, the ravens circling and the eagle preparing itself. But usually the beasts of battle, as in *Brunanburh*, are three: wolf, raven and eagle, and the wolf is missing at this point. The poet has made the Vikings into wolves, a pack of animals hunting and greedily savaging their prey. In all, then, the poet develops a sharp contrast between the anonymous and animalized Vikings, and the humanized, motivated, heroic, socially cohesive band of English warriors.

DEFEAT AND VICTORY

For all this, though, the English were badly defeated in the battle of Maldon. Whose fault was it? One of the implications of the characterization of the Vikings is that these cunning, hateful, bestial, heathen creatures, *en masse*, were merely the occasion of the failure of the English, not the cause. The poet certainly criticizes Byrhtnoth for allowing the Vikings across the causeway, even if the criticism can be found only in two or three lines. Byrhtnoth was guilty of excessive courage and excessive generosity: he granted the Vikings too much land. Byrhtnoth no longer has control of the battle and its progress when he acknowledges, as he makes way for the Vikings, 'Only God knows who will control the battlefield.' The poet takes a pragmatic view, seeing Byrhtnoth's action as mistaken, but he also depicts Byrhtnoth as idealistic, taking upon himself responsibility for the defence of King Æthelred's people and land.

The other most obvious example of blame is the flight of the cowards. After the death of Byrhtnoth, the sons of Odda steal Byrhtnoth's horse and run away from the battle.

> They turned then from the battle, those who did not
> > want to be there.
> The sons of Odda were first in the flight
> from the battle there, and Godric abandoned the
> > good man
> who had often given him many a mare.
> He mounted the horse that had been his lord's,
> and got into the trappings, as was not right;
> and his brothers Godwine and Godwig
> both ran with him. They did not care for battle,
> but ran away from the fight and sought the wood,
> fled to the place of safety and saved their lives,
> and with them more men than was at all proper,
> if they had remembered all the favours
> that he had done for their benefit.

There is an ironic inversion of the heroic gift-giving here: the lord gave gifts to his retainers to ensure their loyalty in battle. But in an act of supreme disloyalty, Godric steals his lord's horse to run from a battle. The two most overly moralistic comments by the poet also occur here: Godric stole the horse *as was not right*; and more men fled *than was at all proper*. Once again the poet strikes the pragmatic note: some men running away is inevitable, but more men fled than should have done. It was simply not fitting that so many should have run. The poet is very forthright in his condemnation of Godric and his brothers. They abandoned all principle and were motivated simply by the instinct for survival. But it is not the poet in his own voice who interprets the significance of the flight of the cowards, it is Offa, Byrhtnoth's second-in-command:

> Godric the cowardly
> son of Odda has betrayed us all.
> Too many men thought when he was riding away
>   on the horse,
> that proud steed, that it was our lord.
> Because of that the army was split here on the
>   battlefield,
> and the shield-wall broken. Curse his trick,
> that he put to flight so many men here!

The responsibility for the now inevitable defeat lies not with the Vikings, who do not merit a mention in these two passages, but with the cowards. It was they who tricked, who put to flight, who split the army, and who broke the shield-wall of the English, not the Vikings.

MORAL VICTORY

There are several different ways of responding to a defeat, whether in battle or these days perhaps in sport. The first is to see defeat as expected and therefore not a disappointment: as King Æthelred's reign progressed, this was the stance taken by the chroniclers, who despaired of any effective resistance. Second is to suggest that 'we' should have won, but adopted the wrong tactics or made significant mistakes: this is partly the approach taken by the poet and the characters in the poem. A third reaction is that 'we' deserved to win because in some way we were better than the opposition, and therefore we had a moral victory. This is the principal tack taken by the poet.

One of the ways the English win a moral victory is in the location of the battle not only in the physical but also the mental sphere. The initial skirmish of the battle is the debate between Byrhtnoth and the Viking messenger, which Byrhtnoth wins. The ultimate victory does not go to those who control the battlefield by brute force, but to those whose hearts and minds remain undefeated even in death. There is a remarkable emphasis throughout the poem on attitude and intention: the mental and physical processes are interwoven. The poem opens with Byrhtnoth commanding his men to concentrate on courage; Offa's kinsman realizes Byrhtnoth will not put up with slackness and signals his intention of not weakening by immediately joining the army. The thread of intention and mental focus continues throughout the poem, especially after Byrhtnoth's death where the warriors need to encourage each other, and each one declares his intention of avenging his lord or of dying in the attempt. Finally, Byrhtwold sums up the whole position:

Resolve must be the firmer, heart the braver,
courage the greater, as our strength diminishes.

This focus is lacking in the cowards: they did not want to be
fighting, they did not care for battle, they did not remember
what Byrhtnoth had done for them. So the loyal retainers win
a moral victory.

But most striking is the way the poet portrays Byrhtnoth.
He is everything he should be in heroic virtue and experience.
His boldness of speech is matched by boldness of action. He is
overconfident and too generous to the Vikings, certainly, and
is criticized for that. But that all is forgiven cannot be doubted,
not only as each of the retainers vows loyalty, but especially as
Byrhtnoth dies. This is the poet's trump card. When he is
dying, Byrhtnoth looks up to heaven and prays to God, asking
that his soul might pass into God's keeping in peace; at the
end of his prayer, it is the heathens who kill him.

He looked up towards heaven:
'Thank you, Lord of the nations,
for all the joys that I have experienced on earth.
Now, kind Lord, my greatest need is that
you grant grace to my spirit,
that my soul might be allowed to journey to you,
travel in peace into your control,
Lord of the angels. I beseech you
that hellish attackers may not be allowed to harm it.'
Then heathen men hacked him to pieces,
and both the warriors who stood beside him.

The death scene is modelled on the death of the saint or
martyr in hagiography. Like St Stephen, the first Christian
martyr in the Acts of the Apostles, and numerous saints

thereafter, Byrhtnoth looks up to heaven and prays; like Christ on the cross he commends his soul to God. Not only that, but the poet adds little details which encourage the audience to think of Byrhtnoth as Christlike: he dies between two others of less significance, as Christ died upon the cross; he effectively sacrifices himself for the sake of his people; and there are twelve named retainers of Byrhtnoth in the poem after his death, which might suggest the twelve disciples of Christ (or then again it might just be an accident, as the poem is fragmentary).

The poem is not unique in this approach, though it takes a more clearly definable form in the verse. Most of the later sources that mention Byrhtnoth see him as a Christian warrior, a pious and devout man who was a great supporter of the monasteries and the Christian cause. The *Book of Ely* records that his head was cut off in the battle, the traditional fate of Christian martyrs. He was buried in Ely cathedral and in later years Archbishop Wulfstan and other saintly confessors were buried alongside. The relics of all were treated with special reverence there. Making Byrhtnoth a saint, or strongly hinting at his sanctity and martyrdom, elevates him and effectively places him beyond criticism. His victory is the ultimate one: he reigns eternally in heaven with Christ, beyond time and chance, above petty tyrannies and reverses. There could be no greater victory, and it is no accident that his retainers pray that they might be able to avenge their lord and kill their enemies. These men have their part in the ultimate victory too.

If the English people were the hero of *The Battle of Brunanburh*, there can be no doubt who was the hero of *The Battle of Maldon*. Byrhtnoth is the man whose character permeates the poem. He is the friendly adviser to his men, calming the fearful, instructing the headstrong. He is the master of words who flays the Viking messenger with his own rhetoric. He is the tactical general who prevents the first attack, then weighs up the options to give away the advantage in the hope of all-out victory. He is the one man the English could not afford to lose, and the one whose loss precipitates the flight of the cowards. It is loyalty to Byrhtnoth which motivates and strengthens the arms of the failing few. He is flawed but glorious. Later tradition makes him larger than life, standing physically taller than anyone else, but his spiritual stature is clear from the start. He is a great man.

A POSTSCRIPT FROM THE CHRONICLES

There are two independent *Anglo-Saxon Chronicle* accounts of the events of 991, the Winchester Chronicle and the Peterborough Chronicle. The differences between them are instructive, and reveal a good deal about how the battle and its aftermath were understood. Winchester was Æthelred's capital, and of course the Winchester Chronicle takes a line strongly supportive of the king. As we have seen in earlier chapters, it has (apart from an extended annal in 1001) very little detail at all about the progress of the later Viking wars, and what detail it does have, is positive. This is its account of the year's events:

> 991. In this year Olaf [Tryggvason] came with 93 ships to Folkestone, and harried the area around it. The fleet went from there to Sandwich, then on to Ipswich, which was overrun, and then to Maldon. Ealdorman Byrhtnoth and his army met them and fought against them. They killed the ealdorman there and gained victory on the battlefield. Peace was made with them after that, and the king took Olaf for confirmation at the bishop's hands *on the*

advice of Sigeric bishop of Canterbury and Ælfheah of Winchester.

The passage in italic type is added in a later hand, and the interesting thing about it is that it appears in the other chronicle accounts; not, however, as the good idea of getting Olaf confirmed, but as the advice which prompted the payment of tribute. The Peterborough Chronicle was copied from a northern original, and this chronicle is persistently critical of King Æthelred and English tactics. It drily records,

> 991. In this year Ipswich was harried, and very soon after that Ealdorman Byrhtnoth was killed at Maldon. In that year it was decided that tribute should be given to the Danes because of the great terror that they created around the coast. The first tribute was 10,000 pounds, and the advice was Sigeric the archbishop's.

The Winchester version takes no account of the tribute. It acknowledges the defeat at Maldon, but counters it with a Christian victory when Olaf is confirmed. Olaf became a notable Christian and missionary king, and for some this would more than offset the loss of pride and hard cash. But in this version there is no terror, no tribute, no bad advice. Governmental spin-doctoring is no great novelty. And by comparison with the Winchester Chronicle's selective and revisionist account of events, the poem of *Maldon* shines with sympathy, honesty and Christian hope.

TWO TURNING-POINTS

These two battles were turning-points in the fortunes of the English in the 10th and early 11th centuries. *Brunanburh* established the West Saxon supremacy throughout England, and the poem is a celebration of heroic deeds and royal victory. Its rhetoric is compelling: the English won the battle and worthily defeated the enemy forces, just as Joshua defeated his enemies and the original Anglo-Saxons defeated theirs. In many ways the year 991 was a turning-point in the second part of the Viking Age. It was the end of the old security, and the start of a serious decline in social and political stability. The code of heroism which every man aspired to, and which gave life its reference points in the days of the Anglo-Saxon conquest of Britain, which fired and inspired King Alfred in his fight against the invading Danish, which gave the fierce exultant tone to the poem on the battle of *Brunanburh* as late as 937, ceased to represent the realities of life in the dreary days of King Æthelred. There were still shining examples of courage and devotion, not least among them the men who died at Maldon. But a significant element of disillusionment sets in after Maldon. In part, this must have been a reflection of the attitudes of King Æthelred himself: the *Anglo-Saxon Chronicle* is full of the warlike deeds of King Alfred and the members of his family, the poem on the battle of *Brunanburh* praises the leadership of King Æthelstan and his brother Edmund – but the references to King Æthelred leading in battle or fighting are very sparse indeed. This absence from battle was something that had to be thought about, preached about and justified from the Bible (Text 13).

No hint of criticism of King Æthelred appears in *The Battle of Maldon*, but in the political morass of Æthelred's reign following this battle, the poet was making a very serious point.

Most of the chroniclers see irresolution and disorganization, cowardice and failure to support one another as typical of both leadership and rank and file. In such circumstances, the example of the leader and men at Maldon would become a bright and shining ideal: an ideal within the grasp of the English even yet if they could put their minds to it, if indeed it could enter their souls as a Christian ideal.

5

THE REVIVAL OF
MONASTICISM

In the period of relative peace between the battles of *Brunanburh* and Maldon, English kings had opportunity to focus on the regeneration of Christian life in England. During this same period, the main movement of Christianity on the European continent was towards the reformation of monasticism following the devastation of the Viking attacks. It is probably no accident that English and French Christianity drew closer together, sharing the same ideals, copying each other's practice, exchanging scholars and scholarship: they had suffered similar humiliations in the preceding years and both now needed to reconstruct a form of faith that would be able to grow in the new conditions. English Christianity drew on its history, and the revived monasticism replicated many of the strengths of past monastic practice, but it also changed its emphasis significantly.

CONVERSION AND MONASTICISM

The conversion of Anglo-Saxon England in the seventh century was achieved mainly by missionaries who were monks living in monastic communities. The great flowering of scholarship, art and building in the eighth century was the result of monastic energies being exercised for the glory of God, and no doubt also for the status of the monastic house. Kings and noblemen were patrons, giving lands and privileges to the monasteries. The culture was enriched in many ways by the presence of the monasteries: before the parish, the hospital, the hotel and the orphanage, monks gave pastoral care and Christian teaching, and the basic practical care needed by the traveller and the unfortunate.

There are many parallels between the conversion period and the period of revival of monasticism in the second half of the 10th century. Scholars have occasionally expressed surprise that the re-establishment of monasticism was the means by which Christianity recovered its hold on the population of England after the first wave of attacks by the Vikings. But the lessons of history were clear to a number of kings. Churchmen generally were in no doubt that the misfortunes of the time were the result of slackness in faith, and to restore the power of the monasteries was also to restore the power of the nation and the crown. Spiritual and temporal power were dependent on each other, and formal theories about the relationship between them were developed during the ninth and 10th centuries in England.

THE 'THREE ORDERS'

In his translation of Boethius's *Consolation of Philosophy*, King Alfred adds a brief comment on the skill and craftsmanship necessary for the adequate performance of the role of king:

> You know *[Boethius says to Wisdom]* that no one can show any skill, nor exercise any power, nor rule, without tools and materials. The material for each skill is that without which the skill cannot

be exercised. The material of the king, and his tools for ruling, then, is the possession of a well-populated country: he must have people who pray, people for the army and people who work. You know that without these tools no king can demonstrate his skill. And this also is his material: he must have provisions for these tools, for the three orders. And their provision, then, is land to live on, and gifts, and weapons, and food, and ale, and clothes, and whatever else is necessary for the three orders. He cannot keep the tools without these things, and without these tools he cannot do any of those things which he is commanded to do.

The notion of the 'three orders', or three types of people – those who work, those who pray and those who fight – became popular in medieval times, but this is one of the earliest examples of the theme. Although heathenism had some kind of priestly class, the emergence of a distinct order of people concerned mostly with prayer was an innovation of Christianity. In the early Anglo-Saxon law-codes, kings were careful to establish a place within the social hierarchy for bishops, clergy and monastics.

In this passage added to Boethius, Alfred gives emphasis to the kind of provision necessary for the secular warriors, but the application of martial imagery to those whose warfare was in prayer would not have been far from his mind. The perception of monks as warriors goes at least as far back as Bede's account of the battle of Chester, sometime before 616, where the heathen Anglo-Saxon king Æthelfrith killed the Welsh monks who were praying for their side's victory, before defeating the Celtic warriors. 'If they cry to their God against us,' said Æthelfrith, 'then they are fighting us even if they do not carry arms, opposing us with their prayers.'

The great homilist of the revived monasticism, Ælfric, developed the idea of the three orders:

> When there is too much evil among humankind, wise men ought to consider with discerning thought which of the pillars of the throne might be broken, and immediately repair it. The throne stands on these three pillars: *laboratores, bellatores, oratores*. *Laboratores* [workers] are those who labour for our sustenance, ploughmen and farmers devoted to that alone. *Oratores* [those who pray] are those who intercede for us to God and who promote Christianity among Christian nations in God's service. They are devoted to this alone, to spiritual warfare, for the benefit of us all. *Bellatores* [warriors] are those who protect our towns and our homeland, fighting against the roving army with weapons. As St Paul the teacher of the Gentiles said in his teaching, 'The warrior does not bear his sword for no purpose. He is God's servant for your benefit, appointed for vengeance on those who do evil.' On these three pillars stands the throne, and if one is broken, the throne immediately falls to the detriment of the other pillars.

In Ælfric's time, which was also the time of King Æthelred 'the Unready', it was becoming clear that the weakest of the three pillars was the warriors, so once again their role is given emphasis. This was a major change from the time of Alfred, when there can be no doubt that the church was the weakest pillar: a time when the great dioceses of the north of England either ceased to exist or were only intermittently able to appoint bishops; a time when the monasteries that had nurtured Bede and Alcuin disappeared to leave only the ruins, 'pillaged and burnt', that Alfred lamented in his dedicatory letter to his translation of the *Pastoral Care*; a time when the idea of monasticism survived better than any ordered practice of it.

EFFORTS TO RE-ESTABLISH MONASTICISM

The Vikings effectively destroyed English monasticism for a century. King Alfred did his best to re-establish it in his reign, after the attacks died down a little. He provided for the foundation of a new monastery at Athelney, the place where he had hidden from the Vikings, but could find no Englishmen to occupy it. So he had to give it to foreign monks under the abbacy of John the Old Saxon, one of the scholars drawn from abroad by the king. Alfred's foundation for women, at Shaftesbury, seems to have met with more immediate and lasting success. Alfred's widow Ealhswith founded the convent of Nunnaminster in Winchester, and by the time of the death of King Eadred in 955, there was a community of women religious at Wilton in Wiltshire as well as one at Winchester.

Several loose communities of secular clerks, that is, clergy often serving in cathedral churches, but not living under specifically monastic vows, grew up. These communities were at least a form of religious life that could be sustained in the difficult circumstances of the time, and which served the needs of the larger churches. But as circumstances changed and the country settled into a pattern of peace, there was a groundswell of opinion that such communities were neither wholly secular nor wholly monastic and should be either one or the other. A constant theme in letters from popes and church dignitaries to English bishops and kings in the ninth and 10th centuries is the scandal (as they see it) of married clerics. Once monasticism of any kind has been re-established, there is pressure for it to be properly monastic. This was the concern at the root of the monastic reform of the 10th century.

The problem of communities which practised a kind of monasticism but without the rigour of a proper monastic Rule was resolved by the work of three reforming prelates and one especially sympathetic king. Much of the groundwork was done by Dunstan, who became archbishop of Canterbury; Æthelwold, Dunstan's pupil and probable author of the *Regularis Concordia*, became bishop of Winchester and did much to implement the reform in the older monastic foundations, and to establish new houses on reformed principles; Oswald, bishop of Worcester and archbishop of York, founded the monastery of Ramsey and probably others, and gradually transformed the community at Worcester into a regular monastic house. The king was Edgar the Peaceable, 959–75, who gave unstinting support to the reform movement. The characters of these three leaders seem to have been complementary. Dunstan was of a slightly mystical bent, though he had the force of character to oppose King Eadwig and reproach him to his face; Æthelwold was a man of action, with considerable financial acumen; Oswald is referred to in all sources with warmth and reverence. A threefold cord is not easily broken.

DUNSTAN
Dunstan was brought up near Glastonbury and introduced to the court of King Æthelstan. His *Life*, which was written in the flowery Latin of the time, about 20 years after his death,

by a man who refers to himself as 'B', illustrates the closeness of the secular and religious powers in late Anglo-Saxon England. Dunstan's career falls into two phases divided by a time of exile under King Eadwig (955–9), during which he went to St Peter's in Ghent and learned the ways of the reformed Benedictine monasticism.

In the first phase of his career, Dunstan built up the monastery at Glastonbury. Having become estranged from King Edmund through some slander, Dunstan was about to leave the country when the king had a close shave in a riding accident. The first thing that came to his mind after his reprieve, apparently, was the disagreement with Dunstan, and he resolved immediately to set it right. Returning from his hunting, the king forthwith took Dunstan to Glastonbury and instituted him as abbot. Dunstan remained at Glastonbury for the next 15 years, gaining experience of the daily problems and joys of the abbot's life which equipped him for his future as bishop and archbishop, and enabled him to implement the reform of the monasteries.

In due course Dunstan became bishop of Worcester. But his career was interrupted after an incident at the coronation of King Eadwig. When the newly anointed king left his corona-tion banquet to cavort with a certain noblewoman and her daughter, Dunstan and one of his ecclesiastical colleagues, a kinsman of his, determined to restrain Eadwig's unseemly behaviour, and all but dragged him back. Not unsurprisingly, this left Eadwig with little love for the bishop, and Dunstan left for Ghent. But Eadwig died in 959, leaving his brother Edgar king of England. Edgar immediately recalled Dunstan, elevated him to the archbishopric of Canterbury, and threw himself into the business of monastic reform and re-establish-ment. Oswald succeeded Dunstan as bishop of Worcester, and Dunstan's friend and pupil Æthelwold became bishop of

Winchester in 963. What Dunstan had begun, with his support the other two carried out, to such effect that by their
deaths late in the 10th century there were about 40 reformed
monasteries in the south of England.

Dunstan was tenacious as well as mystical, and he worked
hard to maintain his close ties with the king. It has been
observed that he signed as witness every one of King Edgar's
charters that were issued during his archiepiscopate. He was
constantly at the king's elbow, therefore. He was, with Edgar,
responsible for the close association of the throne and the
reform movement that resulted in the formulation of prayers
for the royal family. These prayers entered into the liturgy of
the reform, and there has been a close liturgical connection
between the church and the royal family ever since. Dunstan
died in 988, at the age of nearly 80. He was less close to King
Æthelred than he had been to kings Edmund and Edgar, and
for most of the last decade of his life, he seems to have concentrated on pastoral work and personal prayer.

Many of the miracles attributed to Dunstan concern
visions, prophecies and foreknowledge. These are conventional in the saint's life, but the number and variety of them
hint at the quality of Dunstan's spirituality: an ability to see
beyond the superficial. This insight, we might imagine, was
what gave his advice to kings its value, and what led the determined and active entrepreneur, Æthelwold, to do as he was
asked by Dunstan and forego his monastic vegetarianism for a
while for the sake of his health. In later years an acrimonious
argument arose between Glastonbury and Canterbury as to
which of them possessed Dunstan's relics, so eager were they
for his saintly patronage.

ÆTHELWOLD

Æthelwold's *Life* was written by Wulfstan of Winchester in about 996. Ælfric the homilist and abbot of Eynsham used this work as the basis of his *Life of Æthelwold* about a decade later. The stories recorded by Wulfstan show a man who was perceived as being strong, diligent, merciful and personally ascetic, yet scholars have displayed little affection for Æthelwold. Perhaps his characteristics are ones that appealed more to the Anglo-Saxons than they do to us. Indeed, Æthelwold's strength attracted enmity in his own day, and Wulfstan relates that certain clerics so hated the bishop that they tried to poison him. Like King Alfred, he had some lingering illness which no doubt led to impatience and acerbity on occasion.

Æthelwold was, perhaps above all, an ecclesiastical businessman, buying up the lands of former monasteries and encouraging donations so that he could establish and restore the monasteries. Not all of these purchases came to full fruition: sites at Barton-on-Humber (Lincolnshire) and Breedon-on-the-Hill (Leicestershire), both in the Danelaw and both sites of major pre-Viking monasteries, were bought, but no community came into being during Æthelwold's lifetime.

We can learn a little more of the way Æthelwold was regarded from the stories which became attached to him. Of the many saint-stories in Wulfstan's *Life*, several of the less conventional ones relate to building-site accidents. One occurred to Æthelwold himself, where a post fell on him, knocked him into a pit and broke his ribs. Another man, Godus, fell off a roof during the rebuilding of the Old Minster in Winchester, got up immediately, blessed himself and climbed back to his original place. Asks Wulfstan, 'To whom should this miracle be ascribed, unless it is to the one who had commanded him to go and do this work of obedience', that is, Æthelwold. Another story, that of a thief whose arms were bound by Æthelwold's curse until he confessed, touches on matters financial. Just as the miracle story of Dunstan's harp playing by itself in B's *Life* tells us (if indirectly) something about Dunstan's musical ability, so these miracle stories tell us something about Æthelwold's practical craftsmanship, interest in building, and financial probity.

Early in his career, he was about to leave the country for the Continent when he was, like Dunstan, prevented by royal intervention. Eadgifu, mother of King Eadred, urged her son not to let such a man leave his kingdom, so Eadred gave him the run-down monastery of Abingdon, initially with 40 hides of land. In due course, Æthelwold was given the other 100 hides of the monastery's original land which had been used by the king. The king supported Æthelwold in the work he set himself and involved himself personally in Æthelwold's building projects. Although the hide was a variable area of land, it was reckoned to be able to support a family and its dependants. On this basis we can estimate that the estates of Abingdon in Æthelwold's time would have been in excess of 10,000 acres.

There is evidence that Æthelwold got on rather better with King Eadwig, Eadred's successor, than did Dunstan. Although Wulfstan simply writes Eadwig out of Æthelwold's *Life*, we know from other sources that the king married Ælfgifu, the daughter of the woman with whom he had cavorted on the occasion of the coronation banquet. The *Anglo-Saxon Chronicle* records that Archbishop Oda separated the royal couple in 958 because they were too closely related, but a charter from Abingdon under Æthelwold bears the signature of Ælfgifu, designated 'the king's wife', implying that the relationship was acknowledged there.

In fact a good deal of political manoeuvring was going on at this time. The future King Edgar, Archbishop Oda,

Dunstan and the monastic party, were set against King Eadwig, Ælfgifu and her powerful kinsmen, who included Ealdorman Ælfhere of Mercia, the leader of the anti-monastic reaction which followed Edgar's death. It may be to Æthelwold's credit that he did not get embroiled in this politicking; perhaps he accepted the king's marriage, trying to work with him for his spiritual good. It might, though, equally well be interpreted as opportunism.

After his elevation to the see of Winchester, Æthelwold vigorously pursued the cause of reform there, and it was from Abingdon that he drew the monks with whom he replaced the Winchester clerics. The Winchester manuscript of the *Anglo-Saxon Chronicle* records under the year 964 that 'King Edgar drove the priests in the city [of Winchester] from the Old Minster and from the New Minster and from Chertsey and from Milton, and replaced them with monks.' According to Wulfstan, however, it was Æthelwold's zeal that purged the scandal. Wulfstan tells us that the clerics in the Old Minster were living scandalously, and that Æthelwold got permission from the king to expel them (Text 14). The clerics inside the church were singing Psalm 2:11–12:

> Serve ye the Lord with fear:
> and rejoice unto him with trembling.
> Embrace discipline:
> lest at any time the Lord be angry,
> and you perish from the just way.

The monks outside interpreted this as divine encouragement to enter and oust the clerics. Æthelwold did the same at the New Minster, and he further established a regular community of nuns at the Nunnaminster in Winchester before buying the land of Ely from the king and establishing a large community of monks there, renovating the buildings and enriching the foundation.

For all his administrative skills and financial acumen, stories told by Wulfstan give another slant on Æthelwold's character. In the great famine of (probably) 976, Æthelwold spent all his money buying food to feed the starving people. And when that was gone, he sold the church plate, just as King Oswald had given a great silver dish to starving peasants outside his banquet in one of Bede's memorable stories. Two stories relate to Æthelwold's reading, in one of which a valuable manuscript was preserved from damage when a nodding Æthelwold dropped a lighted candle on it. In the other, a monk tried to copy or excel Æthelwold's reading, and an angelic visitant gave him a poke in the eye for his pains! Like Dunstan, Æthelwold had visions. He died in 984, much mourned by rich and poor, monk and nun, and stories of healings at his tomb soon began to circulate.

OSWALD

Less is known of Oswald, the other member of the trio of leaders. A *Life* written by Byrhtferth of Ramsey is concerned as much with the events during his life which affected Ramsey and the other monasteries, as with the man himself. Chief among these events were the anti-monastic reaction following the death of King Edgar, and then the renewal of Viking attacks; but the *Life* also gives details of the murder of King Edward, Æthelred's brother and predecessor. These matters are given full treatment, and the *Life* provides some interesting background on, among others, Byrhtnoth the hero of the battle of Maldon (see chapter 4).

Oswald was related to two archbishops with Scandinavian names: he was nephew of Archbishop Oda of Canterbury, and kin to Oscytel of York. He was descended, according to

Byrhtferth, from a Danish warrior who had been in the army of 'Hinguar', Ivarr the Boneless, who had killed King Edmund of East Anglia. His family was wealthy, and although Oswald spent a good deal of his life away from the Danelaw, he used his connections to promote monastic reform there, principally in the monastery of Ramsey. This monastery he, together with Æthelwine the ealdorman of East Anglia, founded in about 970, and he endowed it with 39 hides of land from his personal wealth. His attempts to re-establish the monastery of Ripon came to nothing, but the former Danelaw was rather dilatory in this respect throughout.

Oswald was professed monk at Winchester, and went abroad to Fleury on the French River Loire, where he observed the reformed monasticism in action. Here Oswald became acquainted with Abbo, one of the outstanding intellects of the day. Abbo visited Ramsey for two years in 985–7, when he was out of favour at Fleury. His teaching at Ramsey is thought to have influenced Byrhtferth, whose scientific and computational work in the *Manual* represents the attempt to pass Abbo's learning on. Abbo picked up information for his *Life of St Edmund* during this time, and the connection between this story of the king's martyrdom at the hands of Hinguar, and Oswald's antecedents may be significant. The litanies of royal martyrs at Ramsey in due course included half a dozen English kings.

Oswald had a hand in founding and reforming many monasteries. He founded Westbury-on-Trym near Bristol in 962, and had a part in the foundation of Deerhurst, Gloucestershire, and the re-establishment of other west Mercian monasteries at Winchcombe, Pershore and Evesham. He became bishop of Worcester in succession to Dunstan in 961, and held that see in plurality with the archbishopric of York from 972 to his death in 992. The existence of numerous

charters granting land to Oswald, or confirming leases of land
by Oswald to others, has led to the suggestion that he was
something of a stockbroker, not over-concerned with ethics so
long as the outcome was favourable, and that this arrangement with regard to the sees of York and Worcester was a
convenience if not a contrivance. Be this as it may, the
arrangement lasted until the end of King Æthelred II's reign,
24 years after Oswald's death.

Despite the detail relating to contemporary events, in the
Life of Oswald Byrhtferth adopts the style of hagiography and
gives only the minimum of dates and names, thus locating the
action in the spiritual realm. The *Life* is also a highly wrought
literary work with extensive allusions to the Bible and theological literature. This tells us something about Byrhtferth,
but perhaps less about Oswald himself. Byrhtferth claimed
that Oswald's reforms of Worcester cathedral were more
leisurely than those of Æthelwold at Winchester. In this he
was contradicted by the 12th-century *Ramsey Chronicle*;
nevertheless, Oswald's leases were witnessed by members of
the Worcester community and there was no 'mass redun-
dancy' involved in the reform. There is, indeed, something
easy-going about Oswald, with his fine physique, his wealth
and connections, his ease at court and his splendid voice. His
devotion to washing the feet of the poor is recorded more
than once, and this particular discipline, widely practised, was
enshrined in the liturgy of Maundy Thursday in the *Regularis
Concordia*. He died in 992, and was particularly venerated at
Worcester.

ROYAL PATRONAGE

The reform movement was heavily dependent upon royal
patronage. According to their biographers, all three of the
leaders were advisers to King Edgar. This closeness to royal

power and patronage is reflected in the *Regularis Concordia* or 'Monastic Agreement', which came out of the synod held at Winchester in the later years of King Edgar. The *Regularis Concordia* was designed to regulate and give consistency to the practice of Benedictine monasticism in England, 'lest by unequal and various use of one rule in one country their holy life should be brought into disrepute', as the preface remarks. It draws extensively on Continental sources, as well as claiming common custom and usage as the source of its practices.

But unlike almost any Continental sources, the *Regularis Concordia* starts and continues with the king. The king prompts the discussion, his wisdom is praised, his advice and consent are sought for such things as episcopal appointments. Prayers and psalms for the royal family are inserted after most of the liturgical hours and after the Mass. The Agreement generally is written in the ornate and mannered style called 'hermeneutic' because it draws on abstruse and difficult words from glossaries. The prayers for the royal family and other collects, however, are in a recognizably liturgical Latin, but more restrained in style, which might give some substance to the claim that they were shaped by custom rather than coined by Æthelwold:

> Almighty God, we beseech thee that thy servant our king, who by thy mercy has undertaken the government of this kingdom, may also receive increase of all virtues; and that furnished in seemly fashion with these, he may have power to avoid the evils of wickedness, to overcome his enemies, and to come to thee, who art the way, the truth and the life. Through our Lord.

THE REGULARIS CONCORDIA
The core of the Agreement is a detailed expansion of the liturgical rites of the Benedictine Rule. The liturgical psalms, prayers, hymns and actions are all set out for the various seasons and days of the year. The *opus dei*, the divine service, is at the centre of the monastic day, and all other activities fit round it. Changes from earlier forms of Benedictinism are evident, many of them added to Benedict of Nursia's practice by his later namesake, Benedict of Aniane. A particular practice was the additional and repeated singing of the seven penitential psalms, but other psalms and offices were also included at various points in the day. The result was that the divine service in Benedict of Nursia's original monasteries, taking about four hours each day, was augmented to occupy most of the monk's waking hours. And the casualty was the time spent in manual labour and reading. Most manual work was now done by servants of the monastery, not by the monks themselves. The division between the *orator* and the *laborator* was more sharply drawn under the *Regularis Concordia* than ever before in English monasticism.

ÆLFRIC'S COLLOQUY
At the end of the 10th century Abbot Ælfric wrote a dialogue for the boys in his monastic school. It was designed to teach them some rather abstruse Latin vocabulary, so it takes the form of a teacher asking questions, as it were interviewing the boys. And the boys play the parts of various tradesmen, who talk about their work and list the things they do. It may be pressing the evidence of the *Colloquy* (as it is called) too far to suggest that it accurately represents the kind of estate-management, commercial interests and cottage industries that the larger monastery maintained, but the dialogue seems to

offer us at least a glimpse of the real life and work of the monasteries. In order to support its spiritual labours, the monastery might well have required a host of ploughmen, shepherds, oxherds, huntsmen, fishermen, fowlers, merchants, shoemakers, salters, bakers and cooks.

Ælfric was too good a teacher to make his *Colloquy* just a list of vocabulary to test whether his boys knew the difference between the Latin words for herring, salmon and sturgeon. The *Colloquy* has some features of drama, with elementary characterization, and it also slips in social and religious comment. The ploughman lugubriously lists all the work he has to do and comments that it is hardship because he is not free, that is, he is a slave. By contrast the shepherd and huntsman are free men, the one doing his relatively menial tasks of guarding the sheep against wolves, milking them and making butter and cheese; the other practising the complex arts of hunting. The shepherd marks his status by saying, 'I am loyal to my lord'; the huntsman does his hunting for the king and the king gives him his clothing, food and gifts of horses or rings – these things indicate that the huntsman is of noble status.

The characterization in this dialogue is elementary, but not without interest. The interviewer comments to the huntsman that he must be a brave man to spear the wild boar, and the huntsman replies with a maxim that could almost have come out of a heroic poem, 'A huntsman must not be timid, because all sorts of wild animals live in the woods.' The qualities of fearlessness and alertness are the qualities of the warrior as much as the huntsman. By contrast the fisherman prefers to catch small fry rather than tangle with whales, and explains this preference as the result of his cowardice. It is not impossible that the noble, fearless hunter and the cowardly sailor-fisherman are deliberately being contrasted by Ælfric, bolstering up the idea of the loyal warrior supporting both the king and the monastery, as against cowardly sailors. But it might be doubted that anybody would make the identification of the fisherman and the Vikings.

The support of the monastery is important in matters of doctrine as well as defence, as is shown by oblique references to some practices that now appear strange. The huntsman does not hunt on a Sunday, a Christian adaptation of one of the Ten Commandments; and the fisherman throws back 'unclean' fish, those that do not have fins or scales, a provision of Deuteronomy 14:10 for the Israelite nation. The poor cook gets short shrift: 'Do we need his skill at all?' asks the interviewer. The cook replies that if he is got rid of, the boys will eat their vegetables green and meat raw, but the retort comes back that they can perfectly well cook for themselves. The cook can only reply that all of them will be slaves then, and none will be lord, and anyway they will still need the skill of cooking. The point of this little exchange seems to be to emphasize the lack of concern in the monastery for the indulgence of the flesh in eating, and a general disdain for culinary expertise. It is aimed at the boys, since the mature monks were not allowed to eat meat at all. All these small touches are aimed at teaching the boys not only their Latin vocabulary, but also the cultural patterns of the monastery.

THE FIRST SHALL BE LAST

Towards the end of the discussion of secular occupations, the characters get a little heated because the focus changes from description of the occupations to deciding which is most important. The late-introduced estate-manager emphasizes the priority of the divine service and hence the occupation of the monk, but the interviewer presses the matter, asking him to assess the secular occupations. The manager says, 'the

ploughman feeds us all', prompting the dissent of the smith
and the carpenter. This gives the manager the opportunity for
a little homily on the theme of each person doing what he
does to the best of his ability:

> Friends and good workmen, let us quickly put aside
> this quarrel, and let there be peace and agreement
> between us. And let us help one another in each
> one's occupation, and let us always agree with the
> ploughman, from whom we have food for ourselves
> and fodder for our horses. And this is the advice I
> give to all workers, that each one should pursue his
> occupation with diligence, for the one who deserts
> his occupation is deserted by [the skill of] his occu-
> pation. Whatever you are, whether it is a monk, a
> mass-priest, a freeman, a warrior, exercise and prac-
> tise it, and be what you are. For it is a great loss and
> shame when a man does not wish to be what he is
> and what he ought to be.

It was hard for a man to change his social role and even
harder to change his rank. Bede's story of Cædmon, who composed noble poems of biblical teaching, is remarkable as much
for the fact that Cædmon the herdsman became a monk, as
for his miraculous ability to compose poetry. Here again is
the idea of the three orders: monk and priest are the *oratores*,
the churl or freeman is the *laborator*, and the warrior is the
bellator, and once more the idea is deployed to encourage
social stability and a sense of vocation. In the 19th century
the idea was a little modified, perhaps a little more cynically
used to keep the poor in their place, in the children's hymn,
'All things bright and beautiful':

> The rich man in his castle,
> The poor man at his gate,
> God made them high and lowly
> And ordered their estate.

Ælfric was unknowingly contributing towards the development of the medieval genre of 'estates satire', which was used almost exclusively to criticize the religious. But there are many curious echoes of the characters and situations in the *Colloquy* in later literature. Disdain for the cook is implied in the General Prologue of Chaucer's *Canterbury Tales*, where the man's abilities are by no means doubted, but Chaucer pointedly mentions the gangrenous ulcer on his leg. And in the same work, the respect for the ploughman as a simple but deeply religious character is evident. The ploughman, who 'gives food and drink to us all' (in Ælfric perhaps a reference to wheat for bread and barley for brewing), becomes a representative of Christ (who gives food and drink in the Eucharist) and of Everyman in *Piers Plowman* and elsewhere. Ælfric's manager specifically contrasts the idea of living with the ploughman and living near the smith: 'what do you give us in your smithy but fiery sparks of iron, the pounding and clanging of sledgehammers, and the blasting of bellows?' The noise of the smithy is made much of in a famous 14th-century poem, *The Blacksmiths* (Text 15).

MONASTIC LIFE
The *Colloquy* is introduced and concluded by questions directed at the boys, and the answers to these certainly give an insight into the life of the monastery. When asked what he did in the day, the boy responds:

I did many things. In the night I got up from my bed when I heard the bell and sang nocturns with the brethren. After that we sang the lauds of the day and of all the saints. After these we sang prime and the seven psalms with litanies and chapter-mass. Then we did terce and the mass of the day. After these we sang sext, had our food and drink and sleep, and then we got up again and sang nones. And now we are here before you, eager to hear what you will say to us.

The two remaining services, vespers and compline, are mentioned later. But the picture given by the *Regularis Concordia*, of a round of almost ceaseless devotion amplified greatly from that of earlier years, is here confirmed. Apart from periods of teaching and learning (and surely the last sentence of the quotation is Ælfric's pious hope more than the genuine voice of the boys), the day is taken up by worship.

MONASTICISM AND LAND

A thread running through the progress of monastic reform is the need of the monasteries for land endowments. The *Colloquy* gives an idea of the population of workers on a monastic estate and the variety of work that went into the support of the monks. Hundreds of charters of the 10th and later centuries refer to leasing and donating lands. The number of these that can be deduced to be forged in order to bolster the claims of later monasteries to lands and privileges is embarrassingly high. But it reveals that one of the more pressing issues which arose with the advent of the monasteries was that of land-holding and distribution.

Monasteries were never purely religious and cut off from the world, even in the ascetic days of the conversion. The *oratores*, the monks, needed land to support and feed them, and the land had to come from somewhere. Usually it came from donations by kings and noblemen, the more pious *bella-tores*. The other order of people, the *laboratores*, the workers, was not so much affected: they paid their dues whichever of the other orders was in control of the land and had the rights. Problems arose when there was a conflict of interest between the monks and the landowners. Bede wrote a letter to Bishop Ecgberht in 734 deploring the fact that monasteries had engrossed so much land that there was not enough left prop-erly to reward the king's retired warriors (Text 16). Bede was an unusually acute observer, but even so, there must have been some widespread disquiet about this matter for him to urge suppression of irregular monasteries.

King Alfred was at least a would-be friend of monasteries. He allocated some of his own revenues for the upkeep of his new monastic houses. But it becomes apparent that he and his successors also leased or gave rights over former church and monastic lands to warriors and leaders so that they could afford to keep soldiers mounted and provisioned for the defence of the kingdom. There is a hint that this was happen-ing in a letter sent from Pope John VIII to Archbishop Æthelred of Canterbury, probably in 878. The letter tells Æthelred to resist the king, Alfred, in some unspecified attack on the rights of the church:

> We ... exhort and warn you, my brother, on account of the necessity of the present time, that you station yourself as a wall for the house of the Lord, laying aside every worldly fear, as a proper servant of God, and, kindled by zeal for him, do

> not cease to resist strenuously not only the king,
> but all who wish to do any wrong against [the
> church], making your service honourable, as long
> as you are permitted by the divine will to discharge
> the supreme episcopate.

It seems unlikely that King Alfred would do any 'wrong against the church' unless it was something that would preserve both church and kingdom, and the expropriation of land might be what is being referred to here.

Certainly, the practice of using church or monastic land for other purposes was still being carried on in the reign of King Edgar. In the 10th-century revival, one of the difficulties confronting Edgar was the fact that some of the former lands of monasteries in the Danelaw had been taken over by Viking settlers and could not now be reclaimed. We have already noted that for the period 972–1016, the archbishopric of York was held in plurality with the see of Worcester. Rather than being the result of political wheeler-dealing, this may have been necessitated by York's poverty. But in Wessex and west Mercia, the English kings were able to endow a growing number of monasteries with adequate estates: the abbots of 18 monasteries attended King Æthelred's court in 993. When King Edgar died in 975, there was a period of civil unrest in which the land-owners whose lands were being squeezed by the monasteries reacted by dispossessing some monks. The leader, mentioned disapprovingly by the poem on the *Death of Edgar* in the *Anglo-Saxon Chronicle*, was Ealdorman Ælfhere of Mercia. Ælfhere died within a few years, and no lasting damage seems to have been done to monasticism. But the legacy of Alfred's appropriation of monastic lands was a bitter one for a time.

One of the most determined defenders of church rights and monastic privileges was Byrhtnoth, ealdorman of Essex and hero of the poem *The Battle of Maldon* (Text 12). The 12th-century monastic records in the *Book of Ely* comment on his resistance to the attempt to restore secular clerks and expel monks from their lands, as well as noting the extensive donations he himself made to Ely. The record of his death at Ramsey, another monastic house, also notes his generous gifts of land. But the *Book of Ely* and the *Ramsey Chronicle* both make reference to the fact that Byrhtnoth's donations were greater to Ely than to Ramsey because, marching south from Northumbria to meet the threat of the Vikings, Byrhtnoth was not given the hospitality his men needed at Ramsey, but was welcomed at Ely. Indeed, the *Ramsey Chronicle* mentions that Byrhtnoth gave 'many and extensive lands [to Ely] some of which he had intended to give to Ramsey on his death'. In this context of land donation, the comment in *The Battle of Maldon* that Byrhtnoth gave the Vikings 'too much land' is particularly striking: it was a misdirected piece of generosity that the English were to regret for a long time.

MONASTIC PRODUCTIONS

Though the forms of monasticism changed in the revival of the 10th century, the revival brought with it a renewed flowering of scholarship, art and building. Utterly different in style and content though they might be, the Lindisfarne gospel-book from the very end of the seventh century is matched by the Benedictional of St Æthelwold from the end of the 10th century in the quality of calligraphy and the technique of its illustration. The list, in Alcuin's Latin poem, *The Bishops, Kings and Saints of York*, of the major authors represented in the pre-Viking library at York runs to 41, even though it may have the gloss or limitations of hindsight, as the poem possibly post-dates his departure to the court of

Charlemagne. Lupus of Ferrières wrote from France to York as late as 850 asking Archbishop Ealdsige for copies of Bede, Quintilian and Jerome. The survival of any of the books referred to is doubtful, principally due to the Viking attacks. Very little is now left of this majestic library. Several ornaments from Viking-Age Scandinavian graves are undoubtedly reworked book-mounts. The libraries of Bede's monastery at Wearmouth-Jarrow, of Whitby or Lindisfarne, all centres of monasticism and scholarship in the seventh and eighth centuries, survive in only the merest shreds. By contrast, the productions of the 10th-century monastic revival survive in considerable numbers.

Many of these later books are not the outright intellectual works that seem to have appealed to the earlier monastics, the commentaries on scripture and discourses of a philosophical nature, though of course these are represented. There is a large number of liturgical books, missals, benedictionals, pontificals, penitentials, psalters, sacramentaries, kalendars (lives of saints and their festival days), hymnals and so on. These met the needs of the new monastic communities for orders of worship and patterns of liturgical devotion. The books are mostly in Latin, but some have glosses in Old English. But the great mass of books written and copied in Old English come from the pens of scribes of the 10th and 11th centuries. The *Beowulf* manuscript, the Vercelli Book of Old English poems and homilies, the Exeter Book of 'various pieces in Old English verse', and the Junius manuscript containing the Old English poetic versions of Genesis, Exodus and Daniel, as well as a poem called *Christ and Satan* – all these were products of approximately the years 950–1050, whatever the date of their composition as poetry.

A continuous translation of the gospels was also composed at this time, and circulated in several manuscripts (Text 17, the Beatitudes). It seems to have had no particular authority, and the manuscripts are functional rather than expensive and elaborate. One or two of the manuscripts have notes in the margin to indicate the day on which the particular passage was to be read, which may imply liturgical use, or at least use of the vernacular translation in support of the Latin liturgical use. The Old English homilies of Ælfric and Wulfstan are found in various manuscripts, and were still being copied in the 13th century. Neither of the homilists used the Old English version of the gospels, but their homilies are tied to the liturgical readings, and once again the use of the vernacular in aiding understanding of the liturgy is clear.

The fact that both the homilists wrote in English as well as Latin might seem to suggest that the Latin learning of the monastic revival was relatively weak. But if we look at some other productions of the revival, we begin to see a deliberate purpose behind this bilingualism. More than one bilingual version of the Benedictine Rule is extant: the one which is in the library of Corpus Christi College, Oxford, written by a single scribe, neatly shows that the letter-forms for each of the two languages were quite different. For this task the scribe needed to be bilingual not only in grammar and vocabulary, but also in orthography, in script. A version of the Benedictine Office in Old English, probably from Worcester, shows in addition a kind of artistic bilingualism: it has the main prayers of the Divine Office in Old English verse, as well as prose instructions and invocations. This is not 'translationese', but careful, fluent, at times graceful writing. Another manuscript, in the British Library, Cotton Galba A. xiv, measuring barely 5.2 x 4 inches, is a collection of prayers; they are predominantly in Latin, from various sources including Celtic ones, but some have Old English translations. And even more significant, there are several prayers in this book in Old English for which

no source is known. One of these, a prayer of penitence or confession, is in strongly alliterating phrases reminiscent of
Wulfstan (Text 18). Another follows the monastic round
of liturgical hours with English prayers on the theme. Writing
in the two languages, then, might show not weakness, but the
concern of the revival to educate the laity, to educate monks
with only functional liturgical Latin, to express spirituality and
devotion in whichever language was most accessible.

A BOOK OF LIFE

A manuscript from New Minster, Winchester, now in the
British Library, shows other sides of the production of the
monastic revival. It is a miscellany written in 1031, with
the focus on listing the names of the monks past and present
in the monastery's *Liber Vitae*, or 'Book of Life'. This lists the
members of the community and is a kind of earthly representa-
tion of the 'the Lamb's book of life' from Revelation, the book
in which those who are to be saved in the final judgement are
numbered. It contains a fine picture on one panel of which
the monks wait in orderly fashion in the presence of the
angels, and the abbot and bishop slightly apart, all looking
towards the triptych on the adjacent page. The triptych, a
series of three drawings, shows St Peter and his huge key dealing with souls after death. In the first Peter opens the door of
heaven and welcomes the just to the heavenly city where
Christ is seated in glory, surrounded by worshippers. In the
second, below the first, Peter uses the key as a weapon to push
away a demon attempting to grab a soul, squashing the
demon's nose. An angel has the Book of Life, and it is bigger
than the book in the demon's hand. To the right, an angel is
ushering a man and a woman away. And in the third picture,
below the second, an angel locks the door on a demon glee-
fully thrusting souls into the yawning mouth of hell.

There is a kind of humorous serenity about this illustration. St Peter is tonsured like the monks, and none of the
people in the hell picture has a tonsure. Hell is like the
mouth of a pig, and the contortions of those locked into this
frame make it clear that it is a horrible fate; but the more
gothic details found in literature and art elsewhere are left to
the imagination. The artist was absolutely confident in his
salvation, and it is clear that any millennial anxiety that was
circulating in England at the time has left him with no
doubts. St Peter wields his extravagantly large key to the evident discomfiture of the demon, while holding firmly on to
the hand of the person whose soul is in dispute, a picture
which illuminates Byrhtnoth's prayer in *The Battle of Maldon*
that his soul might be allowed to go to heaven without harm
from hellish attackers. And in the four-square heavenly city,
Christ is seated in glory, and worshippers adore him with
upraised hands.

This manuscript, Stowe 944 in the British Library, also
includes the will of King Alfred in Old English, a piece on
the six ages of the world, a list of English saints, a list of
kings, an account of the vision of a monk called Eadwine
relating to an agreement between the New Minster and the
Old Minster, part of a charter, lists of relics at New Minster,
and Latin and English versions of a piece on the times for
Mass. The preoccupation with things monastic is evident,
even down to Eadwine's attempt to give St Cuthbert's sanction to Æthelwold's decree that the New and Old Minsters
in Winchester (long rivals in almost everything) should
share services. There is also the connection with royalty,
saints and relics, eschatology, and land for the foundation of
the monastery.

But central to the manuscript, as also to the whole
enterprise of monastic revival, is the serene confidence that

salvation is assured through the monastic life, the life of consecration, the life of faith. When all else is cut away, the monastic revival was about living salvation both here and hereafter.

6

SAINTS FOR HARD TIMES

Battles and revived monasticism were not the only weapons in the Christian armoury for the fight against the Vikings and heathenism. Saintliness was regarded as a powerful force in its own right. In the difficult times of the Viking attacks, Anglo-Saxon Christians could draw on the support of saints from the past, for it is of the essence of hagiography that saints are not bound by time. But they could also draw strength paradoxically from the example of recent martyrs, those victims of the Vikings who willingly gave their lives in hope of the resurrection, of whom the world was not worthy. By their godly lives and the miraculous powers of their relics, the saints reinforced the Christian understanding of the world which the Vikings had shaken: that God was in control of history, and that events were leading to the vindication of his faithful people. In this chapter we will explore the saint's life genre, the boundaries between history and hagiography in Old English literature, and the use that hagiography was put to.

HAGIOGRAPHY

Hagiography, writings about the lives and miracles of saints, is not always a kind of literature that appeals to us as modern readers. There are good reasons for this. One of the simpler ones is that hagiography is not history, and we like to be sure that what we are reading is either fiction or fact. Modern historians tend to exclude much of the miraculous element of the saints' lives from their work, and try to build factual history from what is left. This is perfectly reasonable, but it leaves out of consideration the purpose for which stories of the saints were written and much more. Moreover, in common parlance 'hagiography' tends to mean the cynical manipulation of facts or even fiction to present a person as better than they really are. We not only do not believe such things, we tend to take pleasure in discovering skeletons in other people's cupboards. Hagiography in early literature gives little opportunity for this kind of pleasure, though occasionally competing cults of saints spread gossip about their opponents, squabbled over or even raided each other's relics.

Perhaps the major appeal of hagiography today is that if we can suspend disbelief, we find a world of wonder, a world of spiritual power, a clear divide between good and evil, and the moral certainty that good will win in the end. In short, hagiography is a kind of romance, without the sexual love-interest. Historical circumstances may have changed dramatically between the time when legends of Cuthbert or Guthlac or Oswald or Ælfheah were circulating and now, but the hearers of the legends of these saints (with perhaps a little less effort in the suspension of disbelief) probably found their appeal very much the same.

The word *legend* came out of the context of the circulation

and use of the saints' lives. It was used without prejudice to
the factuality or otherwise of the detail in the stories: it
simply means in Latin 'what is to be read'. And what was read
on the saint's day was the record of the saint's life, death and
miracles. In the revived monasticism of the 10th century,
hagiography had its place in the Night Office. In other words,
it was the main form of bedtime story for the monks. But if
that seems to trivialize hagiography, the serious side of it was
that these stories had significant social influence: they
affected public and private worship, the dedication of
churches, local and national festivities, and the status
of monasteries was intimately connected with the patronage
and relics of the saints.

The process of canonization of a saint was one that was
formalized only late on in the church, but it was becoming
custom in the late Anglo-Saxon period for the Pope to recognize saints and martyrs on the basis of the stories recorded
about them in hagiography. In Anglo-Saxon times what made
saints was the circulation of stories about them, particularly
their miracles and the effectiveness of their relics, and usually
the growth of a centre for their veneration. Since the hagiographical tradition is based on the proposition that saints
continue to be at work in the ordinary world through their
relics at their shrine, a hagiography is never complete, and
stories continue to be added to the saint's life even after an
officially recognized version has been written.

TWO TYPES OF SAINTS' STORIES

There are two basic types of stories about saints. The earlier
form of saint's life was the martyrdom, the *passio*, which
recorded particularly the saint's death. The historical context
for the growth of this genre was the Roman persecution of the
early church from the latter half of the first century through

to the early fourth century. This has obvious precedent in the gospels, where the passion of Jesus himself takes up, on average, one third of the whole gospel narrative. There are very early martyrdom stories, such as the martyrdom of St Stephen by stoning in the Acts of the Apostles; or that of Polycarp, an old man who would not forswear the Lord who had stood by him, and was put to the sword and his body burned in the year 155. The genre became popular in Christian literature, and as it did so, stories emerged about earlier saints as well as later ones.

The later form of saint's life emerged after the effective end of Roman persecution, and this was the *vita*, the life. Here persecution is internalized, and the sufferings of the martyr are replaced by the self-persecution and suffering of the saint, who denies him or herself all luxury, and fights against the world, the flesh and the devil through prayer and virtuous living. Most of the earlier Anglo-Saxon saints' lives are of this type, though the Anglo-Saxons soon adopted a calendar which drew in saints of all kinds. A collection called *The Old English Martyrology*, which includes the main dates of the year with saints' days and brief details of the saints, seems to have circulated as early as the ninth century, and was still being excerpted and copied into the margins of other manuscripts after the Norman Conquest. The saints here, by no means all martyrs, are Greek, Roman, Hebrew, English, Celtic.

Hagiography is very conventional or formulaic. There are individualizing details, but broadly both the *passio* and the *vita* follow a pattern. In the *passio*, or martyrdom, there is an evil authority figure who tries to make the saint forswear his faith on pain of death (this is especially the threat levelled at men), or do something repugnant to his or her faith (women especially are put under pressure to marry or to submit to

sexual advances). Often there is a debate between the two
parties, which the saint wins hands down. But when the saint
refuses to submit to pressure, all kinds of inventive tortures
are applied and heroically resisted. Finally, the saint is killed,
usually by beheading.

In the *vita*, the birth or childhood of the saint is usually
attended by signs which betoken an extraordinary future. In
due course the saint grows up, usually becomes a monk or
nun, develops the piety and insight which shows their nature
as a person chosen by God. Saints practise extreme asceticism, fasting and keeping vigils. Often they see visions
or hear heavenly voices. Their holiness and power is demonstrated by their ability to help other people either in miracles
or in more ordinary ways, such as their example or their
teaching. Often saints have to endure the scorn or opposition of others, but their restraint and persistence put their
opponents to shame. They become famous, and are sought
out for their help and advice, but they prefer the lonely
battles against spiritual forces, and the delight of the companionship of God, to much public acclaim. They frequently
predict the time of their death, and their last words are
always holy and their death serene.

The two forms, *passio* and *vita*, merge after the death of a
saint. Miracles happen at the site of the death, or at the tomb
where the saint's body lies. The authorities decide to move
the body so that the popular veneration can be accommo-
dated, and the body is found to be incorrupt, and often any
wound has healed. The saint is relocated or 'translated' to a
more prestigious site, and the number of stories relating to
the healing powers of the relics increases. The story is finally
written down and used in church and monastery for the
encouragement of believers, and often enough in the claims
of monastic house to land, and power in local and national

politics. Saints are celebrated and remembered on the day of their death, which is their birthday to eternal life.

HISTORY AND HAGIOGRAPHY

The saint's life is located within a broadly historical context, but it is evident that the main preoccupations of the genre are not historical in any scientific way. Each of the formulaic features of hagiography has a symbolic meaning, some relation to miracles or statements in the Bible. It echoes or reflects an earlier saint's power, or has a generally understood conventional significance. The incorruption of the bodies of the saints after death signifies their purity in life, but also fulfils statements in the Psalms and St Paul, that God's holy one will not see corruption (Psalm 16:10) and that 'this corruptible [nature] must put on incorruption' when the dead are resurrected (1 Corinthians 15:53). In the Creeds, the notion of 'the communion of saints' was apparently interpreted to mean that what was true of one saint was also broadly true of the others. The underlying idea is that the saints shared the quality of holiness of life and therefore could potentially share the same way of working after their death. Hagiography, even from so brief a description, can thus be seen to be more of a way of finding and interpreting a divine pattern within a historical framework than a way of recording what happened. Hagiography is more about faith and belief than naked fact.

The Anglo-Saxons themselves were aware of these different modes. It has often been remarked that though Bede used the same terms of respect, and indeed affection, of St Cuthbert and the abbots of his own monastery when he wrote about them, his writings on Cuthbert are hagiography while his account of the abbots is history. There are miracles in quantity in the verse and prose lives of Cuthbert, but none in the accounts of Abbot Ceolfrid and the others. Bede fully acknowledged the pressure he was under to write more miracles, stories of which were still circulating some thirty years after the saint's death, into his prose *Life of St Cuthbert*, although he refused on the ground that his work was complete.

Another Cuthbert present at Bede's own death recorded his words and actions as if in preparation for Bede to become a saint, including Bede's awareness of his approaching death. Indeed this Cuthbert promised a fuller account of the stories already circulating about Bede. But nothing is known of this fuller account, and it is rather later that miracle stories appear. Though York, Durham and (more improbably) Glastonbury claimed his relics and miracles, there was no official *Life* and Bede did not figure in the *Old English Martyrology*.

During the years of the Viking attacks, a period when many met an untimely death, hagiography was close to the minds of writers. Not all the martyrs of the time were killed by Vikings, though. King Edward was killed in 978 by the machinations of his own family, particularly his mother and brother Æthelred, according to Byrhtferth of Ramsey in his *Life of St Oswald*. Edward had a flourishing cult throughout the Middle Ages, and was widely venerated. The northern version of the *Anglo-Saxon Chronicle* commemorates him in rough verse:

> No worse deed was done by English people than this
> since they first came to the land of Britain.
> Men murdered him, but God made him great.
> He was in life an earthly king,
> now after death he is a heavenly saint;
> his earthly kinsmen had no desire to avenge him,
> but his heavenly Father has greatly avenged him;
> the earthly slayers wished to hide his memory in
>   the earth,

but the heavenly Avenger has spread his memory
   in heaven and on earth.
Those who had no desire to bow to his living body
now humbly bend on their knees to his dead bones.
Now we can perceive that human wisdom and
   contrivances
and counsels are of no value against God's plan.

The counterpoint of earth and heaven set out here is one of
the keynotes of hagiography. But, as befits the historical purpose of the *Chronicle*, there is no record of miracles, simply
the assertion that justice, and poetic justice, will be done. It
was noted earlier that one of King Æthelred's law-codes
makes provision for the celebration of Edward's festival.
Perhaps this is the meaning of the writer's references to the
'earthly kinsmen' and those who 'had no desire to bow' to
Edward: popular veneration had forced the king to recognize
his half-brother's holiness.

THE USE OF HAGIOGRAPHY: ÆLFHEAH

Especially in times of persecution, saints were a refuge against
the heathen, their spiritual power countering the naked hostility of the attackers. The saints in Gregory the Great's
Dialogues in various ways countered the attacks of the
invaders of the declining Roman Empire; King Alfred, seeing
the importance of this, had the book translated. But to be
effective, the saints had to be real ones, and hagiography at
this time was not uncritical. There was serious doubt that
Ælfheah, who has come down into modern times as St
Alphege, was a martyr. By considering the various versions of
his life, we can begin to see how the doubt arose, but also how
the life was put to use and how history becomes transformed
into hagiography.

Ælfheah's story is told in the *Anglo-Saxon Chronicle* under the years 1011–12 (Text 19). He was bishop of Winchester, then archbishop of Canterbury. He was instrumental in the settlement between Æthelred and Olaf Tryggvason, whereby Olaf was confirmed and promised never again to come to England with hostile intent. He was captured and eventually killed by the Vikings.

In 1011, the Vikings took Canterbury through the treachery of someone called Ælfmær and held a number of church dignitaries hostage, a habit they had got into when it had proved consistently lucrative in both England and on the Continent. Ælfheah was kept prisoner from September 1011 until the following Easter, April 1012, and whereas the other hostages were released, Ælfheah refused to allow any ransom to be paid. At a drunken feast, the Vikings pelted Ælfheah with bones and the heads of horned cattle, and finally smashed his skull with an axe. Ælfheah's body was taken to St Paul's in London for burial and the chronicler simply remarks, 'and now God reveals the holy martyr's powers there'.

In the year 1023, according to one manuscript of the *Anglo-Saxon Chronicle*, Ælfheah's body was taken via Rochester back to Canterbury with the permission of King Cnut and with suitable ceremony. Clearly, there were stories circulating very early on about St Ælfheah, and the moving of his body constitutes the translation of relics which is one of the procedures for the ratification of a saint's cult.

The sober outlines of Ælfheah's death recorded in the *Anglo-Saxon Chronicle* have the ring of truth. Pelting with bones is recorded in an Icelandic saga of the 14th century, *Hrolf Kraki's saga*, as an unpleasant way of showing contempt for a person. In another saga, *Egil's saga*, Egil sets up a stick and puts a horse's head on it, by way of directing bad luck and insult at Erik Bloodaxe. The nickname of one of the turncoat Danish leaders who started the English flight from the Viking army in East Anglia in 1010, Thurcytel 'Mare's head', is not intended to be flattering (and the alternative given by Henry of Huntingdon, Thurcytel 'Ant's head', and his comment, 'who deserves eternal disgrace', reinforces the insult if not the interpretation of the name).

The details in the *Chronicle* bear a resemblance to what Scandinavians thought themselves capable of doing, and the business with heads of animals is bizarre enough, even if the account is not very specific, to draw attention to it. This detail is recorded independently in the *Chronicle* of Theitmar of Merseburg, a Continental writer who died in 1018, and hence had almost contemporary information. The story is told there of Dunstan, but it clearly relates to the martyrdom of Ælfheah. It is probable, then, that the pelting with bones and animal heads actually happened. The blow with an axe, a typically Scandinavian weapon, also seems perfectly plausible. And verisimilitude is added when the chronicler uses the Scandinavian word for the disorderly 'council', *husting*, into which Ælfheah is brought before his death.

Interestingly, there is no actual record in detail of miracles in the *Chronicle*, simply the statement that they occurred. But the chronicler of the account in the years 1011–12 makes it clear that he thought Ælfheah was a martyr since he uses both the phrase *hi hine gemartyredon*, 'they martyred him' and the term *martir*, 'martyr' of the archbishop. Moreover, the writer took some care in the writing of the annals. There is a patterning of language which to some scholars suggests verse or the rhythmical prose of the great homilists Ælfric and Wulfstan. When Canterbury and Ælfheah are captured, 'there might then be seen wretchedness where before bliss was seen', and when Ælfheah is struck with the axe, 'his holy

blood fell on to the earth and his holy soul he sent forth to
God's kingdom'. Not only is there parallelism and contrast,
but the writer also makes grim play on the word 'head':
Ælfheah was the head of English Christianity, he was pelted
with animal heads before being struck on the head with
the axe. Like the earlier passage concerning Edward, the
chronicler seems to be writing of an acknowledged martyr or
confessor, perhaps even laying the foundation for a later
saint's life. And in the 1023 annal of the Worcester manuscript of the *Chronicle*, the writer constantly refers to
Ælfheah's saintly status and his 'holy body' and merits, calling
him 'the holy martyr'.

It was somewhat later, at the end of the 11th century, when
the question of whether Ælfheah was a martyr or not arose.
The point was argued between the French-born Archbishop
of Canterbury, Lanfranc, and the theologian Anselm. It was
not miracles or the fact that Ælfheah had been killed by the
Vikings that decided the issue. The story of Ælfheah's death
made it clear that he died because he would not allow payment of ransom, rather than for his refusal to forswear Christ.
It was only special pleading by Anselm that kept the saint
in the calendar. His life was written soon after this by
a monk called Osbern, and it is at this point that the
miraculous element comes into the recorded story, along with
some fascinating detail.

Osbern's *Life* has the usual hagiographical trimmings.
Ælfheah at a very early age proved to be unusually wise
and holy; he professed as a monk and confronted the laxity
and negligence of other monks at Deerhurst, before moving
to the stricter regime at Bath; when St Dunstan, the archbishop of Canterbury, had a vision of the Apostle St Andrew
pointing out Ælfheah as the divine choice, he became bishop
of Winchester; he practised extreme asceticism and helped

the poor; he became archbishop of Canterbury in succession to Dunstan, and went to Rome for the willing approval of the Pope; later, he pleaded with the attacking Danes to spare their victims; in his own captivity he did all he could to help his fellow-prisoners; he had a debate with a demon who tried to entrap him; calling on Christ, he was stoned to death by the Danes; after his death miracles started to happen, and some of the Danes were converted; at his translation, his body was found incorrupt; many miracles followed.

The fascinating thing about this account by Osbern is that though it keeps to the historical framework, its focus is extra-historical. The action is on the spiritual plane. The most extreme example of this is the fact that Osbern omits the cattle-heads from the missiles thrown at Ælfheah, being content with stones. The purpose of this is to emphasize the parallel with St Stephen, the first Christian martyr, who was stoned in the Acts of the Apostles in the Bible. Thus in order to demonstrate Ælfheah's saintly status and likeness to the proto-martyr Stephen, Osbern has removed one of the most distinctive and plausible historical details in the early stories.

John of Worcester in the early 12th century, borrowing from Osbern and other sources, gives a very similar account of Ælfheah's death, but elaborates with gory detail the devastation of Canterbury and the dreadful treatment of its citizens (see chapter 1). He records that the traitor Ælfmær was an archdeacon; that the ransom proposed for Ælfheah was 3,000 pounds (of silver); and that the man who hit Ælfheah with the axe, wishing to put him out of his misery, had been baptized by Ælfheah the previous day, and was called Thrum. 'God's wrath', he also tells us, 'broke out against that murderous people, and slew 2,000 of them by means of excruciating disorders of the bowels', a plausible detail if there was the number of bodies lying around that John suggests – nine out of every ten of the city's population were killed in his account. John gives us motives, colour, names, numbers, but his account nevertheless keeps very closely to the historical details of the Chronicle, including the pelting with bones, stones and ox-heads. But there are no miracles. The only details which make it clear that John knew Ælfheah to be a saint are the first reference in the annals for both 1011 and 1023 to 'St Alfeg', and possibly the attention given to the day of his death, 19 April, which is also his festival day.

So in the record of the martyrdom of Ælfheah we have a quite clear distinction between history and hagiography. The Chronicle and John of Worcester (with elaborations) are content with the history. Osbern's story mingles some aspects of the vita and the passio, but it is clearly hagiography; the shocking details of Ælfheah's death in the Chronicle are changed for the hagiographer's purpose.

The distinction between hagiography and history is not always so clear. Bede, the greatest of England's early historians, does not clearly distinguish between the two in his Ecclesiastical History, as will be evident in what follows. But in the modern concern for separating fact and fiction, the purpose of hagiography has often been ignored or undervalued. When we put the Lives of the saints into their historical context, we can appreciate that purpose a little more.

ÆLFRIC'S LIVES OF THE SAINTS

Ælfric wrote his set of homilies, the Lives of the Saints, around the turn of the first millennium. All the lives are composed in a kind of rhythmical prose for preaching. They vary considerably in length, but Ælfric evidently selected material for the purpose of informing and encouraging his hearers. Most of the lives are those of the great martyrs and saints of the early church such as St Basil, St Thomas and St Mark the Evangelist, and he uses an impressive range of sources. Ælfric added several saints of more local interest including St Alban, St Swithun and St Æthelthryth. In this last group he included the lives of two English kings, Oswald and Edmund, for which he had particular sources, and which he treated in particular ways.

ST OSWALD

The main source for the life of St Oswald was Bede's *Ecclesiastical History*, Book III. Bede's overall focus is historical, and he is writing about recent history. He records the bare details of the battle of Heavenfield in 634, between Oswald and the Northumbrians, and the Celtic king of Gwynedd, Cædwalla. Bede relates Oswald's piety and generosity, his appeal to Iona for missionaries to convert the Northumbrians to Christianity, the establishment of a monastery and episcopal see at Lindisfarne in 635, and St Aidan's missionary preaching until his death in 651. He records Oswald's building of churches, particularly York Minster, Oswald's power over the Celtic races around him, his influence in the conversion of King Cynegils of Wessex, and the establishment of the see of Dorchester. And he records Oswald's death at the age of 38 in battle against Penda, the heathen king of Mercia, at *Maserfelth*, near Oswestry, on 5 August 642. All of these matters had great interest and significance to the Anglo-Saxon church, and the historical details can be confirmed from other sources.

Mixed in with these stories, though, are other details which show a deeper significance than the purely historical. The cross which Oswald raised at Heavenfield was left standing there, and people were healed by it, and cattle too. A man with a badly broken arm was healed by moss taken from the

cross. On one occasion when Aidan and Oswald were at a
feast, a message was brought in that people were queuing up
outside for alms: Oswald immediately not only had food sent
out, but also sent the great silver dish on which it was being
served, with orders that the dish should be broken up and
distributed to the poor. At this point Aidan grasped the king's
hand and said 'May this hand never wither with age.' After
Oswald's death his head and his hands were cut off by Penda
as gruesome trophies, but were rescued by faithful Christians
and became relics. Bede records in 731 that the arms were
preserved at Bamburgh and were undecayed in his day, while
Oswald's head was buried in Lindisfarne, and was carried with
them by the community of St Cuthbert on their wanderings
after the Vikings made Lindisfarne uninhabitable.

The bones of Oswald were washed and the water healed
many. Earth from the place where Oswald died healed a mad
horse and a paralysed girl. Some of the earth was put in a bag
by an ecclesiastical traveller, and when the place where he
was staying burnt down, the post on which the bag was hung
remained unburnt. Finally, an Irishman of careless and
dissolute life was near to death from plague, and realizing that
he was on his way to hell, he called for some relic of Oswald's.
Acca, later bishop of Hexham and friend of Bede, happened
to be there, and had a piece of the stake on which Oswald's
head had been impaled. He shaved a piece of the wood off
into holy water and gave it to the Irishman to drink, whereupon he was healed and became a devout and holy man.

All this material is added by Bede to the basic historical
account of Oswald's life. But Ælfric, quite appropriately for a
sermon, has changed the emphasis of the material (Text 20).
He has made a *vita* out of the miscellaneous details Bede
recorded in his *History*. The focus in Ælfric's *Life of Oswald* is
on his virtue, vindicated after his death, rather than on

the historical detail. Ælfric has made very little change to the material that came down to him from Bede. He improves or perhaps clarifies the meaning of Aidan's speech to Oswald at the banquet, making it 'May this right hand never rot in corruption', and it is central to the story that it did not decay. Similarly, he adds the personal pronoun to Oswald's proverbial speech as he dies, 'May God have mercy on [our] souls.' This meaning is implied in Bede, but the *Old English Martyrology* makes it into something more like Christ's prayer of forgiveness to his slayers: 'Oswald ended his life with words of prayer when he was killed; and when he fell to the earth, he said, "God have mercy on the souls"', perhaps implying 'their souls'. The point about this is that Ælfric sees this dying speech as the *commendatio animae*, the saint commending his soul to God.

Ælfric also draws a brief moral from the story of the Irishman, that 'no one should renege on what he voluntarily promised to Almighty God when he was ill, lest he forfeit himself if he denies God what he promised'. The final detail recorded by Ælfric is the removal of Oswald's bones from Bardney in Lincolnshire to Gloucester, for which the *Anglo-Saxon Chronicle* gives the year 909. So it is clear that Ælfric has clarified and interpreted his sources to establish Oswald as a saint and to make him an example for his hearers to learn from and honour.

ST EDMUND, KING AND MARTYR

The story of St Edmund demonstrates even more forcefully how the saint is constructed, the details of his martyrdom perhaps even invented, in order to serve the purposes of religious inspiration and the political manipulation of his cult. The detail of Edmund's story, even in its historical aspect, is not so well authenticated as that of Oswald. The *Anglo-Saxon*

Chronicle baldly records Edmund's death in 869 at the hands of the great Danish army which had been marauding around the east and north of the country since 865:

> In this year the enemy army rode across from Mercia into East Anglia and took winter quarters at Thetford. That winter, King Edmund fought against them, the Danes won and killed the king and overran all the land.

Asser, the historian and biographer of King Alfred, writing within a few years of Edmund's death, records little more than the *Chronicle*, except that the battle was fierce and a large number of Englishmen were killed. The implication of the historical sources is that Edmund died in no unusual way in battle.

Yet by the end of the century there was a thriving cult of St Edmund. We know this because a great hoard of silver was buried in around 905 at Cuerdale in Lancashire and about 1,800 of the coins had been minted in memory of St Edmund. The coins were apparently produced in East Anglia, at this time an independent Anglo-Scandinavian kingdom. Some of them bear the legend *Sce Eadmundi Rex* and it is thought that this inscription is actually addressing Edmund, as in 'O St Edmund, King'. Within 25 years of his death Edmund was being venerated as a saint by his Danish killers.

We can find further confirmation of St Edmund's high standing among the Scandinavians. When Ari Thorgilsson 'the Learned', Iceland's first historian, wrote in the third decade of the 12th century about the settlement of Iceland, this is what he recorded:

> Iceland was first settled from Norway in the days of Harald Finehair, the son of Halfdan the Black.

According to the opinion and reckoning of Teit my foster-father, son of Bishop Isleif, the wisest man I have known; and of Thorkel son of Gellir, my father's brother, who had a very long memory; and of Thorid, daughter of Snorri the Priest, who was both very knowledgeable and accurate: this was at the time when Ivar son of Ragnar Lothbrok had St Edmund, the king of the English, killed, which was 870 years after the birth of Christ, as it is written in his [St Edmund's] saga.

It is probable that St Edmund's 'saga' is Abbo's Life. But the striking thing here is that Ari locates his story in relation to just three historical reference-points: that of Harald Finehair (and the majority of the Icelandic family sagas do that); the birth of Christ (a universal learned reference-point); and the death of St Edmund. The date of Edmund's death is conveniently close to the time of the first settlement of Iceland, but even so, the prominence given to the Edmund story is remarkable.

Ælfric's version of Edmund's story (Text 21) starts with a messenger coming from Hinguar, the Viking leader, to Edmund with the demands of the Viking army. The messenger says that Edmund must give Hinguar half of the treasures of the land and become an under-king, one who will do what the Vikings want. Edmund asks a bishop what he should do, and the bishop tells him that it is probably best to agree to the demands of the Vikings. Edmund is not impressed. He gives the messenger a spirited reply for his audacity, responding that he will only accept the terms if Hinguar first submits to Christ; otherwise, he would rather die. When the messenger passes on this reply, the army hurries to Edmund's hall, where Edmund throws away his weapons, is captured, bound and beaten, then used as a target, and finally beheaded. The king's head is thrown into the bushes where a wolf finds it. Some time later Edmund's people go looking for the head so that they can bury Edmund properly, and as they wander through the forest they call out to each other 'Where are you?' Edmund's head replies, 'Here, here, here', and they find the wolf guarding the head, and take the head back in triumph.

Edmund is buried, a church is built, and miracles start to happen. The body is dug up to be moved to what is now Bury St Edmunds, and is found incorrupt, the wounds healed, with only a thin red line around the neck to show that Edmund was beheaded. A certain widow Oswyn then looks after the body, cutting the hair and nails. Because people honour the saint and make offerings at his shrine, it becomes wealthy, and sometime in the years between 926 and 951, eight thieves try to rob the sanctuary; they are frozen in position by the power of the saint, and are hanged for their pains. A certain man called Leofstan mockingly goes to check that the saint's body is incorrupt, and instantly goes mad before dying horribly.

Ælfric goes to some lengths to explain how he got his information and how Abbo, the writer from whom he borrowed, got his. He gives the circumstances of Abbo's visit to England and his writing of the *Life*, telling us in the preface that in 985, Abbo, from the Frankish monastery of Fleury, visited Archbishop Dunstan, and Dunstan told him the story. The substance of the information was what Dunstan had heard told in King Æthelstan's presence by King Edmund's sword-bearer, who was an eyewitness to the martyrdom. Abbo wrote this into the *Passio Sancti Eadmundi*, and dedicated it to Dunstan (Text 22). Abbo gives the story an impeccable pedigree, and although Ælfric omitted some of the more lurid details of the story in his translated sermon version, he did not omit the pedigree.

Ælfric translated Abbo's *Life* at the end of the 10th century. Many subsequent writers retold the tale and improved upon it. It even appears in the legendary *Saga of Ragnar Lothbrok*, because in Scandinavian tradition, Ivarr the Boneless (Hinguar) and Ubbe (Hubba), among others, were the sons of Ragnar 'Hairy-trousers', a famous Viking adventurer. This part of the tradition becomes significant in the account of the martyrdom given by Roger of Wendover in his 13th-century *Flowers of History*.

We have already noted that the precise details of the martyrdom are not present in the *Anglo-Saxon Chronicle* or in Asser. This is not surprising, for events in East Anglia were not at this time their overriding concern. So how reliable is Ælfric's account of the source of his story? Dorothy Whitelock calculated that if the sword-bearer was (as Abbo says) a very old man and Dunstan a young man, then there is no particular mathematical reason to doubt the transmission of the story through oral telling over the space of more than a century. She writes further,

> The main facts of the martyrdom are likely to be true. On this central theme, Abbo could not drastically have altered what he claimed to have heard from Dunstan, to whom he sent this work. He could not have invented the armour-bearer. Nor is it likely that Dunstan should indulge in motiveless and flamboyant lying. It is one thing to add to one's narrative speeches and moral statements; it is a different matter to turn a death in battle into a cruel execution after the battle. Nor is the account of the martyrdom incredible. The slaying of a prisoner by the Danes, using him as a target can be paralleled by the martyrdom of St Ælfheah in

1012. The removal of the head is a well-evidenced
practice among primitive peoples. There is good
support for making Hinguar the Danish leader at
this time.

We can agree with much of this, and the views of such a scholar
are not lightly to be discounted. But there are flaws in the argument. Perhaps the most significant is the implication that
the only alternative to telling the truth is 'invent[ing]' and
'motiveless and flamboyant lying'. As we have already seen, the
manipulation of stories and events better to represent the saintly
ideal is one of the more significant purposes of hagiography.

The ultimate source of the story in Abbo is Edmund's
sword-bearer. This fact is rather obscured by Abbo's focus on
King Æthelstan and the future Archbishop Dunstan. While
the latter two are unimpeachable witnesses, as Abbo was fully
aware, the sword-bearer is not. Now Professor Whitelock says
the sword-bearer is a person who could not have been
invented, and if we are to believe that Dunstan told what he
had heard and Abbo recorded it accurately, then as a person
he was probably not invented. But the whole notion of a
sword-bearer is foreign to Anglo-Saxon times. Anglo-Saxon
kings carried their own arms and fought their own battles.
Moreover, it is fundamentally improbable that a sword-bearer
in heroic times would have been able passively to watch all
the king's sufferings so as to pass on the story. And if he had,
it is unlikely that such a man would have been given much
credit for watching his king die. The whole idea runs counter
to the most basic ideals of loyalty of the Anglo-Saxons, such
as we find in *The Battle of Maldon*. Indeed, Ælfric and even
Abbo seem to be aware of the difficulty because at the crucial
point they shift the responsibility for the story to 'a certain
man [who] was there nearby, kept hidden from the heathen by

God, who heard all this and told it afterwards just as we have related it here'.

ROMAN MARTYRS AND EDMUND

Once that problem is registered, it is not difficult to see what Abbo was doing with the story. If we are disposed to doubt the eyewitness testimony of the 'sword-bearer', it is not difficult to account for most of the features of Edmund's martyrdom. As we have noted, the focus in the *passio* is on the manner of the martyr's death and often the debate which precedes it, as he or she is offered the chance of life by the tyrannical and often demonic opponent. The saint always turns down the offer, and is tortured horribly before succumbing to death. In a rather subtle way, Abbo and Ælfric have exchanged Hinguar and his messenger for the Roman governor or emperor, but otherwise the details are much as the convention demands. Edmund's courage and kingly dignity are shown to good effect against the boasting and pride of the Viking messenger.

After his capture, Edmund was first beaten with rods or cudgels; then he was tied to a tree, and was whipped; when the Vikings lost patience, they shot at him with arrows and spears. Even at this stage, Edmund was still calling out to Christ, and he was finally beheaded. The details here are those which are traditional for a martyrdom. Roman martyrs were beaten with rods or cudgels, as were St Lawrence and St Bartholomew in Ælfric's homilies. Lawrence was later whipped as Edmund was; and like many Roman martyrs, Bartholomew was beheaded as Edmund was. Examples of these kinds of tortures can be multiplied from Old English poems and stories of the saints, from the *Old English Martyrology*, and from the Bible. And all the martyrs pray and call out to Christ during their torments. The point is that these tortures are known to be the practices of the persecuting Romans and are not known to be the practices of the Vikings.

Next the Vikings shoot at Edmund with arrows. Professor Whitelock offers in Ælfheah's death a parallel for shooting missiles at the martyr but it seems rather distant. Ælfheah's death by pelting with bones is well-attested and quite idiosyncratic in a Scandinavian way, as we have seen. But the specific parallel given by nearly all writers for the use of a martyr as a target is St Sebastian. As Ælfric says, Edmund was entirely covered with the Danes' missiles, like the bristles of a hedgehog. The *Acts of St Sebastian, Martyr* from the fifth century, the *Old English Martyrology* on St Sebastian from the ninth century, Abbo himself, and Ælfric, all give this simile.

And there is another very strong link with a Roman martyr-story relating to a man who died in the persecution of the Emperor Diocletian. When Leofstan the mocker checks to see if Edmund's body is incorrupt, he dies. Once again Abbo draws the parallel with a Roman martyr, St Lawrence, and as Ælfric observes in his version of St Lawrence's *Life*, 'people always wanted to see how he lay ... but God checked them, so that seven people died together in a single viewing there'.

The details of the martyrdom of Edmund in Abbo's account, followed closely by Ælfric, are therefore characteristic of Roman martyrdom stories. This leaves the later miracle-stories. Now these are generic, in the sense that such stories occur throughout the hagiographical tradition. The spiritual order of things breaks through into the ordinary: the incorruption of the body signifies the moral purity of the character; the punitive miracles warn the presumptuous against treating the saint with contempt, and reveal the fact that the saint has heavenly power through his relics to work miracles on earth. Moreover, the later miracle-stories are in some obvious cases based on local tradition rather than the supposed testimony of the sword-bearer. So the account given by Abbo cannot be said to be history, nor was it supposed to be.

SCANDINAVIAN TRADITION

The fact remains, however, that there was a strong tradition which passed on the story of the martyrdom. Among the Danes and their descendants, there must have been an oral tradition since none of the available hagiographical accounts of the martyrdom pre-dates the issue of the St Edmund coinage. This suggests that at least some elements of the story may have been an eyewitness account after all – not by some hidden sword-bearer, but by the murderers themselves. Certainly, something about Edmund's death prompted the veneration of the Danes, and the spread of that veneration through the Scandinavian world. After the much older saints Alban, Botulf and Brigid, St Edmund is the most frequently commemorated saint from Britain in Scandinavian kalendars, litanies, masses and offices: two of these saints are Celtic, Brigid and Alban; Botulf was, like Edmund, an East Anglian saint, with a very widespread cult throughout Scandinavia. If the martyrdom story did originate from the Danes, then what Abbo has done is to remove any authentic detail and replace it with the tried and tested formulas of the Roman martyrdom stories. He has done what Osbern did later with the martyrdom of Ælfheah, and indeed what many hagiographers thought to be their business – he has shown the communion of saints in demonstrating the similarity, not the particularity, of their sufferings and powers.

POLITICAL ELEMENTS TO THE STORY

There is, moreover, a political element to the writing and publication of Abbo's hagiography. The early development of the cult of St Edmund is rather obscure, and it is unknown precisely when the body was translated from where it was initially housed (we are told) in a temporary shelter, to what was to become Bury St Edmunds. The translation of the body, it should be remembered, is the time at which the cult becomes officially acknowledged. There are late traditions which variously date the translation to the early years of the 10th century, and some time before the reign of Æthelstan (924–39), and Abbo himself says the relics were at Bury by the time of Theodred, bishop of London from 926. But, curiously, this detail is unmarked in the early sources. At the time of the translation, assuming it did take place in the first quarter of the 10th century, the Danes had settled in East Anglia and had taken political control; they had in addition been converted to Christianity.

However great or little the part of the local Anglo-Saxons in the origin of the cult (and Abbo and Ælfric make it great), it flourished under Danish overlordship, including the founding of a community. It is often, and reasonably, assumed that the cult was essentially opposed to the Danes and was a focus of resistance. Certainly Abbo emphasizes the heathen nature of the Danes and the cruel treatment the English and Edmund received at their hands. And there is no doubt that such cruelty occurred, though Abbo either did not know or did not care to clarify the details of the battles and harrying that went on around the time of Edmund's death. But there remains the possibility that the cult was encouraged by the Danes, to promote reconciliation between themselves and the conquered people, and to demonstrate the reality of their conversion.

The political context of Abbo's writing, and more so of Ælfric's a little later, is the renewal of Viking attacks in the late 10th century, and this accounts for the strong anti-Danish current in the work. What is still unclear is whether Abbo invented the martyrdom story completely or simply reworked the detail. Whichever it was, the intention of appropriating the cult for the cause of English unity and promotion of Christian resistance to the renewed Viking threat is clear enough. The telling of the tale in the presence of King Æthelstan, the king whose victory at *Brunanburh* was so significant in the political unification of England; and the retelling of the tale by Archbishop Dunstan, whose reform of the monasteries was so significant in the progress of Christianity in the 10th century, locates the story in this political and religious context, quite apart from its subject-matter.

LATER TRADITIONS

Later writers took up the story of King Edmund and greatly elaborated it. The account of Roger of Wendover, writing in St Albans in probably the third decade of the 13th century, is notable (Text 23). Roger's version gives us a tantalizing glimpse of a possible early version of the martyrdom. It gives motivation to the Danish leaders, and has some elements of overlap with the Norse saga of Ragnar Lothbrok, which was only written down later. Lothbrok, in Roger's account, was hawking in a boat, but was struck by a storm which eventually brought him to Norfolk. He was welcomed by King Edmund, and soon asked to learn more of the arts of hunting from the English. The king had his huntsman Bernus show him, but he excelled Bernus and aroused his envy. Bernus killed him and hid his body in the wood. The body was discovered when Lothbrok's faithful dog would not desert it except rarely to eat at King Edmund's table, and was followed back to the body. As a punishment, Bernus was set adrift in Lothbrok's boat. He drifted to Denmark; there he was tortured by Hinguar and Hubba to disclose what had happened to Lothbrok their father, and told them that he had been killed on King Edmund's order. They immediately set off on an expedition of revenge using Bernus as their guide. With some minor variations, the tale then follows Abbo's *Passio.*

Roger's concern is to tidy up the story and give motivation
to the characters. The attacks of the sons of Lothbrok are
prompted by desire for vengeance and by malicious lies on the
part of Bernus. The story is balanced, with the body of
Lothbrok being hidden in a wood and guarded by a faithful
dog, and the head of Edmund being hidden in a wood and
guarded by a wolf. There are parallels as well between
Lothbrok's arrival in the drifting boat, and the punishment
meted out to Bernus.

It is suggested by scholars that this tale originated in
the reign of Cnut, and was prompted by the need to mitigate
the anti-Danish sentiment of the earlier versions. Roger's version evidently had access to Danish sources or traditions, but
it does not much change the outline of Abbo's story of the
martyrdom. In combining the sources, Roger probably opted
for the line of least resistance, as he often did: he retained
most of the written source, and adapted the other traditions
to fit. But we no longer have access to these traditions, except
through Roger's version; whether they included a genuine
alternative, from the Danish perspective, to Abbo's official
hagiography we cannot now tell.

I have suggested that the armour- or sword-bearer in
Abbo's *Passio* might be a useful fiction to give credibility to an
earlier story filtered through the hagiographical traditions of
the church. The attribution to Dunstan himself may simply
have been a way of attaching his authority to this story, and
showing respect for the great churchman. Roger's version
gives us a tantalizing glimpse of this possible alternative,
which might have originated earlier than the reign of Cnut,
and have given a more authentic version of the martyrdom.
But it is impossible to assert anything other than that
Edmund was killed by the Danes, and was very early venerated as a martyr by both Danes and Anglo-Saxons.

The veneration of Edmund among the Danes shown by the St Edmund memorial coinage and the varying traditions of the martyrdom which seem to have Scandinavian sources reveal that the cult was put to use by the descendants of the people who killed the king. The stories gave at least some motivation for the killing, and the veneration of the king was a kind of public repentance and restitution for an acknowledged wrong. In the years following the martyrdom, the saint and his cult and hagiography were used by Anglo-Scandinavians to promote reconciliation and integration. Hagiography, then, is put to different uses by various writers. The official versions by Abbo and Ælfric were used with an overt moral, spiritual, and indeed political purpose.

ÆLFRIC AND ENGLAND

When Ælfric translated the *passio* of Edmund and the *vita* of Oswald, he wanted to teach lessons about virtue and holy living, which is the overall purpose of homilies. He also wanted to reinforce the Christian world-view. At the end of Oswald's life he wrote, 'it is no wonder that the holy king could heal sickness now that he lives in heaven, because he wanted to help the poor and weak when he was here on earth'. But there was another thing that Ælfric wanted to teach, and he made this plain at the end of Edmund's life:

> the English nation is not deprived of the Lord's saints since in England there lie such saints as this holy king [Edmund], the blessed Cuthbert, St Æthelthryth of Ely and her sister incorrupt in body, for the confirmation of the faith. There are also many other saints among the English who

work many miracles, as is widely known, to the
praise of the Almighty in whom they believed.

Ælfric had a nationalistic agenda, writing as he was in a time
when the Danes were again invading, raiding and killing. He
saw in Oswald, as Bede did, a new Constantine, taking the
cross into battle; he saw in Edmund, as Abbo did, a new St
Sebastian, martyred under Diocletian by being used as a
target; and in the same life he compares the fate of the arro-
gant mocker Leofstan with the fate of those who mocked St
Lawrence, seven of whom died. Ælfric saw these English
saints and martyrs as an emblem of hope for his native land, a
sign of the special blessing of God, and an encouragement for
the faith of the English, troubled but not subdued by the fear-
some Vikings. Ælfric saw the English as making a significant
contribution to Christendom as a whole, and as having such
saints as the early church had – those (in the words of
Tertullian, the early Church Father) whose blood was the
seed of the church.

7

ANGLO-SAXON ENDINGS:
FEAR AND FAITH

 The Anglo-Saxons were intrigued by questions of beginnings and endings. Two very popular topics for consideration in verse and prose from throughout the entire period are the Creation of the world, and the End, whether personal or cosmic. Cædmon's *Hymn*, purportedly the first Christian verse in English, is about the creation of the world. Poems and sermons, proverbs and charters all have references to the End, to death, judgement, heaven and hell. In two versions of the same poem (enterprisingly called *Soul and Body*), the soul addresses the body, reproaching the body for indulging itself and not taking enough care of its soul and for leading it to hell. In two versions of another poem (equally enterprisingly entitled *The Judgment Day*), the Day of Judgement is described in detail. Sermons collect and list the biblical signs of the Last Days and focus on the rewards and punishments to come. Manuscript illustrations include graphic pictures of demons forking souls into the gaping mouth of hell, as we have seen in an earlier chapter. Urgent warnings for people to be prepared for the end occur in all kinds of places.

It would be a mistake to suppose that the Anglo-Saxons only started to focus on endings when the Vikings appeared on the scene. For much of this chapter we will examine the way Christian ideas of personal and cosmic endings are related to social conditions throughout the Anglo-Saxon period. But it is clear that the advent of the Vikings made a very significant impact on the way the Anglo-Saxons thought of endings, and contributed to a fearful anticipation of the end of the world. The sense that the land and its people were under God's judgement that we saw in the second chapter arose in the first Viking attacks, but it sharpened into a fear of apocalypse in the second wave of Viking attacks. The specific interpretation of the millennium as the time of the reign of Antichrist would hardly have gripped the imagination of churchmen if all had been tranquil in England. Nevertheless, fear was overcome by pragmatic faith.

THE LAST THINGS

Eschatology, ideas relating to 'the four last things', namely death, judgement, heaven and hell in the Christian scheme of things, was part of the fabric of the Anglo-Saxon world-view. Where life is poor, nasty, brutish and short, the thoughtful person naturally desires some sort of meaning, purpose and justice to it. And in Anglo-Saxon England eschatological ideas were never far from the surface. Sudden death could and did come, whether from natural causes or from external attack. The Vikings played their part in keeping people from becoming smug in the face of death, but that part had been played by others before them. A poem in the Exeter Book of Old English poetry is called *The Fortunes of Men*, but is largely a list of the ways in which people can die, more appropriately 'The Misfortunes of Men' perhaps. But eschatological ideas come in varying packages: people conceive and use ideas in different ways according to a variety of factors, and this chapter will explore some of these before showing how eschatology took a particular turn at the end of the first millennium.

ESCHATOLOGY AND CONVERSION

There is a passage in Bede's *Ecclesiastical History*, Book II, chapter 13, where an unnamed chief addresses King Edwin's council, held in the year 627, to discuss what the religion of Northumbria should be. The chief describes human life as like the flight of a sparrow through the hall in winter; for a while the bird is in the warmth and light, but soon it passes out into the darkness whence it came, and he concludes,

> 'So this life of man appears but for a moment; what follows or indeed what went before, we know not at all. If this new doctrine brings us more information, it seems right that we should accept it.' Other elders and counsellors of the king continued in the same manner, being divinely prompted to do so.

There are certain difficulties for us in accepting this story at face value. One of these is that the chief's claim to ignorance about 'the other world' seems to run counter to the evidence of Anglo-Saxon heathen burial. At more or less the same time as this council was taking place, 150 miles to the south, a ship with rich grave goods was interred in a mound at Sutton Hoo. There is still debate over the purpose of such deposits, and the symbolism of the ship itself. But it all argues for a strong, if possibly residual, concept of an afterlife involving a journey in which such things as weapons and money, food and drink might be needed. Ignorance of what follows or precedes life is in any case contradicted by the chief's next sentence, with the reference to 'more information'. This implies at least some information

already. This was and is a matter on which most people have
their views.

Perhaps we should not press the details too far. But quite
apart from the archaeological and logical problems, there is
the fact that the image of the sparrow's flight itself presents a
rather forbidding notion of the other world, as a world of cold
and storms, dark and terrible. In a purely naturalistic sense
these things are chilling. But they are also characteristics
of hell in Germanic myth and some apocryphal texts of the
biblical tradition. In a popular eschatological vision recorded
by Bede in the last book of his *Ecclesiastical History*, a man
called Dryhthelm sees souls leaping from a burning pit into
one filled with 'raging hail and bitter snow' and back again
without relief of their torment. Bede goes to some pains to
assert that this is not hell itself, lest people should think that
there is some alternative to the biblical fire, but not every-
body who heard the story was quite so discriminating. The
sparrow story, when set in a wider Anglo-Saxon context,
reflects the uncertainty of heathen beliefs (or Bede's knowledge of them) about the before- and after-life, but it also
seems to reflect a Christian perspective on those beliefs.

Wherever he got the story from, and however he processed
it, Bede was concerned to replace the uncertainty, intellectual
inadequacy and variety of pre-Christian eschatological beliefs
with the sure teaching of the Church. And at the same time
he wished to present the intellectual strength of Christian
eschatology as one of the major factors which gave
Christianity its appeal in the conversion of Northumbria, if
not of England.

ESCHATOLOGY AND DYING

When Bede was dying, he was accompanied and helped by a
young man called Cuthbert, later the monastery's abbot, who

recorded Bede's one surviving vernacular work, his *Death Song*. It is a maxim, a kind of proverb:

> Before that inevitable journey no one becomes
> wiser in his thoughts than is necessary for him,
> in order to ponder, before his departure,
> what might be the judgement on his soul,
> whether good or evil, after his death-day.

Christian eschatological certainty is there: death and judgement are inevitable, and preparation essential. The simple contrast of 'good or evil' towards the end is fraught with implications of heaven and hell. In the face of his own death, Bede warns himself and others to fear complacency. No one gives enough thought to the very important question of how he or she will be judged. And if Bede's maxim lodged itself in the memory of scribes and ordinary people, perhaps Bede would have helped some, at least, in their preparation. At any rate, this account of Bede's death by Cuthbert, with its lines of English verse, was very frequently copied. Even if they did not understand the English, scribes on the Continent and down to the 16th century in England recorded the verse, and there are more manuscript copies of this poem in Old English than of any other.

Bede himself probably coined the proverbial-sounding phrases of his *Death Song*. He probably felt that a generalized reflection on the End was an appropriate and pious way to approach his own end. It is striking how many Anglo-Saxon poets and homilists felt that such reflections were appropriate to bring their discourses to a close. A speaker uses various techniques from tone of voice and gesture, to 'markers' of various kinds, to indicate that he or she is finishing. The Anglo-Saxons tended not to use that prompt of false hope,

'Finally ...', but to close by talking of the end of ends, the ultimate, final, personal and cosmic end. At root, this is a simple association of ideas: ending with the End. But it is developed in all kinds of ways, so that while it is in some senses predictable, it is also varied and purposeful.

SOME LOOSE ENDS

The poet of the *Rune Poem* seems to have had a mission to cram as much eschatology into his poem as possible, perhaps because he was aware of the traditional, even pre-Christian origin of his material. This is an alphabetical poem which is something like an adult version of 'A is for apple'. Naturally there is some difficulty in elaborating an eschatological message from the words which represent the characters of the runic alphabet, such as aurochs (an extinct kind of bison) or birch or hail. But in the eschatological view, money (*feoh*) has to be given away to secure God's approval, hardship (*nyde*) can be a source of help and salvation if it is heeded in time, human beings betray each other simply by dying. And at the end of the poem, earth is the destiny of the dead, where the flesh cools, goes livid, and all human bonds are broken.

Similarly, the poem called *The Order of the World* ends on an eschatological note:

> therefore a man must determine that he will obey
>   the Lord,
> each one of the sons of men determine to abandon
>   empty pleasures,
> let every wickedness sink below with fiery sins,
> abandon the transitory joy of life, and aspire to the
>   bliss of joys above,
> journey to the better kingdom.

Part of the poem itself is a contemplation of the sun's rising and setting, and the exhortation here echoes that in part, with sins sinking below, and the soul aspiring to bliss. Certainly the poet is using the inevitability and predictability of the created order to suggest the same of the eternal order, 'the better kingdom' to which he wants his hearers to aspire.

There are two manuscripts of a very small collection of Latin and Old English verse proverbs, where the proverbs basically say that something becomes its opposite. This is a pretty bleak view of life when each of the first set of terms is a good thing. Yet apparently these proverbs were used as translation exercises for the instruction and education of the young. Here again they are left with the reminder of mortality:

> Heat grows cold, white becomes dirty,
> the beloved becomes hated, light becomes dark.
> Everything which is not eternal decays with age.

Two of the Old English elegies which explore the experience of loneliness and exile close with a focus on heaven. For the protagonist of *The Seafarer*, the exile is one voluntarily undertaken for the love of God; it is enforced exile for the protagonist of *The Wanderer*. For both, the consolation is that hardship and all earthly things are transient, whereas heaven is permanent. *The Wanderer* ends with a switch of focus from despairing contemplation of the impermanence of pleasures, relationships and all the trappings of earthly power:

> Well it is for the one who seeks grace,
> comfort from the Father in heaven,
> where for us all security remains.

The protagonist has related in the poem how he perhaps unknowingly experienced the Lord's grace, and how he sought security in his bitter exile: now he seeks grace and finds security. In *The Seafarer*, the idea of heaven as home has particular resonance to the exile who has given up home and family for the love of God:

> Let us consider where we have our home,
> and then work out how we might get to it,
> and then also work so that we arrive there,
> in the eternal blessedness
> where is the source of life, hope in heaven,
> in the love of the Lord.

WULFSTAN

This kind of idea was not only the province of the poets. Late in the Old English period, Wulfstan the homilist and later archbishop annotated a fair-copied manuscript of his own various works, apparently at different times, as thoughts occurred to him. His miscellaneous jottings occupy about two-thirds of a page of a manuscript now kept in Copenhagen. 'Everyone needs spiritual sustenance' is the kind of thought, along with the biblical quotation in Latin, 'man shall not live by bread alone', and it is easy to see how Wulfstan's thoughts were developing these ideas into the bones of a sermon. The middle section of these jottings is a proverbial comparison,

> How can the one who is away from his land and far from home return home if he will not learn how the road lies that leads to his home? How can we find the straight road to heaven unless we get into the habit of asking and eagerly consider how we can get there?

There is a strong similarity between this and the ending of *The Seafarer* quoted above. Wulfstan apparently made a few notes that he might use later, and this proverbial comparison might well have given one of his sermons a dramatic ending, pointing his listeners to their final destiny, and urging them to live and learn in such a way that they would arrive at the right destination.

One of the characteristic ways of describing the fate of souls in hell in Old English is by using the word 'woe'. Wulfstan uses it often. In an eschatological sermon on Luke he describes in detail the horrors of hell and abruptly generalizes, 'Woe to those who have to dwell there in torment'. Another collection of eschatological material made by Wulfstan was of the 'Woes' from Isaiah and Jeremiah. 'Woe to the wicked', says Isaiah (3:11), 'Woe to you who add house to house', 'Woe to those who rise early in the morning to follow drunkenness' (Isaiah 5:8, 11) and so on, describing the nasty habits and comeuppance of people in Isaiah's time, but also and not coincidentally, in Wulfstan's time. In the Old English version accompanying these Latin 'Woes' in another manuscript, there is the doleful refrain, 'Isaiah said yet more which came to pass upon the sinful people'. These 'Woes' are not developed into a coherent sermon, but each is self-contained, perhaps the core of a future homily.

THE END OF AN EPISODE
In Old English poetry, hellish 'Woe' is often contrasted with heavenly 'Well', the similarity of sound marking the opposition of sense. The poet of *Beowulf* uses the phrases to sum up and give judgement on an episode in the history of the Danes early in his poem. The poet tells of the establishment of Hrothgar's kingdom and the building of his hall Heorot. Songs in the hall enrage the monster Grendel who starts

to visit and devour men; the Danes try to kill Grendel, but do not succeed, so in their desperation they try offerings to idols:

> Such was their habit,
> the hope of the heathen. They thought of hell
> in their hearts. They did not know the Lord,
> the Judge of deeds, they were not acquainted with
>   the Lord God,
> and did not know how to worship him, the
>   Guardian of the heavens
> and Lord of glory. Woe it is for the one who must
> through persistent enmity thrust his soul
> into the embrace of the fire, expect no change
> or alteration of any sort. Well it is for the one who
>   is permitted
> after the day of death to approach the Lord
> and to ask for protection in the embrace of the
>   Father.

The grim play on the word 'embrace' here, reinforced by 'Woe' and 'Well', underlines the stark contrast in the two kinds of fates: the embrace of the Father or the embrace of the fire of hell. This passage comes at the end of a verse section, and draws the line under this episode in the Danes' history, allowing the poet to acknowledge that historically his characters were heathen, but that it was not their fault. He treats them throughout with sympathy. There were some Anglo-Saxon preachers who would have condemned the Danes out of hand, but the way the *Beowulf* passage ends on a note of hope is characteristic of the poet's eschatological optimism.

FOLK ESCHATOLOGY

A collection of folk wisdom in verse called *Maxims II* turns
from very miscellaneous observations to concentrate in its last
few lines on the fate of the soul after death:

> The Creator alone knows
> where the soul will go afterwards,
> and all the spirits who go before God
> after the day of death to await judgement
> in the embrace of the Father. The future is
> hidden and secret; the Lord alone knows these
>   things,
> the saving Father; no one comes back
> here under the roofs who can say for sure
> to people what might be the Lord's decree,
> the establishment of the victorious where he
>   himself dwells.

The reflection that leads to this conclusion is 'The wise man
ought to ponder on the conflict of the world; the criminal
must hang to repay properly what he did earlier'. As Dr
Johnson said, 'when a man knows he is to be hanged in a fort-
night, it concentrates his mind wonderfully'. Perhaps one of
the more interesting features of the ideas expressed here,
though, is the way they combine generality and specificity,
certainty and uncertainty. The poet seems to be picking up
ideas from all kinds of sources. While there is certainty about
judgement, the poet takes refuge in the uncertainty of the
outcome. And while he asserts the hiddenness of things and
God's unique knowledge, he nevertheless stresses only the
positive aspects of eschatology, 'the embrace of the Father' (as
in *Beowulf*), 'the saving Father', 'the establishment of the
victorious'. Such a poem provides something of a relief from

the dread warnings and not infrequent doom and gloom of the more rigorous homilists in prose and verse. But it does it by a kind of poetic shrug: 'we can't be sure' – in relation to the unpleasant things, at least.

Eschatology was familiar ground to the Anglo-Saxons, then. In the uncertainty of life, eschatology was an ever-present concern. It was appropriate to the rhetoric of conversion, to pious reflection at the approach of death, to description and depiction of Christian living. It occurs in a great variety of places, but was particularly useful for the purpose of giving a sense of an ending to formal discourse.

ESCHATOLOGY AND APOCALYPTIC

For all the seeming gloom of this insistence on eschatology, it helped people to face the harshness of life with Christian courage, knowing that in heaven, every tear would be wiped away, and there would be no more suffering. The biblical image of heaven as a banquet, explored for example towards the end of *The Dream of the Rood*, was one which combined creature comforts with social pleasures and joyous entertainment. Anyone who went to hell probably deserved the punishment, and not everyone was so sure about hell as they were about heaven, as we have seen. Eschatology was providential, benevolent and inevitable.

Biblical apocalyptic, in the Book of Daniel in the Old Testament or in the Book of Revelation at the end of the New Testament, originated in the miseries and hopes of the oppressed and persecuted, whether Jewish or Christian. It represented a profound mistrust of political power and a desire for the institution of the perfect rule of God. The end was envisioned as convulsive, destructive and comprehensive. Apocalyptic is to do with the end of the world order, the final battle of good and evil, the playing out of the cosmic conflict between God and the forces of evil in which human beings are pawns. In the biblical book of Revelation, beasts, monsters, fires, plagues and wars manifest themselves on earth. In the apocalyptic teaching of Jesus in the gospels, the cosmic upheaval of earthquakes and the failing of the sun, moon and stars, is mirrored in the caving-in of social conventions. Human beings are deceived, plagued, slaughtered; they turn on each other, even within families, to kill and be killed. So whereas in eschatological teaching the ending of personal death and judgement, though fearful, is potentially happy, in apocalyptic visions, new and disturbing ideas are introduced of opposition to God, decay of faith, decline in morals, deception and failure in the church, terror and plague in the world. In other words, the ending threatened by apocalyptic was not simply personal, rather it was about impersonal forces devastating everything earthly: an end of individuality, society, and state.

THE MILLENNIUM

Not unnaturally, this generalized preoccupation with eschatology came into sharper focus at the end of the first millennium. Bede had explained in his chronological works the idea of the Six Ages of the World, and the seventh age that was the eternal reign of Christ and the saints after the Last Judgement. This scheme was based upon the creation story of Genesis, in which God created the world in six days and rested on the seventh or sabbath day. The ages were punctuated by important events in the biblical story: the first age was from Adam to Noah, the second from Noah to Abraham, and so on. The last age, the sixth age of the world, was inaugurated by the birth of Jesus and would be brought to a close by the end of the world and the Day of Judgement.

The Anglo-Saxon scholar knew that he was living in the Last Days. Abbot Ælfric, preaching on Luke 21, warned people in his sermon for the Second Sunday of Advent:

> In the lesson Jesus said, 'nation shall rise against nation, kingdom against kingdom, great earthquakes shall be everywhere and pestilence and hunger' ... Indeed in these new days nations have arisen against nations, and their affliction on earth has happened greater than we read of in old books. Often an earthquake in various places has over-thrown many cities, as it happened in the days of Tiberius Caesar, when thirteen cities fell in an earthquake. With pestilence and hunger we are frequently afflicted ...

The fact that Ælfric does not specify the various earthquakes, but only that they were like the well-documented ones in Tiberius's reign (AD 14–37), might suggest that his desire to warn his people of the signs of the times was greater than his recall of specific events. Later in the same sermon he admits that the signs in the sun, moon and stars predicted in Luke and the other gospels have not been noted yet. Nevertheless, Ælfric knew that he was living in the last days of the world, and the fulfilment of these prophecies was only a matter of time.

A MATTER OF TIME

Bede had also popularized the Dionysian BC/AD dating system, which gave the scholar a grasp of universal chronology. Hitherto, and indeed for long after Bede among ordinary people, the normal system of dating had been according to the number of years the king had reigned. In Bede's day this gave rise to problems, because there were different kings ruling the small kingdoms which made up Anglo-Saxon England. At a stroke, the Dionysian system gave the foundation any serious historian needed: a way of locating events in different places in a consistent historical continuum. Strikingly, however, this was no neutral, purely scientific calculation, because it provided time with a beginning, creation; an essential turning-point, the birth of Christ; and a sense of momentum towards an end, the apocalypse. Before, there was a patchwork of events, one patch similar to another patch, overlapping with some, contrasting with others. The Dionysian system made the patches into a pattern with a meaning. Allied with the idea of the six ages and biblical prophecies about the end of the world, the Dionysian system gave rise to speculation that the end of the first millennium would also herald the end times when Satan was let loose, Antichrist would reign, and the pangs of the apocalypse would begin.

The particular significance of the idea of the thousand years, the millennium, came from Revelation 20, where St John writes,

> I saw an angel coming down out of heaven, having the key to the Abyss and holding in his hand a great chain. He seized the dragon, that ancient serpent who is the devil or Satan, and bound him for a thousand years. He threw him in to the Abyss and locked and sealed it over him, to keep him from deceiving the nations any more until the thousand years were ended. After that, he must be set free for a short time ...

From early in the 10th century there are references to the last days, and individuals reading the signs of the times, from wars and rumours of wars, signs in the heavens, earthquakes, pestilence and famine, betrayal and breaking of family bonds. By the end of the 10th century and into the 11th, there is a spate of apocalyptic and eschatological work. Bede's *Judgment Day* poem was translated into Old English verse at this time. The *Apocalypse of Thomas*, an apocryphal treatise on the Last Judgement, was translated probably on four different occasions. The *Vision of Paul*, another apocryphal work attributed to one of Christ's apostles, was a popular text, and Ælfric felt obliged to condemn it. Adso, a French abbot, had written a letter to his queen around the middle of the 10th century detailing the life and times of the Antichrist, and this book, the *Libellus de Antechristo*, was translated possibly by Wulfstan, and certainly used by him in a series of five sermons composed just before the millennium. Ælfric made extensive use of Julian of Toledo's *Prognosticon Futuri Saeculi*. Visions of heaven and hell appear in the anonymous collections of homilies.

Some rather strange and not always orthodox notions make their appearance around this time. Ælfric thought that at the general resurrection of the dead, people would be 33 years old, presumably because Jesus was that age at the time of his crucifixion and resurrection. Some sources dealing with the nature of hell picture it as alternately hot and cold (see above), an idea which probably originated in the *Vision of Paul* and before that in Job's curse, Job 24:19 (in the Vulgate it reads, 'Let him pass from the snow waters to excessive heat: and his sin even to hell'). The old idea that demons pounce on the soul as it leaves a person's body at death is given a new lease of life. In the version of the *Apocalypse of Thomas* written into the margin of one manuscript, there is the curious claim that after the Last Judgement, Mary the mother of Jesus, St Peter and the archangel Michael will each claim a third of the condemned souls, rescuing them from hell.

Apocalyptic ideas make their appearance in slightly unex-pected places, too. The early crucifixion poem found in runes on the Ruthwell Cross is apparently expanded in the poem now called the *Dream of the Rood*, which includes a set piece on the Judgement Day, and an afterthought on the harrowing of Hell (Text 24). Aldred, the glossator of the Lindisfarne Gospels, working about 960, gives mostly literal, word-for-word translations of the Latin text of the gospels, but at several points he gives brief theological commentary. For the Beatitudes (compare Text 17) in Matthew 5, he adds com-mentary which expands and puts an eschatological spin on the biblical maxims. The marginal glosses, which are added to the literal interlinear gloss, to Matthew 5:4, 'blessed are the meek', Matthew 5:6, 'blessed are those who hunger and thirst for righteousness', and Matthew 5:8, 'blessed are the pure in heart', are as follows:

> For the meek shall possess the land of the living.
> Blessed are those who thirst and hunger for righteousness, for they will be satisfied in eternal life.
> Blessed are the clean in heart without treachery or any deceit, for they shall see God in eternity.

One might have supposed that there was sufficient about the Beatitudes to indicate a duality of interpretation, relating both to the here and now and the there and then; and in these cases, perhaps rather more of the latter. But Aldred notes the millennial factor: the land here and now does not belong to the meek, but rather to those who oppress them, and this will only be set right in heaven, 'the land of the living'; for the same reason those who long for righteousness will only be satisfied in eternal life; and treachery and deceit are apocalyptic signs of the present age that will pass away, before the eternal reign of God is established.

There are some indications that the interest in apocalyptic was not only English. The cross at Gosforth in Cumbria will be mentioned in more detail in the next chapter because it gives an insight into the conversion of the Scandinavian settlers. The iconography of the monument is remarkable: most of it can reasonably be interpreted as Scandinavian apoc-alyptic, depicting the events of Ragnarök, the end of the world. Every face of the cross has a monster or monsters: fantastically interlaced bodies writhe over it and end in wolf-heads with gaping jaws. On the upper east face Vithar, spear in hand, has one foot in the mouth of the apocalyptic wolf Fenrir of Norse mythology. He avenges the death of his father Odin by killing the wolf. On the west face Heimdall, with his horn in one hand and spear in the other, holds two beasts at bay. And below him, Loki lies bound under the fangs of a dragon dripping poison, and Sigyn his wife collects the venom.

These images can be interpreted by reference to the Scandinavian poems of the Edda, and Snorri Sturluson's prose redaction of the myths from the 13th century, and indeed from carvings and artefacts from Scandinavia and elsewhere. Loki, like Satan, is bound until the final cataclysm when he is loosed to fight, with the great earth-serpent and the wolf Fenrir and the terrible dog Garm, against the gods. Heimdall blows his horn to warn the gods of the approaching enemy forces, and in the ensuing fight Loki and Heimdall kill each other. The wolf swallows Odin, and Vithar, with one foot on the wolf's lower jaw, rips the jaws open to kill the wolf. Thor is killed by the huge earth-serpent, and the battle is brought to an end by the burning of the earth. The prelude to the whole event is the breakdown of social bonds, fighting, terrible winter, earth-quakes and the devouring of the sun and moon by monsters.

Snorri's narrative of Ragnarök is much coloured by his Christian world-view, and indeed there is strong evidence that the poem *Völuspá*, from which Snorri drew much of his material, was also influenced by Christian apocalyptic thinking. The ideas became common property, and were used by heathens and Christians alike around the time of the millennium. The fascination of the Gosforth cross is that it expresses a distinctly Scandinavian concern about the apocalypse within the context of a Christian monument.

SOCIAL CONDITIONS

Scholarly interest in the millennium was at least partly prompted by social conditions. If there had been peace and plenty in England at the time, and Ælfric's list of the signs of the last days had been even thinner than the one he gave in his Advent homily, it is doubtful that there would have been much concern about the number. Apart from some people camping out at Jerusalem and Megiddo, the site of the battle of Armageddon mentioned in Revelation, the end of the second millennium passed off without undue apocalyptic excitement. Conditions in the western world were basically stable and comfortable. But it was different at the end of the first millennium.

There had been a period of peace and consolidation after the first wave of Viking attacks and settlement that occupied most of the ninth century. The reign of King Edgar the Peaceable, 959–75, had seen the re-establishment of monasticism and the strengthening of the church. But after Edgar's death there had been an anti-monastic reaction. Monasteries were given privileges which freed them from taxes and services; local magnates naturally objected to being deprived of lands, income and workers, and under the new king, Edward, made life difficult for the monks. The *Anglo-Saxon Chronicle* (written of course by monks) records in 975,

In this year Edward, Edgar's son succeeded to the throne; and soon in the autumn of the same year appeared that star known as 'comet'. The next year came a great famine and very many distur- bances throughout England.

In his days on account of his youth, God's adversaries broke God's laws; Ealdorman Ælfhere and many others hindered the monastic rule and destroyed monasteries, dispersed monks and put to flight God's servants whom king Edgar had ordered the holy bishop Æthelwold to establish; widows were robbed many a time, and many injustices and evil crimes flourished thereafter, and ever afterwards things went from bad to worse.

The chronicler sees in these events the signs of the times which are a prelude to apocalypse: the comet, famine, war, attacks on the church, decline of morals and social bonds. In 978 Edward was assassinated, and Æthelred became king to popular acclaim. He reigned until 1016. Within two years of his accession, the second wave of Viking attacks began, and the sad story of the decline and humiliation of the English has already been recounted.

Æthelred's responses to the conditions in which he found himself were contradictory. He trusted the wrong men and his plan to get rid of the Scandinavian threat in one fell swoop on St Brice's Day in 1002 is passed over in silence by the chroniclers. Unable as he was to defeat the Vikings convinc- ingly in battle, and forced to pay tribute and provide food and lodging for the mobile and dangerous enemy forces who were not over-scrupulous about keeping their truce promises, Æthelred's reign went from bad to worse, as Archbishop Wulfstan was in the habit of saying.

While all this was going on, Æthelred increased his donations to monastic houses and religious causes. Even so, his
popularity did not last, even among the monks, and the
Anglo-Saxon Chronicle compilers who were not in the immediate circle of the court at Winchester became increasingly
critical of Æthelred and his policies.

THE CHURCH'S RESPONSE

The most famous Anglo-Saxon sermon, *Sermo Lupi ad Anglos*,
Archbishop Wulfstan's 'Address to the English, when the Danes
most severely persecuted them, namely in the year 1014 from
the Incarnation of Our Lord Jesus Christ' (Text 5), best encap-
sulates the response of the church to the social conditions.

> Beloved people, recognize what is the truth: this
> world is in haste heading towards the end, and for
> this reason the longer things go on in the world
> the worse it gets. And so it must of necessity
> worsen considerably because of people's sins before
> the coming of Antichrist. Then, indeed, it will be
> fearful and terrible throughout the world.
>
> Face the facts too, that the devil has deceived
> this nation all too completely, and that there has
> been little true faith among the people, though
> they say the right things, and that too many injus-
> tices have prevailed in the land. And there were
> never many people who reflected about remedies
> for these things as they ought; rather, day after day,
> one crime after another has been committed, injus-
> tice has been carried out, and the law often
> violated throughout the nation. So as a result we
> have experienced much injury and insult, and if

we wish to experience any remedy we must deserve
better from God than we have so far.

Wulfstan goes on to list the kind of things the English were up
to, and what was generally going on at this time: false religion,
contempt of the clergy and religious, oppression of the poor,
enslaving people on the merest pretext, loosing of family ties,
sexual licence and perversion, cowardice among the armies,
disregard of social order, abuse of power, cynicism, murder,
theft, whatever people thought they could get away with.
There are three main versions of the sermon, giving increasingly lurid details of the sins of the people; this suggests that
Wulfstan used the sermon more than once, and possibly that
things were getting worse, as the archbishop repeatedly says.

Several things are worth noticing here. Wulfstan emphasizes the incarnational date in his title, 'the year 1014 from
the Incarnation of Our Lord Jesus Christ'. Wulfstan certainly
expected something apocalyptic to happen around the thousand years after Christ's birth or death. Five sermons written
by him just before the millennium are packed with references
to the apocalypse. Among the Anglo-Saxons, however, there
was no rigid interpretation of the date. Written about the
same time as Wulfstan's *Sermo*, Byrhtferth of Ramsey's
Enchiridion or handbook of dates and mathematical calcula-
tions, discusses the six ages of the world in Bede's scheme as
'thousands', and notes that the first 'thousand' lasted 1,656
years according to Jewish scholars, and 2,242 years according
to the Greek writers of the Septuagint version of the Old
Testament. The failure of the Antichrist to appear on the
scene precisely one thousand years from the birth of Christ,
did not mean the end was not nigh.

Wulfstan goes on to stress that the general decline in moral
standards, though bad, is not the worst that can happen. And

although there is a degree of inevitability in the decline as
Wulfstan sees it in the first few lines, the greater part of the
sermon is castigating the English for their errors and sins, and
urging them to do better. So far as Wulfstan is concerned,
the problem is not the enemy, though they are the occasion of
the social breakdown, but the failure of English Christian
morality. Wulfstan makes no easy identification of the
Vikings with the forces of the devil or Antichrist. Indeed, he
holds up the heathen as examples several times: heathens
dare not refuse offerings to their gods and respect to priests,
but the so-called Christian English do. The implication of all
this is that the final apocalypse is avoidable, because the
English can still turn from their wicked ways.

Wulfstan closes his *Sermo ad Anglos,*

> Let us often consider the great Judgement which
> we must all face, and protect ourselves from the
> surging fire of hell's torment, and work to merit the
> glory and joy that God has prepared for those who
> do his will on earth. May God help us. Amen.

Having started his sermon with apocalyptic, Wulfstan slips
almost imperceptibly into eschatology.

And having started his ecclesiastical career with apocalyptic, Wulfstan seems to have spent most of the rest of his time
doing his best to ensure the apocalypse did not happen. He
was appointed Archbishop of York in 1002, the same year as
Æthelred's planned ethnic cleansing on St Brice's Day. The
province of York covered most of the area of England significantly influenced by the Scandinavians. Wulfstan would
certainly have had to deal with the suspicion and distrust of
some at least of his flock in the aftermath of the plot. In his
Sermo Lupi of 1014, he sees the Viking attackers as the

scourge of God on the apostate English, but puts the blame
for the state of the country on his own people. He drafted the
later law-codes of Æthelred in order to restrain the forces of
social breakdown.

When Æthelred died in 1016 and Prince Edmund died the
year after, Cnut, the Danish king and leader of the Viking
forces which had been such a thorn in Æthelred's side,
became king of England and reigned for the rest of Wulfstan's
life. Wulfstan was instrumental in negotiating the reconciliation between Cnut and the English church which led to Cnut
becoming, in legend at least, a most Christian king and benefactor of the church. And as Wulfstan had drafted laws for
Æthelred, so now he drafted them for Cnut. The famous story
of Cnut and the waves, though apocryphal, shows how the
simple re-establishment of royal authority was equated in
the popular mind with piety, goodness and all that was proper.
Cnut was happy to foster this notion, prudently marrying
Æthelred's widow, supporting the church, and going on pilgrimage to Rome. Wulfstan loyally supported him, despite
what he had said earlier about the savagery of the Danes.

By the time of his death in 1023, it is clear that Wulfstan
had become a significant politician, and was using his influence to mitigate the problems of his time, establish just laws
and encourage social stability. He has left a very varied legacy
of literature, but perhaps two mid-11th century inscriptions
are as much monuments to Wulfstan as they are to their dedi-
catees. In the church at Aldbrough in Yorkshire is a dial,
inscribed in a curious pidgin Norse–English with 'Ulf ordered
the church built for himself and for the soul of Gunvor'.
Another inscription, above a door at St Gregory's Minster,
Kirkdale, in North Yorkshire, reads, 'Orm Gamal's son bought
St Gregory's minster when it was all broken and fallen down,
and he had it built again from the ground for Christ and St

Gregory in the days of King Edward and Earl Tostig. Haword made me and Brand, priests.' The names of these people building and restoring churches, together with the priests, are all Scandinavian. These are the descendants of people who had found a home in the church of Wulfstan's time.

Wulfstan did not apparently lose his sense that the apocalypse and the end of all things was nigh. But there is no evidence from Anglo-Saxon England that anyone was sitting around waiting for the end, least of all Wulfstan. He identified the apocalypse as a process that could be if not reversed, then delayed. And he tried by all means possible to delay it. Resistance against the aggressor failed, but as a result of the political process and Wulfstan's diplomacy, peace and prosperity in material and religious terms returned. Reform and renewal in the church and the country took place. The apocalyptic signs of the times which Wulfstan and others saw around the turn of the millennium not only prompted the speculation that the end of the world was nigh. The simple and pragmatic identification of these signs as a moral problem also enabled scholars such as Wulfstan to deal with the failure of the apocalypse to happen. It was a threat, a crisis that was averted.

8

SCANDINAVIAN SETTLEMENT AND CHRISTIANITY

The Vikings changed the face of England. But living in England also changed the Vikings. The curious thing is that the literature of the Anglo-Saxons all but ignores both of these major changes. That the Scandinavians settled the land and became Christians emerges over a process of time – the fact that the Archbishop of York had something to do, for example. But *how* they became Christians, or indeed how they settled is not recorded directly. We have to deduce the processes from a wide range of evidence, not all of which is unambiguously clear. In this chapter we will look at place-names and language and sculpture as well as the literature to see if we can understand how these changes happened.

SCANDINAVIAN SETTLEMENT

The most significant results of the Viking attacks are mentioned almost in passing in the *Anglo-Saxon Chronicle*. In 876 'Halfdan shared out the land of the Northumbrians, and they proceeded to plough and maintain themselves'. In 877 the other part of the Viking army 'went to the land of the Mercians, part of which they shared out, and the other part they gave to Ceolwulf'. In 880 the Viking army from Cirencester 'went to East Anglia and occupied the land and shared it out'. In 890 Guthrum died, who 'lived in East Anglia and first settled the land'. And, by way of summary, in 896 'the Viking army dispersed, part into East Anglia, part into Northumbria, and the ones who had no money got ships there and went south over the sea to the Seine'. The chronicler was not much interested at this point in affairs beyond Wessex. Indeed, in his comments following the last settlement mentioned above, he shrugs off the effects of the previous hundred years with 'the Viking army had not too greatly troubled the English'; according to him, disease had been of far greater concern.

But half of England which had previously been ruled by English kings was now under the Danes. The land was divided along Watling Street between the Danelaw in the north and east, and Wessex in the south and west, a boundary neatly reflected in the place-names, many of which, north of Watling Street, are of Scandinavian type. Although interpretation of the evidence is still open to debate, it is now generally accepted that there was considerable intermarriage and secondary settlement: in effect, a migration from the Scandinavian homelands following the dividing up of English lands in the last quarter of the ninth century.

There are a few hints in the Chronicle as to how things progressed. Plainly there was a change of objective from raiding, to longer-term gains and richer prizes, and then to political domination and settlement. When the army stayed over the winter, in some sense its identity changed. The establishment of Ceolwulf in Mercia was consolidation of land gains with a view to later occupation. The story of King Edmund of East Anglia, unreliable in many details though it is, suggests that Hinguar was looking for a tributary king in East Anglia such as Ceolwulf was in Mercia. And after the initial distribution of lands in Northumbria and East Anglia, it seems that late-comers needed money to set up there since in 896 the ones without money had to go off to the Seine. This implies that to settle in the Danelaw required investment capital, money to buy land from the chiefs and kings settled there after the initial sharing out of land among the army. The later armies in 893 and 895 had so far settled as to have to make arrange-ments for the safety of their women, ships and goods in East Anglia when they went raiding to Chester and later moved between the Lea above London, and Bridgnorth on the Severn.

There is evidence in the *Anglo-Saxon Chronicle* of the estab-lishment of social and political structures, the development of ties of family and trade. This is backed up by archaeological evidence of manufacturing, trade and settlement from excava-tions in such places as York. But the Alfredian chronicler was much more interested in the military aspects, the attacks on Wessex, than in the internal development of Anglo-Scandinavian society. And the later chroniclers were more concerned with the re-establishment of English overlordship than with the kind of people, or their social organization, over whom the English kings gained control.

LANGUAGE AND NAMES

Names, both place-names and also personal names, are there-fore fundamental to the interpretation of the Scandinavian settlement, because there is not much other evidence. The evidence of names can give us only limited information, particularly in relation to the numbers of Scandinavian settlers involved. Some still argue that rather than widespread immigration, the settlers were few in number and constituted a military élite, which imposed its language and social patterns from above. But we can tentatively put together a picture of the process of Scandinavian settlement.

Part of the problem in interpreting the evidence for the Danish settlement is that whereas there was virtually no overlap between Celtic and Anglo-Saxon elements in names, there is quite a bit of overlap between Anglo-Saxon and Scandinavian. The languages are closely related, and for example, the words 'house', *hus*, 'slope', *hlith*, 'island', *ey* or *eg*, 'brushwood', *hris*, are pronounced almost exactly the same and mean almost exactly the same in both languages. Some very common elements are related but have different pronunciations in the two languages: 'dike' is Norse, 'ditch' English; *brigg* and 'bridge', 'kirk' and 'church', *steinn* and 'stone', *skirr* and 'sheer' (bright), follow the same pattern. Some elements, mercifully, are quite distinct: most personal names are different in the two languages, and the characteristic *by*, 'farm, village' and *thveit* ('-thwaite'), 'clearing' terminations are definitely Scandinavian in origin. There is a possibility that some *thorps* are from Old English *throp*, particularly ones outside the Danelaw. Both elements mean 'dependent settlement' or 'outlying farm', but the number and pattern of the settlements so named in the Danelaw is distinctive, and for most of these, derivation from OE *throp* is only a remote possibility. In terms of numbers, in the Domesday Book of 1086, there are 303 names ending in -*by*, 109 with *thorp* and 57 hybrid Norse-English names in the Danelaw. Many more are recorded later.

In Nottinghamshire there are about 100 place-names with the Old English element *tun* 'farm, village'. This normally comes into Modern English as –*ton* and is one of the most common English elements. Some of the names containing this element have a Scandinavian personal name as the first element, as we shall see, so even common English names-types were affected by Viking settlement. But another

common English element, *ham* 'homestead, village', is represented by only eight names, including Nottingham. By way of
comparison, there are 21 names in the county with Danish *by*
'farm, village', and 36 with Danish *thorp*.

The map shows the distribution of parish names of
Scandinavian origin, clearly demonstrating the concentration
of these in the Danelaw.

AN EXAMPLE: LEICESTER AND THE WREAKE VALLEY

What happened when the Danes took possession of the lands
they had conquered? Probably the simplest way to gain some
idea of the patterns of settlement is to look at a map and see
the type of names represented on it. Surrounding Leicester, for
example, we find Thurnby, Oadby, Blaby, Enderby, Kirby
Muxloe, Ratby, Groby, Barkby, all names of a Scandinavian
type. The settlements now inside the city, which were outlying
villages until the middle of the 19th century, all have English
names: Knighton, Aylestone, Braunstone, Glenfield, Birstall,
Humberstone, Evington. If we head from Leicester along the
River Wreake, in a direction roughly north-east towards
Melton Mowbray, we find names such as Thurmaston, Barkby,
Gadsby, Rotherby, Kirby Bellars, Hoby, Asfordby, Dalby,
Thorpe Satchville and Thorpe Arnold. All these are either of
Scandinavian type, or show Scandinavian influence.

This area illustrates a kind of ripple pattern. At the centre
is the oldest name, Leicester, which is from a pre-English
folk name *Legore*, with the Old English element *ceaster* meaning 'Roman fortified town'. Surrounding it are the farms and
villages named after Anglo-Saxons Brant and Eafa
(Braunstone and Evington), fortifications (Birstall), and land-
type (Glenfield means 'open land free of weeds or other
undesirable growth'). Surrounding them are the Scandinavian

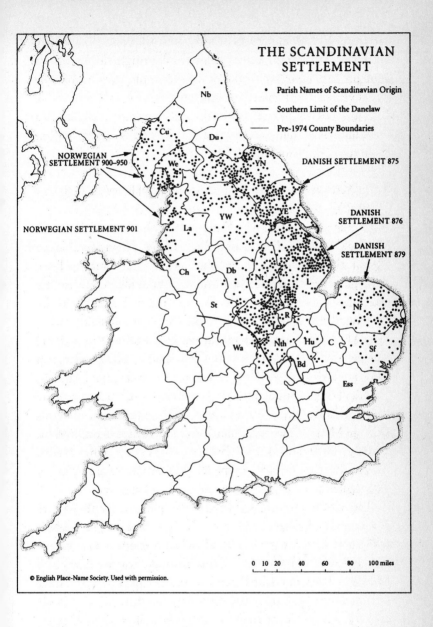

THE SCANDINAVIAN
SETTLEMENT

• Parish Names of Scandinavian Origin

—— Southern Limit of the Danelaw

—— Pre-1974 County Boundaries

NORWEGIAN
SETTLEMENT 900–950

DANISH SETTLEMENT 875

DANISH
SETTLEMENT 876

NORWEGIAN SETTLEMENT 901

DANISH
SETTLEMENT 879

Nb

Cu

Du

We

YN

YW

YE

La

Ch

Db

Nt

L

Nf

St

R

Wa

Nth

Hu

C

Sf

Bd

Ess

0   10 20   40   60   80   100 miles

© English Place-Name Society. Used with permission.

settlement names characterized by the element *by*, 'village, farm', with Scandinavian personal names like Eindrithi in Enderby, and topographical elements like *grof*, 'a pit' in Groby. Thus the earliest pre-English name is at the centre, the English ones reflect the growth of English settlements, and the Scandinavian name-types reflect the growth of later Scandinavian settlement. Then finally, the Scandinavians spread along a minor and twisting river (Wreake is from a Scandinavian word meaning 'twisting'), establishing new settlements where there were few existing English-named farms.

The major centres of population in this part of the east Midlands, Nottingham, Leicester, Melton, Newark, all have English or anglicized names. The Wreake valley has a whole string of tiny settlements with Scandinavian names, with relatively few English names among them. The logical supposition is that these small settlements with Scandinavian names were farms cut out of unused or disused land by the descendants of the Viking armies. The land quality is poor and these settlements would not have supported a large population in the first millennium. Dotted in the offing are the *thorp* names: these are dependent settlements tied to a larger one, smaller generally than the *by*s and in situations even more marginal.

ANOTHER EXAMPLE: NOTTINGHAM AND THE TRENT VALLEY

If we travel from Nottingham towards Newark along a much more important waterway, the River Trent (a British name), we come across Gunthorpe, Gonalston, Thurgarton, Fiskerton, Rolleston and Staythorpes. Most of the names here are English, and the few *by* names are mostly distributed away from the river settlements. Comparing the Trent valley with the Wreake, it appears that the Trent valley was already well-populated by the time the Scandinavians arrived.

The Trent valley also has a series of moderately important, if rather small, settlements with English *ton*, but with Scandinavian personal names, like Thorgeirr in Thurgarton, Hroald in Rolleston, or showing Scandinavian influence like Fiskerton for an Old English *Fisherton*, and Carlton for a possible Old English *Churlton*. These hybrid names suggest that the villages were originally English, but changed hands when the Scandinavians arrived. So instead of being something like Alfredston, 'Alfred's farmstead', the village was named after the Scandinavian leader who took it over, Thorgeirr, and became Thurgarton. An interesting feature of the name Thurgarton is that the earliest spellings of the name show it has been anglicized. This tells us that the village was an early Scandinavian annexation, because later Scandinavian names at the time of Cnut, from 1016 onwards, tend to use Scandinavian forms of spelling, in a resurgence of Scandinavian pride under a Scandinavian king. So within a few miles of each other, we have a Scandinavianized Fiskerton and an anglicized Thurgarton. There was evidently a fair bit of linguistic give and take in the Trent valley.

AN INTERPRETATION OF THE PLACE-NAMES

The explanation of the patterning of names in the east Midlands which best fits the evidence has been proposed by Kenneth Cameron. His argument is that the hybrid names are those of places taken over by Scandinavians in the earliest phase of the invasion and settlement. The Scandinavian leaders naturally occupied or took ownership of the best land. We know of a couple of places that were completely renamed – *Streoneshalch* in North Yorkshire became Whitby, and *Northworthy* in the east Midlands became Derby – but the majority of the villages were partially renamed to reflect their new ownership. The ordinary men in the great Viking army were rewarded with disused or virgin land in the vicinity of the towns and villages where their leaders settled.

When they broke the new land in, these men gave their new homes *by* names, often using their own names as the first element. This process went on for centuries. Then when their children or relatives from Scandinavia came to join them, they carved out parcels of land from the main estates, the *thorps*, or plots for building, the *tofts*, or cleared wooded land for new farms, the *thwaites*.

Once again, comparing the Wreake valley with the Trent, it might seem that the Scandinavian settlement was denser in Leicestershire than in Nottinghamshire. That would probably be a mistaken assumption. The Scandinavian influence on the major names of the Trent valley was limited by the English population that was already living there. But if we look at minor names, we see a very significant Scandinavian element. In Nottinghamshire we have the ancient Fosse Way, but apart from that, the streets and roads use mainly the Scandinavian word *gata*, Modern English 'gate', but meaning 'road'. There are few names with Old English *mersc*, 'marsh', but dozens with Scandinavian *kjarr*, 'carr' as it now is. There are lots of *holms* and few *eys* (both meaning 'dry land in marsh), lots of *becks* and relatively few *brooks* (both meaning 'stream'). Scandinavian terms replaced the common English ones found outside the Danelaw. The Scandinavian settlement appears to have been quite dense, since it changed not only major names in centres of population, a reflection of political power, but also the ordinary, everyday terms for common things, a reflection of interaction between people of equal status. In other words, the Scandinavian settlement changed the ordinary vocabulary of the working man and woman, and to do that there must have been quite a few working men who were Scandinavian. Once these words took root in the local dialect, they were used by people of both ethnic groups.

NAMING FASHIONS

However, it should be pointed out that Scandinavian names and Scandinavian people do not invariably go together. For the most part they do, especially early on in the time of Viking influence. But as the Anglo-Saxon period goes on, the equation of name and ethnic origin becomes less and less secure. There is a charter from 1046 in which a woman called Wulfgyth, widow of a man called Ælfwine, and sister of men called Eadwine and Wulfric, leaves property in East Anglia. All these names are English. But Wulfgyth mentions her sons and daughters: the sons are Elfkitel, Kytel, and Wulkitel, all anglicized versions of Scandinavian names; the daughters are Bote, Gode and Ealdgyth, all English names. It seems that naming fashions are no respecters of ethnicity, and that having a Scandinavian name does not necessarily mean you are Scandinavian, any more than Paul means you are small, or Nigel that you are dark-haired. Recent research on naming patterns reveals that women's names tend to be more conservatively English in this period, while men's names often follow the Scandinavian trend. Which means that with late Anglo-Saxon and early Middle English place-names, we can only safely talk about Scandinavian influence.

NAMES AND THE CHURCH

One of the few habitative name-elements (name-elements, that is, that refer to places where people live) borrowed by the Anglo-Saxons from the Celts was the word for a church, *egles*. This appears in names such as Eccles, Exhall, Eccleshall, Eccleston, Eaglesfield and Ecclesfield, and it hints that the Anglo-Saxons were content to leave the Christian Celts to their worship and Christian buildings. There is a parallel to this in the Kirbys or Kirkbys which dot the area of the ancient Danelaw. Although the name is wholly Scandinavian, meaning 'settlement with a church', it indicates a pre-existing Christian building and, presumably, English congregation. Although some Vikings were baptized and confirmed as Christians in the ninth century, it is entirely improbable that any of these settlements were named after a Scandinavian church.

An interesting feature of these names is the fact that more than half of them have early spellings which are anglicized, as in *chirchebi*, showing the English pronunciation which becomes modern 'church' with the Scandinavian *by* added. But none of them appears in modern spelling and pronunciation as 'Churchby'. So there was a time when the Scandinavian name was given a distinctively English pronunciation by the local people, but that pronunciation was eventually replaced by the Scandinavian one. In addition, it has been noted that the Kirbys are generally found on land which is not as marginal as that on which the other *by*-named settlements are situated. All this suggests that these Kirbys and Kirkbys were in origin, and continued for some time to be, English settlements, reflecting English Christian building, worship and tradition. This was recognized by the Scandinavian settlers. Perhaps these names reflect some give and take in culture and religion between the Scandinavian and English populace. Certainly this confirms the overall picture that the English shared their Christian faith and the Scandinavians shared their language in the process of assimilation over the course of history.

POLITICS AND THE CONVERSION OF THE SCANDINAVIANS

The evidence of names that we have just looked at shows that settlement went on, and the Scandinavian settlers mixed with their English neighbours. It does not tell us everything that we want to know about the process of assimilation. But it reveals that it went on as soon as the Vikings were domesticated by settled living. This enables us to see that what must have been a calculated gamble on King Alfred's part paid off. He was able to use both Christianization and settlement together effectively as a way of dealing with the Vikings under Guthrum. But when he tried to use just one of these two means with Hæsten, he failed. So did Æthelred when he tried much later to broker a treaty with the Vikings. Æthelred had neither the character nor the options that King Alfred had, and the final phase of Viking assimilation was brought about when Cnut was able to join land and law with Christianization once again.

KING ALFRED'S POLICY WITH GUTHRUM

The baptism and subsequent behaviour of Hæsten and Guthrum shows how Christianity was allied with polity in long-term war. In 876, Healfdene settled in Northumbria, and the following year Mercia was settled. King Alfred was defeated and Wessex itself was occupied early in 878. But the brother of Hinguar and Healfdene was killed together with 840 of his men in Devon. According to some versions of the *Chronicle* a special war-banner called 'Raven' was captured from the Vikings, and the *Annals of St Neot's* picturesquely records that the raven on the banner would predict the outcome of the battle, drooping if defeat was forthcoming. At the battle of Edington later in 878, King Alfred routed the Viking forces and pursued them to their fortress. After the battle, the

Anglo-Saxon Chronicle records,

> The Viking army gave him preliminary hostages
> and swore great oaths that they intended to leave
> his kingdom; and they also promised that their
> king intended to receive baptism, and they fulfilled
> that promise. After three weeks, King Guthrum
> came to him at Aller in a company totalling 30,
> the most worthy of the men in the Viking army.
> Aller is close to Athelney. And King Alfred stood
> sponsor to him at his baptism there; the loosing of
> the chrism was at Wedmore [eight days later], and
> he spent 12 days with the king, who honoured him
> and his companions with gifts.

It is evident that Alfred treated Guthrum and his men with
royal hospitality on this occasion. Alfred also negotiated a
treaty with Guthrum sometime after the latter's baptism and
before 886. The treaty between Alfred and Guthrum clearly
defined the respective territories of the English and
Scandinavians, set out the equality of men on both sides in
terms of compensation for death and injury, and forbade all
men to change sides in unscrupulous pursuit of personal
advantage (Text 1). The wisdom of this last provision is best
illustrated by the antics of Ealdorman Eadric in the reign of
King Æthelred, whose disloyalty and opportunism led to the
defeat of the English and the accession of King Cnut, as we
have seen earlier.

Alfred's treaty put the former Vikings under the sanctions
of law, religion, and loyalty to a generous and competent
godfather. Before the restoration of Alfred's fortunes by his
victory at the battle of Edington in 878, these terms would
have been unimaginable. The significance of the military

victory is not to be diminished. But the key to the whole agreement was that the Vikings were ceded land: not West Saxon land, but the lands of the Danelaw as it was soon to become. A settled army would need a bridge between themselves and the local population, a role in which Christianity would prove very useful; law (itself a Scandinavian word) would be necessary to regulate relations between individuals; and some kind of agreement would need to be established between the settled people on either side of the border.

We should not miss perhaps the most remarkable feature of the agreement between Alfred and Guthrum:

> ... if a man is killed, we all consider English and Dane to be equally valuable, at eight half-marks of refined gold; that is except the peasant who occupies rented land, and Danish freedmen, who are considered to be equally valuable at 200 shilling for either of them.

Alfred agreed laws with Guthrum which provided for compensation in the event of cross-border slaying. At this point, when the Viking wars were still in progress, when groups of men were still killing each other formally in battle and informally in guerilla warfare and presumably in various other less obvious ways, when marauding was still an option for the summer – such a law can only seem like the triumph of hope over experience. But it is testimony to Alfred's vision and ambition, his will for order to prevail. For Alfred and Guthrum, killing is to become subject to the sanctions of law, and there is not to be a return to the anarchy of the earlier Viking days. Alfred was thus able to control and domesticate the Vikings by tying them to the land.

KING ALFRED'S POLICY WITH HÆSTEN

Alfred later tried the same tactics with Hæsten as he had with Guthrum, but with a less happy outcome. In 892, Hæsten arrived in Kent with a reported fleet of 80 ships and camped at Milton Regis, while another force of 250 ships was based at Appledore. Alfred camped between them in 893, and throughout that year there was a series of minor skirmishes. The Viking armies then moved to Benfleet in Essex, from where Hæsten carried out a series of raids. An English army attacked the fortress when Hæsten was out raiding, destroyed the ships there and captured Hæsten's wife and two sons. The *Anglo-Saxon Chronicle* records:

> Hæsten's wife and sons were brought to the king and he gave them back to him, because one of them was his godson, the other the godson of Ealdorman Æthelred. They had sponsored the sons for baptism before Hæsten had come to Benfleet, and he had given Alfred hostages and oaths, and the king had given him generous gifts, as he also did when he returned the boy and the woman. But as soon as they came to Benfleet and built the fortress, Hæsten harried his kingdom, the very part which Æthelred his son's godfather had to rule. And another time he was out harrying in that same kingdom when his fortress was destroyed.

Alfred had taken personal responsibility for the baptism of Hæsten's sons, and given him gifts. The chronicler very obviously disapproved of Hæsten's behaviour in the face of Alfred's repeated generosity. But Alfred was unable to contain Hæsten, despite having hostages and having joined with Ealdorman Æthelred in sponsoring the boys at baptism. The chronicler's emphasis that the focus of Hæsten's raiding was on the parts of Mercia ruled by Ealdorman Æthelred may be a hint that Hæsten had his eye on those lands for himself. Because Alfred was unable and unwilling to give them to him, Hæsten remained free from the ties of land and law, and apparently also of some of the ties of religion. He later left for the Continent, and he does not appear in the *Anglo-Saxon Chronicle* again.

KING ÆTHELRED'S POLICY

King Æthelred faced some of the problems that Alfred encountered with Hæsten. The Viking army under Olaf, Josteinn and Guthmund that arrived in 991 was essentially a marauding army, looking for spoil, which they found as they raided around the coast. But they were also competent, defeating the Essex levies led by Ealdorman Byrhtnoth at the battle of Maldon in August that year. The king had the threat of a highly mobile and efficient army to deal with, and he tried to come to terms.

Piecing the story together from divergent accounts, it seems that Æthelred tried the same formula that Alfred had used. The Winchester Chronicle tells us that after the battle of Maldon the king stood sponsor to Olaf Tryggvason at his baptism. Other versions of the *Chronicle* record that tribute was paid, just as in some cases King Alfred had paid tribute. Somewhere around the same time in 991, a treaty was drawn up between the Vikings and Æthelred (Text 25). It proposed similar things to Alfred's treaty with Guthrum: compensation for killing was to be the same for people of both races, and neither side was to harbour fugitives from the other. But whereas the emphasis in Alfred's treaty was on land and law and equality, the emphasis in Æthelred's is on ships and fleets, trading and harrying. In trying to contain other large-scale attacks, Æthelred rather implausibly requested the support of the army he had only just bought off in return for food. And making provision for dealing with minor disturbances in towns, Æthelred seems to be trying to promote trade and avoid the people provoking the Vikings.

So Æthelred was attempting what King Alfred had attempted more successfully in the case of Guthrum. He applied the sanction of religion, and Olaf Tryggvason became a notable missionary. He tried to engage the loyalty of the Viking army with tribute and treaty. By offering food to the men if they would fight for him, Æthelred was also offering to be their lord. The laws to regulate trade and to distinguish it from robbery, and to put the resolution of grievance under the customary legal processes of oath-swearing and ordeal, were an attempt to appeal to the commercial interests of the Vikings. But clearly this was a treaty made in the shadow of a defeat for the king. The Vikings did not all embrace baptism, they certainly did not confuse tribute with gift-giving, and raiding remained for them an attractive alternative to trading. Without the Vikings being tied to the land, religious, social and commercial sanctions could have little effect. Such a treaty was doomed to failure. Just as King Alfred could not pin Hæsten down without giving him land, neither could King Æthelred pin down this army.

EVIDENCE OF SCANDINAVIAN ASSIMILATION

The Scandinavian militiamen who did stay seem to have settled quickly and with relatively little disturbance into the population of Anglo-Saxon England. Monastic estates were taken over wholesale, and some English villages changed hands from one lord to another. But if the place-name evidence has been rightly interpreted, there was virtually no displacement of the indigenous people other than monks. After the initial conquest, settlement and expansion was by means of breaking in new land for agriculture, rather than dispossessing the English.

In the fighting, men had been killed and the intermarriage of Scandinavian men and English women was inevitable. Political structures changed, with the Scandinavian wapentake replacing the hundred, the English equivalent, in the Danelaw: this was effectively the local court and district council, and though the name changed it is not possible to say what else did.

Scandinavian names appear on coins. Some methods of calculation changed: in the treaty of Alfred and Guthrum referred to above (Text 1), the *mark* was a Scandinavian weight, as was the *ora*. As well as names, the English language adopted many Scandinavian words. Many of these have completely replaced their English equivalents: the verb 'take' for example, replaced the Old English verb *niman*. But the Scandinavians also introduced new pronouns which replaced their Old English counterparts, 'they', 'their' and 'them', as well as 'she'. The list of vocabulary would be tedious to read, but many words are characterized by the Scandinavian *sk* sound: skirt, scab, sky, skill, scare, scowl, scrub, skin and so on. The Scandinavians were not sheltered from the ordinary trials and joys of life either, since they gave the language 'birth', 'dirt', 'steak', 'law' and 'die'.

Compared with this wealth of material, the lack of evidence for the continuation of Scandinavian heathenism is remarkable. Roseberry Topping in Yorkshire, earlier called *Othenesberg*, 'hill of Odin', may be dedicated to the chief of the Norse gods, but it may simply be big and impressive like Wansdyke, 'Woden's dyke', and have little to do with worship of any kind. Similarly, Elloughton in East Yorkshire may represent 'hill with a heathen temple', but it could mean 'Helgi's hill'. Quite a few place-names derive from the Scandinavian word *haugr*, 'mound, burial mound', but some of these have been found to be natural, and upon excavation of the artificial ones, some have been found not to have been used for burial. The archaeological evidence is sparse overall, though minor grave goods and weapons have been found from Saffron Walden in Essex, Hesket-in-the-Forest in Cumbria, Ingleby in Derbyshire, Santon Downham in Norfolk, and elsewhere.

SCULPTURE AND CHRISTIANITY

Alongside this evidence, we have to put a significant number of Scandinavian-style sculptures distributed over the Danelaw. Styles of decoration similar to those on the Danelaw sculptures can be found in the Scandinavian homelands and from areas conquered, settled or visited by the Vikings, particularly the Isle of Man. What is surprising in these sculptures is the fact that they are often found in churches or in contexts which are Christian in some sense. This raises all kinds of issues with regard to their interpretation. Distinctions between Christian, pre-Christian and heathen imagery are all, apparently deliberately, confused.

The Scandinavian settlers introduced an entirely new type of monument, the hogback, 11 of which were found in the restoration of the church of Brompton in North Yorkshire, and 19 in fragmentary form at Lythe in the same county. In shape, the hogback resembles a large kerbstone, such as those used along urban English roads. It is carved with interlace or other decoration, and the top usually has a slightly convex curve. As this type of sculpture is not found in the Scandinavian homelands, and is found predominantly in areas of England affected by Vikings from Ireland, it was probably introduced from the west. It is generally accepted that these hogbacks represent the form of a Viking-style house, influenced by Irish reliquaries which carried or displayed the relics of a saint. But though the hogbacks may be grave-markers or funerary monuments, and though they are found in Christian contexts, they are no longer associated with saints.

Some sculptures were crude or are damaged now, but several of them are executed with consummate skill. A panel of a sarcophagus from St Paul's churchyard, London, now in the Museum of London, has a beautiful example of a Scandinavian Ringerike beast. This is a highly stylized horse-like creature looking over its shoulder, with a smaller snake-like animal entangled with it. Tendrils with tightly curled ends fill the rectangular space. From Kirk Andreas on the Isle of Man, a stone cross-panel, now broken, clearly has depicted within it the god Odin being swallowed by the wolf Fenrir, a Scandinavian mythological and apocalyptic image. A cross fragment from Leeds has a picture from the Scandinavian and English legend of Wayland the Smith, who among other things made a flying machine to escape from captivity. The more brutal aspects of Wayland's activities, cutting off the heads of two princes and making drinking-bowls from them as his vengeance on the king who had enslaved him, are recorded on the front panel of an English whalebone casket, the Franks Casket, now in the British Museum. The panel is divided in two, with the left-hand side being occupied by Wayland, and the right-hand side having the Adoration of the Magi.

The Gosforth cross from Cumbria is a quite extraordinarily elegant, slim, beautifully carved and obviously Christian monument; some of its imagery has already been mentioned

in the previous chapter. It has a developed, sophisticated
Christian iconography, with a crucifixion scene on the east
side. The east is associated with the altar and the Eucharistic
sacrifice in church building, and here with Christ's sacrifice.
In the Anglo-Saxon Christian tradition, the crucifixion scene
is depicted most often with Mary the mother of Jesus on
the left of the cross, and John the apostle on the right. But
sometimes the spearman, in extra-biblical tradition called
Longinus, is shown piercing Christ's side and another figure,
in extra-biblical tradition called Stephaton, holding the
sponge soaked in vinegar which was offered to Jesus (John
19:29). The Gosforth cross has Longinus in a panel below
Jesus with his spear penetrating up into the crucifixion panel,
but a female figure on the right-hand side. This female figure
has a Scandinavian pigtail, and is carrying what appears to be
a horn. The closest parallels to the figure are the pigtailed
women who greet warriors as they ride to Valhalla on
Scandinavian picture-stones from Gotland. It may represent
Mary of Bethany with her jar of ointment ready to anoint
Jesus at his death, the specific association made in John 12:7,
or one of the other Marys who went to anoint the body after
the crucifixion in Mark 16:1.

Occasionally warrior figures appear on Christian monuments, as at Gosforth, where they represent characters in
the crucifixion story. But the Scandinavians seem to have
introduced armed warriors outside of the context of the crucifixion. One of the clearest of these is at Middleton in North
Yorkshire, where a near-complete cross portrays a man in a
peaked helmet, a single-edged knife or scramasax across his
waist, with a spear alongside to the right, an axe in the left-
hand bottom corner, a sword and shield in the left-hand
top corner. The warrior has foreshortened legs, and it is
thought that he may be sitting with the scramasax across his

lap, possibly on his high-seat in the hall. He appears on the cover of this book. Above the warrior panel is the cross proper, decorated with simple interlace. On the other side of the cross is a Jellinge-style (a distinctive, relatively plain style of decoration) Scandinavian beast with a tendril of the decoration surrounding it passing through its jaws. Other fragments of crosses at Middleton have warriors in the same style of dress and equipment. A warrior on the cross from Sockburn, County Durham, is equipped in a similar style to the Middleton warrior, but he holds his spear and lacks the shield, sword and axe. He is marching rather than sitting.

QUESTIONS OF STYLE AND MEANING

The striking thing about these images is the obvious assimilation of Scandinavian style and Christian context. They invite the viewer to ponder the implications of seeing Christianity expressed in or alongside a different or unconventional stylistic code. What is to be made of the fact that many of the hogbacks have bear-like beasts at each end? Are the beasts attacking the 'house', like some apocalyptic monster? Are the images of the Ringerike beast at St Paul's, Odin on the Kirk Andreas cross, and Wayland on the Leeds cross (and indeed on the Franks Casket) set in *contrast* with their context, or subordinated within it? Is the Mary-Valkyrie figure on the Gosforth cross an aid or a hindrance to Scandinavian understanding of the crucifixion scene? The Middleton man adopts a posture which is familiar from manuscript pictures of Christ sitting in glory and judgement, one that is given magnificent treatment in the very modern tapestry of Coventry Cathedral. Is the Middleton man sitting under Christ, as represented by the ring-headed cross above him, but bearing a sword as God's servant like earthly judges in Romans 13:4? Or is he just a warrior remembered as such in the local Christian style on a cross?

These are questions impossible to answer unequivocally. We simply do not know. But Scandinavian style and Christian context are too frequently linked for the pattern to be entirely accidental. To use a linguistic metaphor, the language is recognizably Christian, but the dialect is Scandinavian with traces of distant heathen meanings in the vocabulary.

Dating these monuments precisely is a little difficult. But most are dated to the 10th and 11th centuries, when more datable finds also appear. The dial at Aldbrough and the inscription at St Gregory's Minster, Kirkdale, with their Scandinavian names representing benefactors and ministers in the church, are datable to the first half of the 11th century and to the reign of King Edward the Confessor (1042–66) respectively (see above, chapter 7). The Aldbrough inscription is in a hybrid Norse-English dialect. A later, 12th-century, inscription is even more curious. The Bridekirk font from Cumbria has an inscription in Scandinavian runes spelling Middle English words, and containing a French name, Richard. All these sculptures plausibly record an increasingly close relationship between the new Scandinavian settlers, their later descendants, and the church. The reaction of the indigenous population to this relationship and its artistic representations can only be guessed at.

CONVERSION

Of the actual process of conversion we know very little. We can guess, as above, that once they were settled, the Scandinavians warmed to Christianity. Guthrum issued coins minted with his baptismal name Æthelstan, some of which are found in the Cuerdale hoard that gave us so many examples of the St Edmund memorial coinage. This surely indicates that Guthrum, for one, took his baptism seriously.

No church mission to convert the Scandinavians is recorded, and it is perfectly possible that they simply adopted the habits of the indigenous people in due course.

Not, seemingly, straight away. At some time before his death in 888, Ealdorman Alfred (probably) of Surrey bought the great and splendid gospel-book known as the Codex Aureus, the 'Golden Book', now kept in Stockholm. This eighth-century manuscript is known as the Golden Book because much of the writing is in gold on pages of vellum stained purple. On folio 11 Alfred's donation is recorded:

> In the name of our Lord Jesus Christ. I, Ealdorman Alfred and my partner Werburg obtained these books from the heathen army with our pure money, that was with pure gold. We did this for love of God and for the good of our souls, and because we had no intention that these holy books should remain any longer in heathendom. And now we wish to give them to Christ Church [Canterbury] to the praise and glory and worship of God, in thanksgiving for his passion and for the use of the religious community which daily lifts up God's praise in Christ Church ...

The gospel-book was redeemed by pure money out of heathendom as an act of piety. Clearly the booty taken from the monasteries in earlier years was being sold off at a good price. Equally clearly, the Danes had no use for such items at this stage. But in the next few years, the picture changed somewhat.

The evidence for the very early veneration of St Edmund King and Martyr among the Danes of East Anglia is discussed in chapter 6. It is clear that sometime before the end of the ninth century, there was a cult of the English East Anglian king flourishing in the Danelaw, as shown by the issue of his memorial coinage. And by the end of the first quarter of the next century, that is sometime around 925, a Scandinavian, Oda, was appointed bishop of Ramsbury. Oda was reputedly the son of a warrior who fought with the Viking army of Hinguar and Hubba.

In 942 Oda was translated to Canterbury and served as archbishop with distinction in the difficult years of the mid-century until his death in 958. He was related to other notable ecclesiastics: Archbishop Oscytel of York, predecessor and uncle of St Oswald, and Abbot Thurcytel of Bedford. King Eadwig made a grant to Oda of land at Southwell, which later became the core of the Nottinghamshire diocese. St Oswald, one of the leaders of the Benedictine reform, was trained by Oda. Oda himself was no provincially minded cleric: he professed as a monk at Fleury, and was warmly disposed towards the reform movement and St Dunstan. Byrhtferth of Ramsey recorded Oda's life and miracles in the *Life of St Oswald*, and he was also known as Oda 'the Good'.

The date of Oda's promotion to Canterbury may be significant, for it was in 942 that a major advance was made in the recapture of the Danelaw. King Edmund had been faced with having to re-establish control over much of what his brother Æthelstan had gained at the battle of *Brunanburh* in 937. Olaf Sihtricsson, the defeated Irish-Norse king or chieftain, had quickly reneged on his pledges and had taken control of Northumbria. An essential step in the process of stamping his authority on the Danelaw was for Edmund to advance towards Northumbria. This he did by taking the formidable group of Danish strongholds in eastern Mercia known as the Five Boroughs. The poem recorded in most manuscripts of the *Anglo-Saxon Chronicle* in 942, known as *The Capture of the*

Five Boroughs, gives an insight into how the Anglo-Saxon royal court thought of what the campaign achieved:

> In this year King Edmund, the lord of the English,
> protector of kinsmen, beloved instigator of heroic
>   deeds,
> conquered Mercia, bounded by Dore,
> Whitwell gate and the broad sea stream,
> the river Humber. He conquered five fortresses:
> Leicester and Lincoln,
> Nottingham and Stamford likewise,
> and also Derby. Before this, the Danes were
> under the Northmen, forcibly subjected
> in the chains of captivity of the heathens
> for a long time, until King Edmund,
> the son of Edward, the defender of warriors,
> redeemed them for his honour.

The implication of the poem is that the Danes were by this time Christian and the Norwegian king from Ireland was oppressing them, even though one version of the *Chronicle* notes that Olaf was *chosen* as king of Northumbria. The poem uses the ambiguous word *alysan* for Edmund's action, a word which had both theological and secular meanings, 'redeem, set free'. These five towns were the core of Danish Mercia, and whether or not the Anglo-Scandinavian population felt they had been freed or redeemed, this was a major step in the retaking of the Danelaw. The appointment of a man of Scandinavian extraction, namely Oda, to the see of Canterbury might have allayed some fears of the Anglo-Scandinavian Mercians, then, and have shown Edmund's determination to assimilate rather than subjugate them in his Christian kingdom.

The same version of the *Chronicle* records the presence of
Archbishop Wulfstan I (not the later homilist who figured
largely in the events of the reigns of Æthelred and Cnut)
with King Olaf when in 943 he tried to counterattack.
He stormed and captured Tamworth, the capital of western
Mercia. King Olaf and the archbishop escaped by night from
Leicester when Edmund trapped them there. In the next year,
Edmund had so far advanced his cause that Olaf and Ragnald
Guthfrithsson, both Irish-Norse kings of Northumbria,
accepted baptism and confirmation respectively, with Edmund
as sponsor. In 944 Edmund regained Northumbria and
expelled the two kings. Æthelweard in his *Chronicle* mentions
that Wulfstan was instrumental in the expulsion of the two
from York as 'deserters' or 'traitors'. Precisely what this means
is difficult to say, but it may refer to the breaking of promises
made at the time of baptism and confirmation, whether of
loyalty to Edmund or to the church. The archbishop and the
Northumbrian ealdorman used a firm hand, whatever might
have been the case. Again we see Christianity taking its place
alongside the politics of power. But the vision was ultimately
social and religious cohesion.

INTEGRATION

Reviewing the various kinds of evidence presented in this
chapter, we can discern a process of Christianization going on
among the settlers of the Danelaw, particularly in the course
of the first half of the 10th century. It was unspectacular for
the most part, involving the integration of the settlers into
the populace, the sharing of cultural values, the judicious
use of political pressure. The evidence of people with
Scandinavian names taking a leading part in the church, and
indeed the reformation of the church, is important. It offsets

to some degree the habit of the chroniclers in referring to the Scandinavians generically as 'heathen'. When the heathen did come again, early in King Æthelred's reign, there were men in the English armies with Scandinavian names or Scandinavian parentage, fighting for their land, their lord and their faith. And when these attacks were over and Cnut became king, land and people were united in faith, in politics, in loyalty. If Cnut did not stem the tide of the sea, he achieved something that might have seemed at least as difficult: he brought two peoples together in a single Christian kingdom.

CONCLUSION

The Viking attacks on England paradoxically had many positive effects. By the time of the Norman Conquest, England was a single political entity, a united kingdom with one king. The old days of internal wars between the different English kingdoms were over, and it was the Viking attacks which reduced the number of English kingdoms. That power to unify was also demonstrated in relation to Europe more widely, and to Christendom in particular. It was at the height of the Viking attacks, curiously, that the Anglo-Saxons showed an increased sense of their position in a greater civilization. They were aware that the Viking fleets that had been ravaging England had gone over to the Frankish lands and were ravaging there. Kings who had been dispossessed of their lands went to Rome as a kind of halfway house before their last journey to heaven. The reconstruction of civilization involved calling in scholars from distant lands – Wales, Saxony and elsewhere. The reform of monasteries borrowed heavily from Frankish patterns and practices. Even the development of a notion of the king as God's instrument on earth, with consecration and coronation being joined together, was borrowed from Continental models. The Anglo-Saxons discovered a common cause with Christians elsewhere in Europe, a relationship based on shared faith, shared fears, shared needs and shared ideals.

The fears were real enough. Before they converted to Christianity (and indeed after), the Vikings killed many Anglo-Saxons, and more deliberately martyred others. Initial responses to the Vikings made the fight against them one of good against evil, Christian against heathen. This spiritual confidence in the English cause, this faith that even if God was purging his people of sin, they would nevertheless come through, stronger and purer, shines through the literature of the time of the first Viking attacks. Faith in God, faith in themselves and faith in the rightness of their cause came together as King Alfred united the English against the Viking threat and as his successors reconquered the settled Danes in England. The survival of Christian faith in the face of disruption and direct attack gave the church confidence to rebuild its institutions as war gave way to peace.

Fear of the Vikings erupted again in the reign of King Æthelred. But the vacillation of the king and the inadequacy of his policies and his leaders undermined the faith of the English. They were now far more mixed ethnically than they had ever been, having intermarried with the Scandinavians, and they had moreover embraced cultural patterns from abroad in the monastic reform. These factors naturally made it difficult for people to be as confident in the rightness of their cause as they had been under King Alfred, and the sense of their Christian Englishness had also diminished. The growth of millennial speculation also fuelled unease and fear. The response of faith as we have it in the literature was more complex than it had been earlier. It was more fearful, generally less self-justifying. It focused on the few, mostly the saints, who had made an impact. But it was effective. And the unremarkable, quiet but steady growth of Christianity among the former Vikings in England continued.

The story of later Anglo-Saxon England, then, is one of fear and faith. Both factors shaped the nation. But it is true to say that faith outlasted fear, and it was faith on both sides that enabled the Vikings to be integrated into a new kind of Englishness, and to make the contribution to civilization in England that they did.

TEXTS IN TRANSLATION

The texts translated here are those that were too long to fit into the main text, but which nevertheless merit reading in full. Editions are given in the next section, 'Sources and Further Reading'. All translations are my own unless otherwise stated.

TEXT 1
THE TREATY OF ALFRED AND GUTHRUM

This is the peace that King Alfred and King Guthrum, and all the council of the English and all the people who are in East Anglia, have agreed and established with oaths, on behalf of themselves and on behalf of their descendants, both those who are born and those yet unborn, who care for God's mercy or for ours.

First about our boundaries: up the Thames, then up the Lea, and along the Lea as far as its source, then straight on to Bedford, then up the Ouse as far as Watling Street.

Then, if a man is killed, we all consider English and Dane to be equally valuable, at eight half-marks of refined gold;

that is except the peasant who occupies rented land, and Danish freedmen, who are considered to be equally valuable at 200 shillings for either of them.

And if a king's thane is accused of killing, and if he dares to exculpate himself by oath, he shall do that with 12 king's thanes. If someone lower than a king's thane is accused, he shall exculpate himself with 11 men of equal rank and one king's thane. And so it is to be in every suit which is greater in value than four mancuses. And if the man does not dare to exculpate himself, he is to pay three times the compensation, according to how the case is valued.

And next, that each man should know who is his surety when he buys men or horses or oxen.

And we all agreed on that day when the oaths were sworn that no slave nor freeman be allowed to travel with the army of the Danes without permission, and none of them with us. If it then turns out that any of them by necessity wishes to trade with us, or we with them, in cattle or goods, that is to be tolerated on the condition that hostages are given in pledge of peace and to make it clear, so that everyone knows, that nothing underhand is going on.

From the Old English.

TEXT 2
THE BATTLE OF BRUNANBURH

King Æthelstan, the lord of noblemen,
treasure-giver of warriors, and also his brother
Prince Edmund, gained lasting glory
in battle with the edges of swords
5 around Brunanburh. The sons of Edward
split the shield-wall, hacked the lime-wood shields
with the hammered swords. For thus it was natural to
    them
from their family descent often to defend the land,
their treasure and homes, in battle
10 against every enemy. The attackers fell,
the Scottish people and the sailors
fell doomed. The plain darkened
with the blood of warriors after the sun,
glorious heavenly body, bright candle of God,
15 the eternal Lord, rose up in the morning,
glided over the vast expanse, until the noble creation
sank to its setting-place. There lay many a warrior
destroyed by spears, Northern men
shot over their shields, likewise also Scotsmen,
20 weary, had had their fill of battle. The West Saxons
advanced in troops for the entire day,
pursued in their tracks the hateful peoples,
fiercely hacked those fleeing from the battle from behind
with milled-edged swords. The Mercians did not withhold
25 hard battle-play from anyone among the warriors
– those who had come to the land with Olaf
in the ship's bosom over the heaving water,
doomed to death in battle. Five young kings
lay dead on the battlefield,

30 snuffed out by swords, likewise also
   seven chiefs of Olaf's, and innumerable warriors,
   both Vikings and Scots. There the prince of the Norsemen
   was put to flight, driven by necessity
   to the prow of the ship almost alone.
35 He shoved the ship out into the water, the king went out
   on the dark flood and saved his life.
   Similarly the old man, Constantine,
   the grey-haired warrior, by flight returned
   north to his own land. He had no reason to rejoice
40 in that meeting of swords: he was shorn of his kinsmen,
   deprived of friends, robbed in battle
   at the place of meeting, and abandoned his young son
   on the field of death cut to pieces by wounds
   in the battle. The grey-haired warrior,
45 the cunning old devil, had no reason to boast
   of the clash of swords, nor Olaf any more reason:
   with the survivors of their armies they had no reason to
      gloat
   that they proved better in the business of battle
   on the field of conflict, in the clash of standards,
50 in the coming together of spears, in the encounter of
      warriors,
   in the exchange of blows, after they had played
   with Edward's sons on the field of slaughter.
   Then the Norsemen, the blood-stained survivors of the
      spears,
   left in their nailed ships on Dingesmere,
55 went to Dublin over the deep water,
   back to the land of the Irish, ashamed.
   Likewise the two brothers, king and prince
   both together left for their homeland,
   went to the land of the West Saxons, rejoicing in the
      battle.

60 They left behind them to divide the corpses
    the dusky-coated one, the black raven
    with the horny beak, and the dun-coated
    white-tailed eagle, the greedy war-hawk,
    and the grey animal, the wolf of the forest,
65 to enjoy the carrion. There was never
    a greater number of the dead, those killed in the army
    by the edges of the sword, on this island
    before this up to the present, of which books, ancient
        witnesses,
    tell us, since the Angles and Saxons
70 came up from the east here
    over the spacious sea to find Britain;
    proud craftsmen of battle, warriors eager for battle,
    they conquered the Welsh and gained a homeland.

From the Old English poem in the *Anglo-Saxon Chronicle*, 937.

TEXT 3
A CHARTER OF ST FRIDESWIDE'S
MONASTERY, OXFORD

In the year of our Lord's incarnation 1004, the second indiction, in the 25th year of my reign, by the arrangement of God's providence, I, Æthelred, ruling the whole realm of England, by royal authority and for love of the Omnipotent, have established with the liberty of a privilege a certain monastery situated in the town called Oxford, where the blessed Frideswide rests. And the territories which adjoin the monastery of Christ, I have restored to it by means of a new title-deed. And to all who look upon this document I will explain in few words the reason why this was done. For it will be known, and quite agreed by all living in this land, what I with the advice of my chief nobles and ealdormen have issued by decree: that all the Danes who have come up in this island, sprouting like tares among the wheat, were to be destroyed by a completely lawful testing, and this decree was to be carried out to the extent of death. The Danes living in the above-mentioned town, attempting to escape death, gained access into this sanctuary of Christ, having broken by force the doors and bolts. Inside, they intended to make a sanctuary and defence for themselves against the people of the town and the suburbs. But when, compelled by necessity, all the people in pursuit tried to force them out, without success, it seems that they set fire to the planks and burnt this church, with its books and charters. With the help of God it was repaired by me and my people, and as I have said earlier, strengthened with the dignity of a new privilege in the name of Christ ...

From the Latin. The reference to the St Brice's Day massacre of 13 November 1002 is clear, but also the savagery of the attacks which did not spare people, church or books, and had no respect for rights of sanctuary.

TEXT 4
THE LOSS AND RECOVERY OF
THE LINDISFARNE GOSPELS

[St Cuthbert] appeared in a vision to ... Hunred, and ordered that when the tide went out they should look for the book which ... had fallen out of the ship into the midst of the waves, and perhaps contrary to anything they themselves might hope, they would by God's mercy find it. For their minds were troubled with the greatest sadness on account of the loss of this book. To these words he added the following: 'Rise up quickly and show the bridle, which you will see hanging from a tree, to the horse, which you will find not far away. It will come to you at once of its own accord and you should take care to bridle it. After that it will pull the cart on which my body is carried, and you will be able to follow it with lightened labour.' When Hunred had understood these things he awoke suddenly from sleep, and told of how he had seen the vision. Soon he sent several of his comrades to the sea which was nearby, to look for the book which they had lost. Now at this time they had come to a place called the White House or by the common people Whithorn.

So they came to the sea and saw that it had receded much farther than normal. When they had walked three miles or more they found that same holy book of the gospels, which retained its enrichment of gems and gold on the outside, as on the inside it showed the former beauty of its letters and pages, as if it had not been touched by the water at all. This event filled their minds with no small measure of joy, and it was now impossible to doubt the aforementioned man as to the other things which he had heard. He went on and found the bridle hanging, as he had learned in his dream, from a tree; and then he looked around and a little way off he saw a horse of reddish colour – where it had come from and how it came to be in that lonely place he could by no means discover. As he had been instructed he raised his hand and showed it the bridle, and it came swiftly to him and presented itself to be bridled at his hands. When he had led it to his companions, they rejoiced to labour afterwards all the more to protect the body of father Cuthbert, now that they knew for certain that his help would never fail them in their need. Harnessing the horse to the vehicle on which they were carrying that heavenly treasure encased in its chest, they followed it wherever it went, all the more safely because they were using as a guide the horse provided for them by God.

Now the aforementioned book is today preserved in this church which has merited to have the body of that same holy father, and in it (as we have said) there is no sign that it has been harmed by the water. This circumstance is believed certainly to be due to the merits of St Cuthbert himself and also of those who had been the makers of the book, that is: Bishop Eadfrith of venerable memory, who wrote it with his own hand in honour of St Cuthbert; his own successor, the venerable Æthelwald, who ordered it to be adorned with gold and gems; and also St Billfrith the Anchorite, who executed Æthelwald's wishes and commands with a craftsman's hand, producing an outstanding piece of work. For he was distinguished in the goldsmith's art. These men, who were all fervent in their love of the confessor and bishop beloved of God, left in this work something through which all those who come after them may appreciate their devotion towards the saint.

From Symeon of Durham's Latin *Libellus de Exordio atque Procursu istius hoc est Dunelmensis Ecclesie* in the translation of David Rollason.

TEXT 5
ARCHBISHOP WULFSTAN'S
ADDRESS TO THE ENGLISH

Beloved people, recognize what is the truth: this world is in haste heading towards the end, and for this reason the longer things go on in the world the worse it gets. And so it must of necessity worsen considerably because of people's sins before the coming of Antichrist. Then, indeed, it will be fearful and terrible throughout the world.

Face the facts too, that the devil has deceived this nation all too completely, and that there has been little true faith among the people, though they say the right things, and that too many injustices have prevailed in the land. And there were never many people who reflected about remedies for these things as they ought; rather, day after day, one crime after another has been committed, injustice has been carried out, and the law often violated throughout the nation. So as a result we have experienced much injury and insult, and if we wish to experience any remedy we must deserve better from God than we have so far. For we have richly deserved the miseries that oppress us, and with great merits we may be allowed to obtain remedy from God, if things henceforth shall improve.

We know very well that a great crime demands a great compensation, and a big fire demands not a little water if it is to be put out at all. It is absolutely essential for every man that he henceforth earnestly heeds God's laws and properly pays God's dues. Among the heathen peoples they do not dare withhold great things or small from what is appointed for the worship of false gods. And everywhere we withhold God's dues all too frequently. And they do not dare among the heathen peoples here or abroad to diminish any of those things that are brought and offered as sacrifices to false gods. And we have utterly despoiled God's houses here and abroad. And the servants of God are nearly everywhere deprived of respect and protection. And among the heathen peoples no one dares in any way to mistreat the ministers of false gods in the way that God's servants are now all too widely mistreated, where Christians ought to keep God's laws and protect God's servants.

But it is true what I say: the remedy is much-needed, because God's dues have diminished for too long among this nation in every district, and the laws of the people have deteriorated all too much, and sanctuaries are widely violated, and the houses of God have been utterly stripped of their ancient privileges and plundered of all that is seemly from inside. And widows are wickedly forced into marriage, and all too many have been reduced to poverty and totally humiliated. And poor men are grievously betrayed and cruelly deceived and widely sold out of this land into the possession of strangers even when perfectly innocent. And widely throughout this nation children in the cradle are enslaved for minor theft through savage injustice. And the rights of free men are taken away, the rights of slaves are pared away, and charitable obligations are diminished. And, to put it briefly, God's laws are hated, and his counsels despised. For this we constantly have disgrace because of God's anger, let it be acknowledged, and the injury will spread everywhere throughout this nation, though no one expects it, unless God protects us.

So it is clear and evident in us all that heretofore we have broken the law more often than we have made amends, and therefore this nation is the subject of much assault. It has not been successful for a long time either here or abroad, but there has been devastation and hunger, burning and bloodshed in pretty well every district, again and again. Theft and murder, plague and pestilence, murrain and disease, malice and hatred, and the ravages of robbers have very severely harmed us, and rapacious taxes have severely oppressed us, and storms have very often caused crops to fail. So now in this land, as it may seem, for many years there have been everywhere among the people many injustices and wavering loyalties. It is all too common that a kinsman protects his kinsman no more than a stranger, nor father his son, nor one brother the other. Nor has any one of us conducted himself as he ought, neither the religious according to the rule, nor the layman according to the law. But more often than not we have made pleasure our law, and have kept neither God's nor man's law nor counsel as we should have. No one has had as right and loyal intentions towards others as he ought, but by word and deed nearly everyone has deceived others; indeed, nearly everyone stabs the other in the back with shameful assault, and more, if he can.

So here in the land there is great treachery before God and the world, here in the land there are many and various betrayals of allegiance. The greatest betrayal in the world is that a man betray his lord's soul; and a very great betrayal also in the world is that a man bring about his lord's death, or drive him from the land while alive; and both of these have happened in this country. Edward [the Martyr] was betrayed and then killed and after that burned; and Æthelred was driven from his country. And widely throughout the nation too many god-children and godparents have destroyed each other. And all too many holy foundations have perished because previously [unsuitable] people have been lodged there, as ought not to be the case if proper respect were to be shown towards the sanctuary of God. And all the time too many Christian people have been sold out of this country. All this is hateful to God, believe it who will.

It is shaming to talk about what has occurred far too widely, and terrible to know what far too many people do who practise the crime: these people club together and buy a woman for themselves out of the common fund, and one after the other, practise disgusting sin with that one woman, taking turns like dogs, disregarding the filth. And then for the right price they sell God's creature, the purchase which he bought so dearly, out of the country into the hands of enemies. We also know well enough where the crime has been committed that a father sold his son for a price into the hands of strangers, and a son his mother, and a brother his brother. And all these are great and terrible deeds, let him understand it who will. And yet there is a greater and also more multifarious thing that injures this nation: many break their oaths and tell great lies, again and again pledges are broken – and it is evident among this nation that God's wrath violently oppresses us, let him who will recognize this.

O! How can greater shame come upon people from God's wrath than frequently comes upon us because of our own deeds? If some slave runs away from his master and abandons Christianity and becomes a Viking, and it happens in due course after that, that the thane and slave fight together in battle: if the slave kills the thane, he will lie and all his kin will get no compensation. But if the thane kills the slave he formerly owned, he will have to pay a thane's wergild.

Base laws and scandalous extortions are common among us, and many mishaps happen to this nation time after time because of the wrath of God, let him acknowledge it who will. This nation has not been successful for a long time either here or abroad, but there has been devastation and hatred in pretty well every district again and again; and now for a long time the English have been utterly defeated and much disheartened because of God's wrath. And the Vikings have been so powerful with God's consent that often in battle one of them puts 10 to flight, sometimes more sometimes less, all because of our sins.

And often 10 or 12, one after the other, offer disgraceful insult to the wife of a thane, or sometimes his daughter, or close kinswoman, while he looks on – one who considered himself important and powerful and brave enough before that happened. And often a slave tightly ties up a thane who was his master before, and makes him a slave, because of the wrath of God. Alas for the misery, alas for the public disgrace which the English now have because of the wrath of God!

Often two, or perhaps three sailors drive bands of Christian men huddled together out through this nation from sea to sea, to our utter disgrace – if truly we could appreciate it aright. But all the insult that we so often suffer we repay with respect to those who disgrace us. We constantly pay them, they daily humiliate us; they harry and burn, plunder and rob and carry it off to their ships. And what else is it in all these events but the wrath of God clear and evident?

No wonder things go wrong for us because we know full well that for many years now people have not cared at all what they have said and done. Rather, it seems that this people has become deeply corrupted by many sins and wicked deeds, by murders and crimes, through covetousness and greed, through theft and robbery, through selling people as slaves and heathen vices, through treachery and deception, through breaking civil and spiritual laws, through assaults on kinsmen and killings, through injuries against the religious and adultery, through incest and through promiscuous fornication. And there are many more lost and perjured than ought to be, far and wide as we said before, through oath-breaking and breach of contract and miscellaneous lies; and again and again people fail to observe festivals or fasts.

And also in this land there are degenerate apostates and all too many fierce opponents of the church and cruel oppressors of the people, and widely there are those who proudly despise just divine laws and Christian virtues, and throughout the nation stupid people contemptuous most often of those things relating always and properly to God's law.

So now far and wide the evil situation has arisen that people feel more ashamed of the good things they do than of the bad, for too often now good deeds are treated with contempt and God-fearing people are derided all too much. And especially those who love the right and have respect for God in any degree are all too frequently blamed and are treated with scorn. And because people do this, abusing what they should praise and hating too much what they should love, because of this, they lead all too many into wicked thoughts and perverse deeds, so that they have no shame even though they sin greatly and offend even against God himself; but because of empty abuse they are ashamed to repent of their wicked deeds as the books teach, like those fools who will not protect themselves from injury before it is too late because of their pride, even though they would do anything afterwards.

It seems that here in this country there are too many injured by the ravages of sin. Here there are killers and kin-slayers and priest-murderers and persecutors of monasteries; here there are perjurers and murderers; here there are prostitutes and infanticides and many foul adulterous fornicators; here there are witches and valkyries; here are robbers and plunderers and ravagers, and to put it briefly, innumerable crimes and wickedness of all kinds. And we are not a bit ashamed of it, but it is evident among this wretched corrupt nation that we are more ashamed to begin the process of atonement as the books teach.

Alas, many people could remember still more besides which a single person could not readily consider, how wretchedly things have turned out all the time throughout this nation. And let each one earnestly examine himself without any undue delay. But in God's name, let us do as is necessary for us, protect ourselves as best we can lest we all perish together.

In the time of the Britons there was a learned man called Gildas, who wrote about their sins, how they so very greatly angered God by their sins that he at last had the army of the English conquer their land and destroy the power of the British altogether. That happened, according to Gildas, because of robbery on the part of the powerful, coveting of ill-gotten gains, because of injustice on the part of the people and unjust judgements, because of sloth on the part of bishops, and because of the base cowardice of God's messengers who kept silent about the truth more often than not, and mumbled into their beards when they should have shouted. Through disgusting luxury and gluttony and numerous other sins, they forfeited their land and perished themselves.

Let us do what is necessary for us: let us take warning of such things. It is true what I say: we know of worse doings among the English than we ever heard of among the British. So it is a priority for us that we examine ourselves and earnestly intercede with God himself. Let us do what is necessary for us, namely, return to justice and abandon injustice as far as possible, and fully atone where we formerly transgressed. And let us love God and obey his laws, and fulfil very earnestly what we promised when we received baptism, or what they promised who brought us to baptism. And let us conduct ourselves justly in word and deed, and earnestly purify our thoughts, and carefully keep our oaths and pledges, and have some loyalty between ourselves without deceit.

And let us often consider the great Judgement which we must all face, and protect ourselves from the surging fire of hell's torment, and work to merit the glory and joy that God has prepared for those who do his will on earth. May God help us. Amen.

From the Old English.

TEXT 6
A LETTER FROM BONIFACE AND
THE ANGLO-SAXON MISSION IN GERMANY
TO KING ÆTHELBALD OF MERCIA

To his dearest master, King Ethelbald, cherished in the love of Christ above all other kings and holding glorious sway over the realm of the Anglians, Boniface, archbishop and legate of the Roman Church in Germany, and his fellow bishops, Wera, Burkhardt, Werbert, Abel, and Willibald, send greetings of unfailing love in Christ.

We acknowledge before God and the holy angels, that when we have heard through trustworthy messengers of your prosperity, your faith in God, and your good works before God and man we have returned joyful thanks to God, praying and beseeching the Saviour of the world to keep you forever safe and steadfast in faith and works before God and in the leadership of the people of Christ. But when we hear that any harm befalls you, be it in the conditions of your government or the event of war or, worse yet, some peril to your soul's welfare, we are afflicted with pain and sorrow; for by God's will we rejoice with you in your joy and grieve with you in your sorrow.

We have heard that you are very liberal in almsgiving, and congratulate you thereon … We have heard also that you repress robbery and wrongdoing, perjury, and rapine with a strong hand, that you are famed as a defender of widows and of the poor, and that you have established peace within your kingdom. In this also we have rejoiced … But amidst all this, one evil report as to the manner of life of Your Grace has come to our hearing, which has greatly grieved us and which we could wish were not true. We have learned from many sources that you have never taken to yourself a lawful wife. Now this relation was ordained of the Lord God himself from the very beginning of the world and was repeatedly insisted upon by the Apostle Paul ... If you had willed to do this for the sake of chastity and abstinence, or had refrained from women from the fear and love of God and had given evidence that you were abstinent for God's sake we should rejoice, for that is not worthy of blame but rather of praise.

But if, as many say – but which God forbid! – you have neither taken a lawful spouse nor observed chastity for God's sake but, moved by desire, have defiled your good name before God and by the crime of adulterous lust, then we are greatly grieved because this is a sin in the sight of God and is the ruin of your fair fame among men.

And now, what is worse, our informants say that these atrocious crimes are committed in convents with holy nuns and virgins consecrated to God, and this, beyond all doubt, doubles the offence. Let us take, by way of illustration, the punishment due to a rascal who has committed adultery with the wife of his lord and consider how much more he deserves who has defiled a bride of Christ, the Creator of heaven and earth, with his filthy lust ...

We therefore, beloved son, beseech Your Grace by Christ the son of God and by His coming and by His kingdom, that if it is true that you are continuing in this vice you will amend your life by penitence, purify yourself, and bear in mind how vile a thing it is through lust to change the image of God created in you into the image and likeness of a vicious demon. Remember that you were made king and ruler over many not by your own merits but by the abounding grace of God, and now you are making yourself by your own lust the slave of an evil spirit, since, as the Apostle says, whatever sin a man commits, of that he becomes the slave.

This is held to be a shame and disgrace, not by Christians only but even by pagans. For the pagans themselves, although ignorant of the true God, keep in this matter the substance of the law and the ordinance of God from the beginning, inasmuch as they respect their wives with the bond of matrimony and punish fornicators and adulterers. In Old Saxony, if a virgin disgraces her father's house by adultery or if a married woman breaks the bond of wedlock and commits adultery, they sometimes compel her to hang herself with her own hand and then hang the seducer above the pyre on which she has been burned. Sometimes a troop of women get together and flog her through the towns, beating her with rods and stripping her to the waist, cutting her whole body with knives, pricking her with wounds, and sending her on bleeding and torn from town to town; fresh scourgers join in with new zeal for purity, until finally they leave her dead or almost dead, that other women may be made to fear adultery and evil conduct. The Wends, who are the vilest and lowest race of men, have such high regard for the mutual bond of marriage that the wife refuses to survive her husband. Among them a woman is praised who dies by her own hand and is burned upon the same pyre with her husband.

If, then, heathen who know not God and have not the law do, as the Apostle says, by nature the things of the law and have the works of the law written upon their hearts, know you, beloved son, who are called a Christian and a worshipper of the true God – if in your youth you were ensnared in the filth of wantonness and involved in the mire of adultery and sunk in the whirlpool of lust as in an abyss of hell – it is now high time that you should remember your Lord, should rouse yourself from the snares of the devil, and wash your soul clean from the filthiness of lust. It is time for you in fear of your Creator no longer to venture to defile yourself by repeating such sins. It is time for you to have mercy upon the multitude of your people who are perishing by following the example of a sinful prince and are falling into the abyss of death ...

Wherefore, beloved son, beware the pit into which you have seen others fall before you! ... The riches of this world are of no avail in the day of requital if a man comes to the end of his life while still making bad use of them; for after the death of the body he shall fall into eternal punishment of the soul. Take these warnings to heart, my dear son, and, I pray you, yield to the prudent words of God's law and reform your life. Turn away from your vices and make an effort to acquire the sacred virtues; so shall you prosper in this world and receive eternal reward in the world to come.

May Almighty God so turn your life to better things that you may be worthy of the grace of our Lord himself for evermore.

From the Latin of Boniface in the translation of Ephraim Emerton. The details Boniface gives of the treatment of adulterous women on the Continent among the Germanic and other races are interesting in themselves, but in the context are an obvious way of deflecting direct attention from Æthelbald's – i.e. the man's – sin. Below is the accompanying letter to Herefrith:

> I most earnestly beg your gracious friendship to be mindful of me in your holy prayers although, from the accounts of those who come from you, I have no doubt that you have done so and will continue so to do ...
>
> We eight bishops, whose names are given below, meeting together, urgently request you, our dearest brother, to convey to Ethelbald, king of the Mercians, our letter of admonition, to read it to him with your explanations, and, in the same form and order in which we wrote and sent it to you, to call his attention to each point with your exhortations. For we have heard that in your fear of God you fear not the person of man and that at times the said king has been willing to give some little heed to your warnings. Let Your Goodness be assured that these admonitory words of ours were sent to that king from no other motive than pure affection for him and because, being born and bred of that same English stock, we sojourn here by the orders of the Apostolic See. The well-doing

and the fair fame of our race is our joy and delight; their sins
and their evil repute fill us with grief and sorrow. We suffer
from the disgrace of our people whether it be told by
Christians or pagans that the English race reject the usages of
other peoples and the apostolic commands – nay, the ordinance of God and refuse to hold to one wife, basely defiling
and mixing up everything with their adulterous lusts, like
whinnying horses or braying asses.

Wherefore, beloved brother, if this, the greatest of vices,
really exists, let us all with one accord urge the king to reform
himself and his people with him, lest the whole race perish
with its prince both here and in the life to come. Let him
amend his own life and, by his example, guide his people into
the way of salvation, so that whereas before he incurred guilt
he may henceforth merit an eternal reward.

We are sending you, as a token of sincere affection and of
our blessing, a napkin with a little incense. May the Holy
Trinity preserve you in lasting health and in all holy endeavour
as you go forward in the way of your well-proven character.

TEXT 7
SWEDISH RUNE-STONES

Some 25 Swedish rune-stones mention England. They are
carved on standing stones in the characters of the Scandinavian runic alphabet. Hundreds of such stones survive, but
the ones from the Viking Age give a glimpse of the pride with
which the Scandinavians regarded their foreign exploits.

One stone in Yttergärde in Uppland commemorates Ulf:

> Ulf has taken three gelds in England: first was the
> one Tosti paid, then [the one] Thorkel paid, then
> [the one] Cnut paid.

Another from Väsby commemorates Alle, who was no shrink-
ing violet:

> Alle had this stone put up in his own honour. He
> took Cnut's geld in England. God help his soul.

A stone from Lingsberg commemorates Ulfrik:

> He took two gelds in England.

TEXT 8
KING ALFRED'S DEDICATORY LETTER TO HIS TRANSLATION OF GREGORY'S PASTORAL CARE

King Alfred commands Bishop Wærferth to be greeted affectionately and lovingly by means of these his words. And I command it to be made known to you that it very often comes into my memory what wise men there were formerly among the English, whether in religious or secular orders, and how then there were happy times among the English. And how the kings who had rule over the people obeyed God and his ministers, and they maintained their peace, morality and authority at home, while they also extended their territory abroad. And how they prospered both in war and in wisdom. And also how eager the religious orders were in both teaching and learning, and also in all the services that they had to do for God. And how wisdom and teaching were sought here by people from abroad. And how we would have to get wisdom and teaching from abroad now, if we were to have them at all.

So completely had wisdom declined among the English that there were very few this side of the Humber who understood their services in English or could translate even one letter of Latin into English, and I do not imagine there were many the other side of the Humber. There were so few scholars that I cannot think of even a single example south of the Thames when I came to the throne. Almighty God be thanked that we now have any supply of scholars at all.

And so I urge you that you do as I believe you wish to: namely, that as often as you can you disengage yourself from secular affairs so that you apply the wisdom that God has given you wherever you can. Think what torments came to us in this world when we neither loved wisdom ourselves, nor passed it on to others. We loved only the name of Christians; very few loved Christian practices.

When I remembered all this, I also recalled how I had seen the churches throughout England full of treasures and books and also a very great number of God's servants, before everything was ravaged and burnt. And they had very little benefit from those books because they could not understand them at all, since they were not written in their own language. It is as if they said, 'Our predecessors, who ruled these religious foundations in the past, loved wisdom, and by that means gained wealth and passed it on to us: their track is still visible here, but we are unable to follow their traces. And as a result we have now lost both wealth and wisdom, because we did not wish to set our hearts on following the trail.'

When I remembered all this, then I wondered greatly at the good scholars who used to be among the English in the old days, who had fully studied all the books: it amazed me that they had no wish to translate any part of them into their own language. But immediately I answered myself and said, 'They never imagined that people could become so careless and learning so decline. They left this task undone deliberately, desiring that there should be the greater wisdom in the land, the more languages we knew.' Then I remembered how the Law was first drafted in Hebrew, and when the Greeks learned it later, they translated it all into their own language together with all the other books. Similarly the Romans, after they had learned the books translated them into their own language through wise interpreters. And all other Christian nations likewise have translated some part of them into their own language.

Therefore it seems better to me, if you all agree, that we translate into the language we can all understand those books that are most necessary for all people to know. And that we arrange it, as we very readily may with God's help and if we have peace, that all the young free-born men now among the English who have the means to apply themselves to it, be set to work on learning until such time as they are able to read English writing well, while they are not needed for other employment. Those who wish to learn more and progress to a higher order can be taught more in Latin after that.

Then when I remembered how knowledge of Latin had declined before this in England, yet many were able to read English, I began to translate the book called *Pastoralis* in Latin and 'Shepherd's Book' in English. Among all the many and various affairs of the kingdom I began to translate this book, sometimes word for word, sometimes idea for idea, as I learned it from Plegmund my archbishop, from Asser my bishop, and from Grimbold and John my mass-priests. After I had learned the book so that I understood it and was able to render it most meaningfully, I translated it into English. I intend to send one copy to each bishopric in my kingdom. With each one there will be an *æstel* worth 50 mancuses. And I command in the name of God, that no-one separate the *æstel* from the book, nor the book from the minster: it is not known how long there may be such learned bishops as now there are, thank God, almost everywhere. It is for this reason that I desired that they should always be at that religious foundation unless the bishop wishes to have them with him, or the book is loaned out, or being copied.

From the Old English.

TEXT 9
CYNEWULF AND CYNEHEARD

[757] In this year Cynewulf and the West Saxon council deprived Sigeberht of his kingdom, with the exception of Hampshire, because of his unlawful deeds. He ruled that area until he killed the ealdorman who stayed with him the longest. And then Cynewulf exiled him to the Weald forest; and he stayed there until a swineherd stabbed him to death at the stream of Privett, and the swineherd avenged Ealdorman Cumbra.

The aforementioned Cynewulf often fought great battles against the British. And after about 29 years from the time he started to rule the kingdom, he wished to exile a certain prince who was called Cyneheard, and that Cyneheard was the aforementioned Sigeberht's brother. And then Cyneheard found out that the king was visiting a woman at *Merantun* with a small retinue. And he rode there and surrounded the chamber before the men who were with the king discovered him. And then the king noticed that, and he went to the door and courageously defended himself until he saw the prince Cyneheard, and then he rushed out at him and severely wounded him. And they all kept fighting the king until they had killed him.

And then the king's thanes discovered the disturbance from the woman's cries, and they ran there as quickly and as soon as they could get ready. And Prince Cyneheard offered to each one money and life, and not one of them wished to accept the offer. But they kept on fighting until they all lay dead, except one British hostage and he was badly wounded.

Then in the morning the king's thanes who were following him behind heard that the king had been killed. Then they rode to *Merantun*, Osric his ealdorman and Wigfrith his thane and the men he had left behind him earlier. And they encountered the prince at the fortification in which the king lay dead, and they rode up to it (the gates had been locked against them). Cyneheard then offered them their own judgement of money and land if they would grant him the kingdom, and told them that their kinsmen were on his side and had no intention of deserting him. And the king's men replied that no kinsman could be dearer to them than their lord, and they had no intention of ever following his slayer. And the king's men offered their kinsmen a safe-conduct if they were to leave the fortification. And the kinsmen in the fortification replied that the same offer had been made to the companions of the king's men who had been with the king earlier; they then said that they would pay no more attention to it 'than your companions did who were killed with the king'.

And they continued fighting around the gates until they broke into the fortification and killed the prince and all the men who were with him except for one, who was the godson of Ealdorman Osric. He saved his life, but he was nevertheless often wounded.

And the aforementioned Cynewulf reigned for 29 years, and his body lies at Winchester, the prince's lies at Axminster. Their direct paternal line goes back to Cerdic.

And in the same year King Æthelbald of the Mercians was killed at Seckington, and his body rests at Repton: he reigned 41 years. And Beornræd succeeded to the kingdom, and ruled for only a little while and unhappily. And in the same year Offa succeeded to the kingdom and reigned for 39 years. And his son Ecgfrith ruled for 141 days. The aforementioned Offa was the son of Thingfrith, the son of Eanwulf, the son of Osmod, the son of Eawa, the son of Pybba, the son of Creoda, the son of Cynewold, the son of Cnebba, the son of Icel, the son of Eomær, the son of Angeltheow, the son of Offa, the son of Wærmund, the son of Wihtlæg, the son of Woden.

[786] In this year Cyneheard killed King Cynewulf and was killed there himself, and 84 men with him. Beorhtric then succeeded to the kingdom of the West Saxons and reigned for 16 years, and his body lies at Wareham, and his direct paternal line goes back to Cerdic. *Up to this time King Ealhmund ruled in Kent.*

From the Old English of the *Anglo-Saxon Chronicle*, in the Winchester manuscript. The words in italic were entered in a later hand. The chroniclers' habit of giving the king's genealogy going back to Woden (as here) highlights the different one recorded for King Æthelwulf.

TEXT 10
THE VOYAGE OF OHTHERE

Ohthere told his lord, King Alfred, that he lived furthest north of all the Norsemen. He said that he lived in that land, Norway, northwards by the Atlantic coast. He said, nevertheless, that the land extends a great way north from there, but that it is all deserted except in a few places here and there where the Lapps camp, hunting in the winter and fishing in the summer in the sea.

He said that on one occasion he wanted to find out how far the land extended due north, and whether anyone lived north of the wasteland. He travelled north along the coast for three days, having the wasteland to starboard all the time, and having the open sea to port. At that point he was as far north as the whale-hunters go at the furthest. He travelled still further due north, as far as he could sail in another three days. Then the land turned east, or the sea penetrated into the land, he was not sure which, but he was sure that he waited there for a west-north-westerly wind, and then sailed as far east along the coast as he could in four days. Then he had to wait for a full northerly wind because the land turned southwards (or the sea penetrated the land, he was not sure which). From there he then sailed as far south along the coast as he could in five days. A great river went up into the land there, and they turned up into the river because they did not dare sail beyond it without permission, as the land was fully populated on the other side of the river. He had not encountered any populated land before, in the time since he had left his own home; there had been wasteland constantly to starboard and open sea to port, except for fishermen, fowlers and hunters, and they were all Lapps. The Beormas had very fully populated their land, but the Norsemen did not dare travel there. But the land of the Terfinnas was completely deserted except where the hunters, fishermen and fowlers camped.

The Beormas told him many stories about their own land and about the lands around them, but he was not sure of the facts, because he did not see everything himself. The Lapps and the Beormas seemed to him to speak a similar language. He had travelled there mainly for the walruses, apart from wishing to see the land, because they have very fine ivory in their tusks and their hide is very good for ship-ropes. (They had brought some tusks to the king.) This whale is much smaller than other whales, not longer than seven ells long. The best whale-hunting is in Ohthere's own land, where they are 48 ells long, and the biggest 50 ells. As one of a party of six, he said he had killed 60 of these in two days.

He was a very wealthy man in the goods of which their wealth consists, namely in wild deer. He still had unsold 600 tame deer at the time when he had left to visit the king. They call the deer 'reindeer', and six of them, very valuable among the Lapps because they catch wild deer with them, were decoy-reindeer. Ohthere was among the chief men of the land, but he had no more than 20 cattle, 20 sheep and 20 pigs, and he ploughed the little land that was arable with horses.

The wealth of Ohthere's people is mostly derived from the tribute that the Lapps pay them, however. The tribute is animal pelts, bird feathers, whalebone and ship-ropes made of walrus-hide or seal-hide. Each one of the Lapps pays according to his status: the highest in rank has to pay 15 marten-skins, five reindeer-skins, one bear-skin, 10 measures of feathers, a bear- or otter-skin coat, and two ship-ropes. Each of the latter has to be 60 ells long and be made of walrus- or seal-hide.

Ohthere said the land of the Norsemen was very long and very narrow. Whatever of it can be used for grazing or

ploughing all lies along the coast. Even that is very rocky in
some places, and wild mountains lie to the east and above, all
along the cultivated land. The Lapps live in the mountains.
The cultivated land is most extensive in the south, and the
further north it goes, the narrower it becomes. In the south it
can be 60 miles wide, possibly more, in the middle region 30
miles or more wide, and in the north, at the narrowest point,
he said it might be three miles from coast to mountain. From
there on, the mountainous area is so extensive in some places
that it would take two weeks to cross it, in other places it
would take six days.

On the other side of the mountains along the land to the
east is Sweden, which borders it up to the north, and in the
north, it borders the land of the Cwenas. The Cwenas sometimes harry the Norsemen from across the mountains, and
sometimes the Norsemen harry them. There are large fresh-
water lakes throughout the mountain region, and the Cwenas
carry their boats over the land to the lakes, and harry the
Norsemen from these. They have very small, very light boats.

Ohthere said that the area where he lived was called
Halgoland. He said that no one lived to the north of him. In the
south of the land there is a trading-port called Sciringsheal, and
he said that it was barely possible to sail there within a month, if
one camped at night and had a favourable wind during the day.
You have to sail along the coast all the way, and to starboard
first of all is Ireland, and then the islands between Ireland and
this land, and then this land until you get to Sciringsheal;
Norway is to port all the way. To the south of Sciringsheal, a
great sea goes up into the land, wider than anyone can see
across; Jutland is on the other side, and then Sillende. This sea
goes up into the land for many hundreds of miles.

Ohthere said that he sailed from Sciringsheal to the trading-port called Hedeby in five days. Hedeby stands among the

Wends, the Saxons and the Angles, and belongs to the Danes. Sailing there from Sciringsheal, Denmark was to port and open sea to starboard for three days; then two days before he arrived at Hedeby, he had Jutland and Sillende and many islands to starboard – the Angles were living in these lands before they came to this land – and to port for two days he had the islands that belong to Denmark.

From the Old English of the Alfredian translation of Orosius's *Histories Against the Pagans*. The *ell* is an obsolete measurement of just under four feet. Ohthere's best whale catch would be about 200 feet or 65 metres long.

TEXT 11
THE VOYAGE OF WULFSTAN

Wulfstan said that he travelled from Hedeby, and with the ship running under sail all the way, he arrived in Truso within seven days and nights. Wendland was to starboard, and Langeland, Lolland, Falster and Skåne to port. All these lands belong to Denmark.

'Then we had Bornholm to port, where they have their own king. Then after Bornholm there were the lands that are called first Blekinge, then Möre, Øland and Gotland to port. These all belong to the Swedes. Wendland was on our starboard all the way to the mouth of the Vistula.'

The Vistula is a very great river which divides Witland and Wendland. Witland belongs to the Este, and the Vistula flows out of Wendland and into Estmere. Estmere is at least 15 miles wide. The Elbing flows from the east into Estmere from the lake on the shore of which Truso stands; the Vistula from the south in Wendland, and the Elbing from the east, together flow into Estmere. The Vistula then takes over from the Elbing, because from then on it is known as the Vistula, and it flows north-west to the sea.

Estland is very large and there are many fortified towns, and in each town there is a king. There is a great deal of honey and fishing. The king and the most powerful men drink mare's milk, and the poor and slaves drink mead. There is a good deal of fighting among them. No ale is brewed among the Este, but there is plenty of mead.

There is a custom among the Este that when a man is dead, he lies uncremated in his house among his kinsmen and friends for a month or sometimes two. The kings and other noble men lie uncremated and unburied in their houses sometimes for half a year, the longer the more wealth they have. All the time that the body lies in the house there is drinking and gambling, until the day when they cremate him. That same day when they intend to put the body on the pyre, they divide the man's money into five or six parts, sometimes more, depending on how much there is – whatever is left after the drinking and gambling. They set down the biggest part about a mile from the town, then the next biggest, then the third, until it is all set out within the mile. The smallest part is nearest to the town in which the dead man lies.

Then all the men who own the fastest horses in the land are assembled some five or six miles from the money. They race towards the money, and the man who owns the fastest horse gets to the first and biggest part, and so it goes on one after the other until all the money is taken. The one who gets the part closest to the town takes the smallest part. Each one then rides away with the money, and is allowed to keep it all, and for this reason, fast horses are extremely valuable there.

When the man's wealth has all been spent in this way they carry him out and cremate him with his weapons and clothes. They dissipate most of his goods on the lying in of the dead man and what they set out by the road for strangers to ride up to and take away. And it is a custom among the Este that men of every tribe must be cremated, and if a single bone is found not completely burnt, they must greatly atone for it.

There is a tribe among the Este who can make cold, which is why the dead men lie so long without decaying, because they make the cold on the man. And if someone puts in two containers [one] full of water and [the other] beer, they can make it so that one of them is frozen over whether it is summer or winter.

From the Old English of the Alfredian translation of Orosius's *Histories Against the Pagans*. See above, Text 6, for the low opinion of the Wends held by their Germanic neighbours.

TEXT 12
THE BATTLE OF MALDON

... was broken.
Then he commanded that each of the warriors release
    their horses,
drive them away, and march forward,
think of arms and have good courage.
5 When Offa's kinsman first understood
that the nobleman had no intention of tolerating
    slackness,
he had his beloved hawk fly from his hands
to the wood, and advanced to the battle.
From that it was obvious that the young man had no
    intention
10 of weakening in the fight when he took up his
    weapons.
Likewise Eadric wished to support his lord,
his leader, in the fight. He carried forward
his spear to the battle; he had good concentration
as long as he could wield his shield and broad sword
15 with his hands; he fulfilled his boast
when he had to fight in front of his lord.
Then Byrhtnoth rode around
and advised there, arrayed his men
and instructed them how to keep in position,
20 and asked them to hold their shields properly
fast in the hand, and not to be at all afraid.
When he had properly organized the troops,
he dismounted among the people where it most pleased
    him to be,
where he knew his close retainers to be most loyal.
25 Then the messenger of the Vikings stood on the bank

and called out sternly, vauntingly announced
the message of the seamen, spoke the words
as he stood on the shore to the nobleman:
'Bold seamen have sent me to you,
30 have commanded me to tell you that they give you
      permission to send quickly
treasures in return for protection. And it is better for you
      all
that you buy off this assault of spears with tribute,
than that we should share out such fierce battle.
There is no reason why we should destroy each other if
      you are wealthy enough for the purpose:
35 we want to establish peace with the gold.
If you who are the most wealthy here decide
that you wish to redeem your people
and give to the seamen money according to their own
      assessment
in return for peace, and take peace from us,
40 we want to walk back to our ships with the payment,
to sail away on the sea and maintain peace with
      you all.'
Byrhtnoth spoke formally, angry and resolute
raised his shield, shook his slender spear,
spoke words and gave him answer:
45 'Do you hear, sailor, what this army has to say?
They want to give you all tribute of spears,
lethal points and old swords,
war-gear that will not serve you in the battle.
Messenger of the Vikings, announce in reply
50 and say to your people a much more hateful message
      than they expect,
that here stands a nobleman of untarnished repute, with
      his army,

who intends to defend this country,
the people and land of Æthelred
my lord. The heathen must

55 fall in battle. It seems to me too shameful
that you walk back to ship with our payment
unfought, now that you have come
this far here into our land.
You must not in such an easy fashion gain treasure:

60 point and edge, spear and sword, grim battle-play
must first arbitrate before we give tribute.'
Then he commanded the warriors to march carrying their
    shields
so that they all stood on the riverbank.
The two companies were not able to get at each other
    because of the water.

65 The flood-tide had come running in after the ebb,
and the tidal streams had joined together. It seemed to
    them too long a time
before they could carry their spears at each other.
The East Saxon vanguard and the Viking army
stood along the River Pante in military array.

70 None of them could harm another
except whichever of them was killed by the flight of an
    arrow.
The tide went out. The sailors stood ready,
many Vikings eager for battle.
Then the protector of warriors commanded a hardened
    warrior

75 who was called Wulfstan to hold the causeway.
He was as brave as the rest of his family, the son of Ceola,
    and he killed with his spear the first man
    who most boldly stepped on to the causeway.
    Undaunted warriors, Ælfhere and Maccus

80   the brave pair, stood there with Wulfstan,
     with no intention of starting a flight from the ford,
     but they resolutely defended themselves against the
          enemy
     as long as they were able to wield weapons.
     When they perceived and understood clearly
85   that they had encountered fierce guardians of the
          causeway there,
     then the hateful strangers began to practise trickery:
     they requested that they might be allowed to have space
          to land,
     be allowed to cross the ford and bring over their troops.
     Then the nobleman granted the hateful people
90   too much land because of his overconfidence.
     The son of Byrhthelm then called
     over the cold water and the warriors listened:
     'Space has been made for you: proceed quickly to us,
     warriors to battle. God alone knows
95   who will be allowed control over the place of slaughter.'
     Then the wolves of slaughter, the Viking army,
     advanced west over the Pante, regardless of the water.
     They carried their shields over the bright water,
     the sailors bore their limewood shields to dry land.
100 Byrhtnoth and his warriors stood ready
     against the fierce attackers. He commanded them
     to make the shield-wall and stand fast
     in the army against the enemies. The fight was near
          then,
     and glory in battle, the time had come
105 when doomed men would have to fall there.
     The roar of battle went up there; ravens circled,
     the eagle ready for carrion; there was uproar on earth.
     They let fly the file-hard spears, grimly sharpened,

from their hands then, and the spears flew.

110   Bows were busy, and the shield received the points.
The onslaught of battle was bitter: warriors fell
on all sides, young men lay dead.
Wulfmær, Byrhtnoth's kinsman was wounded:
he chose rest in death; the son of Byrhtnoth's sister

115   was cruelly hacked about with swords.
Recompense was given to the Vikings there:
I heard that Edward struck one
powerfully with his sword, did not hold back the stroke,
so that the doomed warrior fell at his feet.

120   His lord said thanks to his chamberlain
for that when he had the chance.
In this way the resolute warriors
supported each other in battle, warriors with weapons
concentrated eagerly on who first

125   was to be able to take
the life of a doomed man. The corpse fell to the ground.
They stood steadfast; Byrhtnoth encouraged them,
commanded that each warrior concentrate on battle
who intended to gain glory against the Danes.

130   A man fierce in battle advanced, raised his weapon,
held his shield in protection and stepped towards that
      warrior.
Just as resolute, the nobleman went towards the peasant.
Each of them intended evil for the other.
Then the warrior from the sea sent a spear of southern
      manufacture

135   in such a way that the lord of warriors was wounded.
He thrust with the shield then so that the shaft
      splintered
and the spear cracked so that it sprang out.
The warrior was enraged: he stabbed with his spear

the proud Viking who had given him the wound.

140   The warrior was experienced: he had his spear pass
through the young man's neck; his hand guided it
so that he took the life of the sudden attacker.
Then he quickly pierced another
so that his mailshirt split; he was wounded in the chest

145   through the chainmail; the lethal point
was fixed in his heart. The nobleman was happier then;
the brave man laughed and said thanks to the Lord
for the day's work that the Lord had granted him.
Then one of the Danish warriors sent a spear flying

150   from his hand so that it went all too far
through the noble man, Æthelred's thane.
Beside him stood a young man not yet full-grown,
a boy in the battle, Wulfstan's son
Wulfmær the younger, who very bravely

155   pulled the bloody spear out of the warrior,
and sent the hardened spear flying back:
the point penetrated so that the one who had severely
      wounded
his lord before lay dead on the earth.
Then a warrior adorned in arms went towards the noble-
      man:

160   he intended to take the warrior's treasures,
his armour and arm-rings and decorated sword.
At that, Byrhtnoth drew his broad and bright-edged
      sword
from its sheath and struck at the man's mailshirt.
All too quickly one of the sailors prevented him

165   when he injured the nobleman's arm.
The golden-hilted sword fell to the earth then:
he was no longer able to control the hard sword,
wield the weapon. Still the grey-haired warrior

spoke the word, encouraged his young men,
170 commanded that the good companions should
    advance.
He was no longer able to stand firm on his feet.
He looked up towards heaven:
'Thank you, Lord of the nations,
for all the joys that I have experienced on earth.
175 Now, kind Lord, my greatest need is that
you grant grace to my spirit,
that my soul might be allowed to journey to you,
travel in peace into your control,
Lord of the angels. I beseech you
180 that hellish attackers may not be allowed to harm it.'
Then heathen men hacked him to pieces,
and both the warriors who stood beside him.
Ælfnoth and Wulfmær both lay dead
when they gave their lives beside their lord.
185 They turned then from the battle, those who did not
    want to be there.
The sons of Odda were first in the flight
from the battle there, and Godric abandoned the good
    man
who had often given him many a mare.
He mounted the horse that had been his lord's,
190 and got into the trappings, as was not right;
and his brothers Godwine and Godwig
both ran with him. They did not care for battle,
but ran away from the fight and sought the wood,
fled to the place of safety and saved their lives,
195 and with them more men than was at all proper,
if they had remembered all the favours
that he had done for their benefit.
It was just as Offa had said to him earlier in the day

at the assembly-place, when he had called the
    meeting,
200 that many spoke bravely there
who would not endure when necessity arose.
The leader of the army, Æthelred's nobleman,
had fallen then. All the retainers
saw that their lord lay dead.
205 Then proud men, undaunted thanes,
advanced, pressed forward there.
All of them intended one of two things:
to lose their lives or avenge the one they loved.
So Ælfric's son, Ælfwine then spoke,
210 a warrior young in years, he spoke out bravely,
encouraged them forward, made a speech:
'Remember the times when we often spoke over the
    mead,
heroes in the hall, we made boasts
about fierce battle when we were on the benches.
215 Now it will become evident who really is brave.
I want to declare my noble lineage to all,
that I was from a great family among the Mercians:
my grandfather was called Ealhelm,
he was a wise ealdorman and prosperous.
220 Thanes of that people must not taunt me
that I wish to leave this army
and return home, now my leader lies dead
and hacked about in the battle. That is the greatest of
    injuries to me –
he was both my kinsman and my lord.'
225 He advanced then, intent on the feud,
so that he injured one, a sailor among the host,
with the point of his spear, so that he lay dead on the
    ground

destroyed with his weapon. He encouraged his
  companions then,
friends and associates, to advance.
230 Offa shook his spear and spoke:
'Ælfwine, you have encouraged us all,
thanes to do what is necessary. Now our lord, the
  nobleman,
lies dead on the earth, it is absolutely necessary for all
  of us
that we encourage each one
235 as a warrior in battle for as long as he is able to hold
and make use of his weapon – the bitter blade,
the spear and good sword. Godric the cowardly
son of Odda has betrayed us all.
Too many men thought when he was riding away on the
  horse,
240 that proud steed, that it was our lord.
Because of that the army was split here on the
  battlefield,
and the shield-wall broken. Curse his trick,
that he put to flight so many men here.'
Leofsunu raised his shield, the protecting board,
245 and spoke. He answered the warrior,
'This I promise: that I shall not flee
a foot's space from here, but I shall rather advance
to avenge my beloved lord in the conflict.
Solid heroes around Sturmer will have no cause
250 to taunt me with the words that I returned home
lordless, turned away from the battle,
now my friend has fallen. Point of spear and iron sword
must rather take me.' He advanced in utter rage,
fought steadily, scorned flight.
255 Dunnere the simple farmer then shook his spear

and spoke, called out over everything,
asked that each one of the warriors avenge Byrhtnoth:
'He who intends to avenge his lord in the army
cannot ever flinch or care about his life.'

260   Then they went forward, not caring about life,
the retainers, hostile spear-carriers,
fought fiercely and prayed to God
that they might be allowed to avenge their dear lord
and bring death to their enemies.

265   They were eagerly supported in this by the hostage.
He was from a brave family in Northumbria,
the son of Ecglaf, Æscferth by name.
He did not flinch at all in the battle-play,
but rather he shot forth many an arrow;

270   sometimes he hit the shield, sometimes he pierced
     the warrior;
from time to time he gave a wound
for as long as he was able to control his weapons.
Edward the Tall still stood in the front line
ready and eager. He spoke with proud words

275   that he had no intention of fleeing even a pace
backwards when his superior lay dead.
He broke out of the shield-wall and fought against the
     warriors
until he had honourably avenged his treasure-giving
     lord
on the seamen, before he himself lay dead among the
     corpses.

280   Æthelric the noble companion, Sibyrht's brother,
did likewise. Ready and eager to advance,
he fought with serious intent, as did many others:
they split the decorated shield and defended themselves
     bravely.

The rim of the shield sprang loose and the mailshirt
    sang
285 a song of terror. Offa struck a sailor
in the battle so that he fell to the earth;
and Gad's kinsman fell to the ground there.
Offa was rapidly hacked to death in the fight,
yet he had achieved what he had vowed to his lord
290 when earlier he had boasted in the presence of his
    treasure-giver,
that they must both ride back to the town
unharmed to their home, or both fall among the Viking
    army
to die of wounds on the place of slaughter.
He died like a true thane beside his lord.
295 Then there was the crunch of shields. The sailors
    advanced,
enraged by the battle. The spear often passed through
the vitals of the doomed man. Wistan, Thurstan's son,
advanced and fought with the enemy warriors.
He was the death of three of them in the press of battle
300 before he, the descendant of Wigelm, lay among the
    corpses.
It was a fierce encounter there; the warriors stood
resolute in battle; fighters fell
exhausted from their wounds; the dead fell to the earth.
Oswald and Eadwold, two brothers,
305 both constantly encouraged their friends and kinsmen
the warriors: they spoke words urging
that they endure as was necessary,
and make use of their weapons without weakening.
Byrhtwold raised his shield and spoke formally.
310 An old retainer, he shook his spear;
he instructed the warriors with great boldness:

'Resolve must be the firmer, heart the braver,
courage the greater, as our strength diminishes.
Our leader lies here, all hacked to death,
315   the good man in the dirt. The one who thinks to
          turn away
from this battle-play now will always have reason to
          regret it.
I am old; I have no intention of leaving here,
but I intend to lie beside my lord,
beside the man so dear to me.'
320   Æthelgar's son Godric likewise
encouraged them all in the battle. Often he sent forth a
          spear,
a deadly spear to fly among the Vikings.
He likewise went to the front of the defending force,
hacked and slew until he fell in the fight.
325   That was not in the least that Godric who fled the
          battle ...

From the Old English of a now-lost manuscript, transcribed by David
Casley at the end of the 17th century.

TEXT 13
WYRDWRITERAS

Historians who write about kings tell us that ancient kings from former times used to consider how they could relieve themselves of some of the burdens of rule, because one man cannot be everywhere and take everything upon himself, though he might have the authority to do so. The kings, as assistance for themselves, established ealdormen under them, and often sent them to battles, just as it is written in heathen books and in the Bible. And the ealdormen subdued the aggressive enemies as we wish to tell by certain examples from Latin books so that we cannot be contradicted.

The famous King David, though he was bold, sent out his general just as it says in Latin in the Books of Kings and just as we declare here in the Latin language so that we may be believed ... King David sent out his general, called Joab, and he fought against Ammon, and he and all his army put his enemies to flight. ... Later David sent Joab out in the next year against the Ammonites and he conquered them with the king's army, and gained victory there as the story tells us. ... Seba was the name of one of David's thanes who had stirred the people against King David with hostile speech, saying that they must not follow David nor do what he said. Seba fled away and made his escape, but Joab the general got his head from the citizens of the town where he had been born.

... Once again, war came about against Israel, and there was a certain amazing giant involved in the war who wanted to kill King David. But Abishai his thane, the brother of Joab, immediately came to his aid and killed the giant, for he saw how he had lain in wait for David, and had tried to insinuate himself among the king's thanes. Then the king's thanes all swore, saying to him thus, 'You must not come out with us into battle ever again, risking your life, lest you extinguish the lamp of Israel' (by which they meant David himself).

Constantine, the first emperor who converted to Christianity, had a general called Gallicanus, whom he sent out frequently on difficult expeditions against violent nations who fought against the emperor, and he always reduced them to obedience to the will of the emperor. That Gallicanus afterwards became so holy that he performed miracles and was martyred for Christ, as I wrote once in an English sermon.

Gratianus was the name of a certain illustrious emperor who trusted greatly in God, as the book *Tripartita Istoria*, that is the *Threefold Account*, tells us. The uncivilized heathen fought against him, but the emperor immediately sent out Theodosius his general against them, and he fought against the heathens, killing many thousands of the heathen men. Because of that great victory he later became emperor as the book tells us; anyone can check it if they wish.

The emperors wished to discover the brave men and provide them with forces and also promote them and develop them for the benefit of all the armies, and wished to honour them after they had gained victory, just as we have said about Theodosius. The younger Theodosius, the noble emperor, often sent out his generals to various conflicts for the defence of his people, as the story tells us. He himself would sing his prayers and entrust his army to God, and God helped him and also defended his army, just as we wrote in a sermon some time ago.

We could make a lengthy list about this matter if we wished to relate what the books from which we gain wisdom and guidance tell us. They tell us how often victorious generals were sent out to many a battle for the protection of their people. The kings themselves sat at home, nevertheless, concerned with other business necessary to their people. The famous Moses, who was able to talk with God, sent out Joshua against Amalek as Exodus tells us; meanwhile Moses discussed with God and drew forth victory for him from the righteous God. Saul avenged this battle later on Amalek, when by God's command he ravaged the land and killed the heathens and destroyed their race, because they contended wickedly against Moses.

Guidance and protection for us must come from God, and we must look single-mindedly to God for our policy, and speak as we mean, so that our vow that we vow to God may be firm and true, more solid than a wall of stone. For God is truth, and he loves truth, and he brings to nothing all those things that liars say. As it stands written in these words in Latin, *Perdes omnes qui loquuntur mendacium,* 'You will destroy all those who speak a lie.'

From the Old English of Ælfric.

TEXT 14
ÆTHELWOLD OUSTS THE CLERICS FROM THE OLD MINSTER

Now at that time there were in the Old Minster, where the bishop's throne is situated, cathedral canons involved in wicked and scandalous behaviour, victims of pride, insolence, and riotous living to such a degree that some of them did not think fit to celebrate mass in due order. They married wives illicitly, divorced them, and took others; they were constantly given to gourmandizing and drunkenness. The holy man Æthelwold would not tolerate it. With permission from King Edgar, he lost no time in expelling from the monastery such detestable blasphemers against God. He replaced them with monks from Abingdon, to whom he was thus both abbot and bishop.

From Wulfstan of Winchester's Latin *Life of St Æthelwold* in the translation of Michael Lapidge and Michael Winterbottom. The inflammatory nature of Wulfstan's language against the clerics is evident from even so brief an extract.

TEXT 15
THE BLACKSMITHS

Dirty smoke-stained smiths grimed with smoke
drive me to death with the din of their
    hammering.
Such noise in the night no man ever heard:
what cries of knaves and clanging of blows!
Creatures deformed in face and body shout out for
    coal and more coal,
and blow their bellows so that their brains all
    burst:
'Huff, puff!' says one, 'Huff, paff!' says the other.

From the Middle English (14th century). The poem goes on for longer
about the smiths and their work, but this first part is enough to show the
general idea.

TEXT 16
BEDE'S CONCERNS ABOUT
FALSE MONASTERIES

Though it is shameful to speak of it, such people have made
so many places to pass under the name of monasteries, when
they themselves are utterly lacking in the monastic life (as
you know well), that there is no place where the sons of the
nobility or retired warriors can be given possessions of their
own.

From Bede's Latin, *Letter to Ecgberht*, section 11.

TEXT 17
THE OLD ENGLISH BEATITUDES

Truly, when the Saviour saw the crowds he climbed up the mountain, and when he sat down his young followers approached him. And he opened his mouth and taught them and said: Blessed are the spiritually poor for theirs is the kingdom of the heavens; Blessed are the kind because they will possess the earth; Blessed are those who now weep because they will be consoled; Blessed are those who hunger and thirst for righteousness because they will be filled; Blessed are the gentle-hearted because they will find gentle-heartedness; Blessed are the pure-hearted because they will see God; Blessed are the peaceful because they will be called God's children; Blessed are those who endure persecution for righteousness because the kingdom of the heavens is theirs. Blessed are you when they abuse you and persecute you and, lying, say every evil against you, because of me. Rejoice and be glad because your reward is great in the heavens.

From the Old English Gospels.

TEXT 18
A PRAYER OF CONFESSION

In the name of the holy Trinity, Father, Son and Holy Spirit, whom I confess to be almighty and eternal God, ever living and dwelling forever in eternity. To him I entrust the keeping of my soul and body, my words and deeds and thoughts, my heart and my mind, my limbs and my joints, my skin and flesh, my blood and bone, my thought and memory and all my intellect, and anything that bodily or spiritually belongs to me that I am able properly to submit.

And by the Lord's holy body, and by the Lord's holy cross, and by St Mary's virginity, and by Christ's birth, and by his holy baptism, and by his holy fasting, and by his sufferings, and by his resurrection, and by his ascension into the heavens, and by the Holy Spirit and the great Judgement that is now approaching for all humankind, and by his holy gospel and all the miracles that are contained therein – by these things I entrust myself to my Lord the almighty God. And I also pray him by all these things that I have just listed, that he, merciful God, will forgive me all my sins and also grant me glory with his saints after this world.

And also by all these things in God's name I entrust myself to the nine orders of angels and to holy St Michael and all the saintly souls whom I entreat in God's name by all these things that they will intercede for me, both here in this world and in eternity, with almighty God; and also by all these things that I have now listed in God's name, I entreat that they restrain enemies visible and invisible for me, so that they may not be allowed to injure me in this world nor afterwards in eternity.

From the Old English of a prayer book, British Library Manuscript Cotton Galba A. xiv.

TEXT 19
THE MARTYRDOM OF ÆLFHEAH

1011. In this year between the Festival of the Nativity of St Mary and Michaelmas, the Viking army surrounded Canterbury. They got into it by treachery, because Ælfmær, whose life Archbishop Ælfheah had saved, betrayed it to them. There they seized the Archbishop Ælfheah and Ælfweard the king's reeve and Leofwine the abbot and Godwine the bishop. They allowed Abbot Ælfmær to go free. In the city they seized all those in holy orders, men and women, and it is impossible for anyone to say how great a part of the people it was. They stayed in the town after that as long as they wished to, and when they had searched all through it they returned to the ships, and led the archbishop captive with them:

> He who formerly was the head of the English
> and of Christendom was then a captive.
> There might then be seen wretchedness
> where before bliss was seen
> in the wretched town whence to us first came
> Christianity and prosperity before God and in the
> world.

And they had the archbishop in their power up until the time when they martyred him.

1012. On the Saturday before the Easter of the year 1012, the Viking army became enraged against the bishop, because he did not wish them to be given any money and forbade that anything should be given in ransom for him. They were also very drunk, because wine from the south had been brought there. They took the bishop and led him to their meeting on the Saturday evening of Easter week, and there pelted him to death with bones and with skulls of cattle. One of them struck him with an iron axe on the head, so that he fell down from the stroke, and his holy blood fell on to the earth. His holy soul he sent forth to God's kingdom.

Bishops Eadnoth and Ælfhun and the citizens of Canterbury received his holy body in the morning and carried it to London with all honour, and buried him in St Paul's minster. And now God reveals the holy martyr's powers there.

When the tribute was paid and the oaths of peace were sworn, then the Viking army dispersed as widely as they had been gathered. Forty-five ships of the Vikings then submitted to the king, and promised him that they would defend this land on condition that he fed and clothed them.

From the Old English of the *Anglo-Saxon Chronicle* in the Peterborough manuscript.

TEXT 20
ÆLFRIC'S
LIFE OF ST OSWALD

After Augustine came to England there was a certain noble king called Oswald in the land of the Northumbrians who believed very much in God. He travelled in his youth away from his friends and family to Ireland by sea, and was baptized without delay there, together with the friends who travelled with him. Meanwhile, his uncle Edwin the Christian king of Northumbria was killed by the British king, Cædwalla, and two of his successors, within the space of two years. And this Cædwalla killed and shamefully treated the Northumbrian people after the death of their lord until the blessed Oswald put an end to his wickedness. Oswald came against him and fiercely fought against him with a small company. But his faith strengthened him, and Christ came to his aid in the slaying of his enemies. Oswald raised up a cross to the honour of God immediately before he went into battle, and called out to his companions, 'Let us fall down before the cross and pray the Almighty that he might save us from the savage enemy who wishes to slay us. God himself knows that we fight justly against this savage king to save our people.' They all fell to prayer there with Oswald and afterwards in the morning went to the battle and gained the victory, just as the Lord granted it to them because of Oswald's faith, and they laid low their enemies, the proud Cædwalla, with his great host, who thought that no army could withstand him.

The same cross which Oswald raised up there, remained for worship, and many sick people and also cattle were healed, as Bede has told us. A certain man fell on the ice with the result that his arm was broken, and he lay in bed, severely ill, until someone brought him a portion of moss, with which it was overgrown, from the aforementioned cross. And the man was healed in his sleep that very night, through the merits of St Oswald.

[Oswald invites Aidan to preach to his people and the story of the dish of food given to the poor is told.]

It happened on one occasion that Oswald and Aidan sat together on holy Easter-day. They were served the royal food on a silver dish, and at that moment one of the king's thanes who was responsible for alms distribution came in and said that there were many poor people sitting in the street who had come from all around to the king's alms-giving. Then the king immediately sent the poor people the silver dish, with all the food, and commanded the dish to be cut up and given to the poor, each of them to have a piece. And it was done. Then the noble bishop Aidan, in great joy, seized the king's right hand, and cried out in faith to him, 'May this hand never rot in corruption!' And it so happened, even as Aidan had prayed for him, that his right hand is sound to this day.

[Oswald prospers, building York Minster, and helping to convert Cynegils, the heathen king of Wessex.]

King Oswald ruled his kingdom gloriously in the world and with great faith, and in all he did he honoured his Lord, until he was killed in defence of his people, in the ninth year of his reign, when he was 38. It came about because Penda, king of the Mercians, fought against him. Penda had earlier helped Cædwalla kill his kinsman Edwin, and Penda was utterly ignorant of Christ, and the Mercians had not yet received baptism. They both assembled for battle at Maserfeld and got to grips with each other until the Christians fell and the heathens approached to the holy Oswald. He saw his death approaching and prayed for his army who were there falling dead, and commended their souls and his own to God, crying thus as he fell, 'God have mercy on our souls!' Then the heathen king ordered his head to be struck off, and his right arm, and for them to be set up as a trophy.

[The arm is rescued and performs miracles: when the monks of Bardney will not receive the relic, it is put in a tent and a mysterious light shines from it in the night. It is then received, washed, and the water heals many. Animals too are healed. The story of the Irishman is told.]

Now says the holy man Bede, who wrote this book, it is no wonder that the holy king heals illness when he lives in heaven, because he wanted to help those who were poor and weak and give them sustenance when he was alive here. Now he has honour with Almighty God in the eternal realm because of his goodness … Holy Oswald's bones were many years later brought to Mercia, to Gloucester, and God there showed many times, many miracles through the holy man. For this let there be glory to Almighty God, who reigns in eternity for ever and ever. Amen.

From Ælfric's Old English.

TEXT 21
THE MARTYRDOM OF KING EDMUND

A certain very learned monk came from the south over
the sea from St Benedict's foundation [Fleury, in France] in
the days of King Æthelred, to Archbishop Dunstan. This was
three years before Dunstan died, and the monk was called
Abbo. They spoke together then until Dunstan related the
story of St Edmund to him, just as Edmund's sword-bearer had
told it to King Æthelstan when Dunstan was a young man
and the sword-bearer was a man of a very advanced age. Abbo
the monk then recorded the entire story in a book, and when
within a few years the book came to us, we translated it into
English, just as it is in what follows. Abbo the monk then
went home to his monastery within two years, and was immediately appointed abbot in the same monastery.

King Edmund of the East Angles, the blessed, was wise and
honourable, and constantly honoured almighty God by his
life of noble virtue. He was humble and good and so single-
mindedly constant that he never wished to stoop to shameful
vices, nor did he ever deviate from his virtuous ways. But he
always remembered the true teaching, 'If you are a leader of
men, do not raise yourself up, but be among men as one of
them.' He was liberal to the poor and widows like a father,
and always guided his people with benevolence into ways of
goodness, and restrained the violent, and lived happily in the
true faith.

In due course it happened that the Danish people with a
fleet travelled far and wide through the land, harrying and
killing, as is their habit. The most important leaders of the
sailors were Hinguar and Hubba, united through the devil.
They landed with their ships in Northumbria, and laid waste
the land and killed the people. Then, having won victory

through savagery, Hinguar turned east with his ships, and left Hubba in Northumbria. Hinguar arrived by rowing among the East Anglians in the year that Prince Alfred, who later became famous as the king of the West Saxons, was 21. And the aforementioned Hinguar suddenly crept like a wolf upon the land, and struck the people, men, women and innocent children, and shamefully oppressed the innocent Christians.

Soon after that, he sent a vaunting message to King Edmund, demanding that he should offer his allegiance to Hinguar if he valued his life. The messenger then approached King Edmund and quickly gave him Hinguar's message, 'Hinguar our king, who is brave and victorious by land and sea, has power over many nations, and has come now with his army suddenly upon this land, so that he may make his winter base here with his army. Now he commands you to share your secret treasures and your ancestral valuables quickly with him, and be his tributary king if you want to live. For you do not have the power to be able to resist him.'

At this, King Edmund called a bishop who was conveniently near and discussed with him how he should reply to the savage Hinguar. The bishop was struck with fear because of the sudden turn of events and the threat to the king's life, and said that it seemed to him the best thing if the king were to submit to Hinguar's demands. The king kept silent and looked at the earth, and then said to the bishop in regal manner, 'Bishop, the wretched inhabitants of this land are shamefully mistreated, and I would now rather die in battle if my people might be allowed to enjoy their land.' The bishop said, 'O dear king, your people lie slain and you do not have the resources to be able to fight; and these sailors will come and capture you alive unless you save your life by means of flight or by submitting to them protect yourself.' Then Edmund, full of courage as he was, said, 'This is what I ask for and the desire of my heart: that I do not survive after my beloved thanes with their children and wives have been suddenly slain in their beds by these sailors. It was never my way to take to flight, but I wished rather to die, if I had to, for the sake of my own land. Almighty God knows that I have no intention of ever turning aside from worship of him, or away from his true love whether I live or die.'

After these words, Edmund turned to the messenger that Hinguar had sent to him, and boldly said, 'Truly you deserve death now, but I do not wish to sully my clean hands with your filthy blood. For I follow Christ who gave us an example in this. I will gladly be slain by you if that is what God ordains. Go now, with all speed, and tell your cruel lord, "Never will Edmund, alive, submit to Hinguar the savage general, unless he, Hinguar, first submits in faith to the Saviour Christ in this land."'

The messenger went quickly away, and on the road he met the savage Hinguar hurrying towards Edmund with all his army. And he told the wicked man how he was answered. Hinguar then arrogantly commanded his Vikings to look out especially for the king who had rejected his offer, and immediately bind him.

So King Edmund stood in his hall when Hinguar came, and mindful of the Saviour, threw down his weapons. He wished to follow Christ's example, who forbade Peter to fight with weapons against the savage Jews. So the wicked men bound Edmund and abused him insultingly, and beat him with rods, and afterwards took the faithful king to a firmly rooted tree, and tied him to it with strong ropes, and then scourged him for a long time with whips. Between strokes, he kept calling out in true faith to the Saviour Christ. Because of his faith, and because he kept calling for help to Christ, the heathens became madly enraged. They shot at him, for their amusement, until he was covered with their missiles like the bristles on a hedgehog, just as St Sebastian was. Hinguar the wicked sailor saw that the noble king had no intention of renouncing Christ, but kept calling out to him with resolute faith. So he ordered him to be beheaded, and the heathen did it. Even while he was still calling upon Christ, the heathen led away the holy man to his death, and with a single blow cut off his head, and his happy soul passed to Christ. A certain man was there nearby, kept hidden from the heathen by God, who heard all this and told it afterwards just as we have related it here.

Then the seamen went back aboard ship and hid the head of the holy Edmund among the thick brambles so that it could not be buried. After a while, when they had gone away, the surviving countryfolk came out to where their lord's body lay headless, and they were sadly grieved in heart for his death, and especially that they did not have the head for the body. The observer who had seen it all said that the sailors had had the head with them, and that it seemed to him that they had hidden the head somewhere in the wood; this turned out to be truly the case. They went all together to look in the wood, searching everywhere among the thorns and brambles, to see if they could find the head anywhere.

It was another great marvel that a wolf was sent by God's guidance to guard the head day and night against other animals. So as they went searching, they kept calling out (as is the habit of those who go about in the woods), 'Where are you now, friend?' And the head answered, 'Here, here, here!' And so it constantly called out answering them all whenever any of them called, until they all came upon it, guided by means of those cries. There lay the grey wolf watching over the head, and its two feet clasped the head. It was greedy and hungry, yet for God's sake it did not dare taste the head, but

protected it from the other animals. They were amazed at the
wolf's role of protector, and took the holy head home with
them, thanking the Almighty for all his marvels. As if it were
tame, the wolf followed with the head until they came to the
town, and then went back to the woods.

Then the countryfolk afterwards brought the head to the
holy body and buried him as best they might when such haste
was necessary, and quickly built a church over him. After a
while, after many years, when the raiding was over and peace
was restored to the troubled people, they got together and
built a church in noble fashion for the saint because many
miracles were being done at his grave, at the prayer-chamber
where he was buried. They then wished to carry the holy body
with popular honour to lay it in the new church. It was a great
marvel, then, that Edmund was just as whole as if he had been
alive, his body was pure and his neck healed where it had
been cut through, and the wound was like a red silk thread
around his neck to show how he had been killed. Likewise the
wounds which the savage heathens had inflicted with their
repeated shots were healed by heavenly God, and he lies thus
uncorrupt to this present day awaiting resurrection and eternal glory. His body, which lies without decay, demonstrates to
us that he lived without fornication here in the world, and
undefiled in life passed to Christ.

A certain widow called Oswyn lived by the saint's grave,
spending her life in prayer and fasting for many years. Each
year she would cut the saint's hair and modestly and lovingly
would cut his nails and keep them in a shrine as relics on the
altar. In this way the countryfolk honoured the saint faithfully, and Bishop Theodred greatly enriched the church with
gold and silver in honour of the saint.

Then one time some unhappy thieves, eight of them,
came one night to the honoured saint intending to steal the

treasures that people took there, and attempted skilfully to break in. One hit the hasp smartly with a hammer, another of them filed away at it with a file, another dug under the door with a spade, another of them intended unlocking the window up a ladder. But their efforts came to nothing, and things went badly for them in that the holy man miraculously fixed them, each one as he stood with his tool, rigidly in place, so that none of them could perform the criminal deed nor move away, but remained there until morning.

People were amazed at this, seeing how the criminals hung there, one on a ladder, one bent in the act of digging, and each one stuck fast at his labour. They were all taken to the bishop, and he commanded that they all be hung on the high gallows. He did not recall, however, how merciful God announced through his prophets the words given here, 'Do not forbear to deliver those who are led out to death'; and the holy canon also that forbids those in holy orders, whether bishops or priests, to be concerned about thieves, for it is not fitting that those who are chosen to serve God, if they are God's servants, should consent to the death of any man. Then Bishop Theodred looked again at his books, and afterwards regretted with sadness that he had given such a severe judgement on the unhappy thieves, and to the end of his life he lamented it. He earnestly asked the people to fast with him for fully three days, praying that the Almighty would have mercy on him.

There was a certain man called Leofstan in that land, rich in the eyes of the world but ignorant before God. He rode to the saint with great arrogance and very insolently commanded them to demonstrate to him whether the holy saint was incorrupt or not. But as soon as he saw the saint's body he immediately went mad and raved savagely and wretchedly died an evil death. This is similar to what the faithful Pope Gregory said in his writing on St Lawrence who lies in the city of Rome: people, good and bad, kept wanting to see how he lay, but God restrained them so that seven men died together at one showing; then the others stopped looking at the martyr with human error.

We have heard of many marvels about St Edmund from the talk of the people that we do not intend to record in writing here, but everyone knows them. This saint, and others like him, makes it clear that God Almighty – the One who preserves him whole in body until the great Day, though Edmund was made from dust – is able to raise man up again incorrupt from the earth at the Day of Judgement.

The holy place deserves honour because of the venerable saint, and that it be well provided with the pure servants of God for God's service, because the saint is greater than people can imagine. The English nation is not deprived of the Lord's saints since in England there lie such saints as this holy king [Edmund], the blessed Cuthbert, St Æthelthryth at Ely and her sister incorrupt in body, for the confirmation of the faith. There are also many other saints among the English who work many miracles, as is widely known, to the praise of the Almighty in whom they believed. Christ reveals to people through his glorious saints that he is Almighty God who does such marvels, even though the wretched Jews utterly rejected him because they are accursed as they wished to be. No marvels are done at their graves for they do not believe in the living Christ; but Christ reveals to people where true faith is when he performs such marvels through his saints widely throughout the earth. For this, glory be to him, with his Heavenly Father and the Holy Spirit for ever and ever. Amen.

From Ælfric's Old English.

TEXT 22
SELECTIONS FROM ABBO'S
ACCOUNT OF ST EDMUND

Here begins the Dedicatory Epistle accompanying the Passion
of Saint Eadmund, King and Martyr.

For Dunstan, Lord Archbishop of the holy metropolitan
Church of Canterbury, ripe, sooth to say, in character as in age,
Abbo of Fleury, a monk in deacon's orders, though unworthy,
bespeaks the news of the blessing of Christ the Lord above
and below. After I had departed from you, venerable father,
with much cheerfulness of heart, and had returned with haste
to the monastery that you wot of, the brethren, with whom,
being detained by their fraternal kindness, I have hitherto
been staying as a guest, began to press me urgently to comply
with their saintly desire, that I would reduce to writing the
Passion of the miracle-worker, Eadmund, king and martyr.
This, they declared, would be edifying to future generations,
and acceptable to you, as well as a serviceable memento of my
humble self among the English churches. They had heard,
indeed, that the story of this Passion, which is unknown to
most people, and has been committed to writing by none, had
been related by your Holiness, as collected from ancient tradition, in my presence to the Lord Bishop of Rochester, and to
the Abbot of the monastery which is called Malmesbury, and
to other brethren then assembled in accordance with your
practice, whom you cease not to nourish with the food of
God's word, alike in the Latin and in the mother tongue. To
them you averred, while the tears ran from your eyes, that you
had in your youth learned the history from a broken-down
veteran, who in relating it, simply and in good faith, to the
most glorious English king, Athelstan, declared on his oath

that, on the very day on which the martyr laid down his life
for Christ's sake, he had been armour-bearer to the saintly
hero. In view of the great reliance which you placed on the
old man's assertions, and which led you to store up his words
in their entirety in the receptacle of your memory, to be
uttered at a later date with honeyed accents to a younger
generation, the brethren insisted strongly, notwithstanding
my diffidence, that I would satisfy their earnest desire, and
to the best of my ability preserve from utter oblivion so
important a series of events. I felt that I could not with due
self-respect refuse their request, and therefore, postponing for
the moment the study of secular literature, I betook myself as
it were to the esoteric wisdom of the spirit, and undertook to
describe the good deeds of the king, who addicted himself on
the throne of his kingdom to the truest philosophy, but especially those which, unparalleled in the world's history, were
wrought after his death; to which none would give credence
were they not vouched for by the irrefragable authority of
your assertion. In truth, when you, the snows of whose head
compel belief, made mention of the still continuing incorruption of the king's body, one of those present anxiously raised
the question whether such things were possible? In order to
clear up the doubt involved in that question, you alleged,
from the ample stores of your experience, the instance (which
still more powerfully struck the astonished minds of your
auditors) of Cuthbert, the Saint of the Lord, and incomparable Confessor and Bishop, who not only to this day awaits
with body incorrupt the day of the first resurrection, but continues to be suffused with a gentle warmth. In this I found an
admirable proof, which led me with more assurance to the
careful relation of the holy king's actions, inspired as I was
with full trust in his and your incomparable merits. And so, in
dedicating to you the first fruits of my labour, I humbly

beseech you to be so good as to bestow upon me, if it be but one day of your leisure in so worthy a cause, retrenching what is in excess, and supplying what is in defect, since, with the exception of the last miracle of the series, I have in every particular composed the narrative, as you delivered it, faithfully following a faithful informant, and exhorting all to the love of so eminent a martyr. Farewell, my Father in Christ.

[Chapter 3 of the *passio* given below, details Edmund's character.]

III. [Prince Eadmund] was sprung from the noble stock of the Old Saxons, and from his earliest childhood cherished most sincerely the Christian faith. Descended from a line of kings, and endued with a high character, he was, by the unanimous choice of all his fellow-provincials, not so much elected in due course of succession, as forced to rule over them with the authority of the sceptre. He was in truth of a comely aspect, apt for sovereignty; and his countenance continually developed fresh beauty through the tranquil devotion of his most serene spirit. To all he was affable and winning in speech, and distinguished by a captivating modesty; and he dwelt among his contemporaries with admirable kindness, though he was their lord, and without any touch of haughtiness or pride. The holy Eadmund did indeed already carry in his countenance what afterwards was made manifest by God's will; since even as a boy he grasped with whole-hearted endeavour the ladder of virtue, the summit of which he was destined by God's mercy to reach by martyrdom.

[Chapters 5–15 deal with the attacks of the Vikings and the martyrdom.]

V. [The devil] despatched one of his own satellites as an adversary to Eadmund, in the hope that, stripped of all his possessions, the king might be goaded into an outburst of

impatience, and in despair curse God to His face. This adversary was known by the name of Inguar; and he, with another
called Hubba, a man of equal depravity, attempted (and nothing but the divine compassion could have prevented them) to
reduce to destruction the whole confines of Britain. And no
wonder! seeing that they came hardened with the stiff frost of
their own wickedness from that roof of the world where he
had fixed his abode who in his mad ambition sought to make
himself equal to the Most High. In fine it is proverbial,
according to the prediction of the prophet, that from the
north comes all that is evil, as those have had too good cause
to know, who through the spite of fortune and the fall of the
die have experienced the barbarity of the races of the north.
These, it is certain, are so cruel by the ferocity of their nature,
as to be incapable of feeling for the ills of mankind; as is
shown by the fact that some of their tribes use human flesh
for food, and from the circumstance are known by the Greek
name Anthropophagists. Nations of this kind abound in great
numbers in Scythia, near the Hyperborean Mountains, and
are destined, as we read, more than all other races, to follow
Antichrist, and to batten without compunction on the agonies of men who refuse to bear on their foreheads the mark of
the beast. Hence it results that they can observe no truce in
harrying the worshippers of Christ, and this is true especially
of the Danes, who, dwelling fatally near to the western
regions, indulge continually in piratical raids upon them. Of
this nation were the generals Inguar and Hubba, whom I have
mentioned above. They set out in the first instance to attack
the province of Northumbria, and overran the whole district
from one end to the other, inflicting upon it the heaviest
devastation. None of the inhabitants could resist these
abominable onslaughts, but suffered the too well merited
chastisement of the divine wrath through the instrumentality

of Hubba the agent of iniquity. Having raked together their booty, Inguar left on the spot Hubba, his associate in cruelty, and approaching [East Anglia] suddenly with a great fleet, landed by stealth at a city in that region, entered it before the citizens were aware of his approach, and set it on fire. Boys, and men old and young, whom he encountered in the streets of the city were killed; and he paid no respect to the chastity of wife or maid. Husband and wife lay dead or dying together on their thresholds; the babe snatched from its mother's breast was, in order to multiply the cries of grief, slaughtered before her eyes. An impious soldiery scoured the town in fury, athirst for every crime by which pleasure could be given to the tyrant who from sheer love of cruelty had given orders for the massacre of the innocent.

VI. At length when the impious Inguar had slain such numbers that he had, I will not say satisfied his Achimenian madness, but from weariness deferred for a while its complete gratification, he summoned a few poor wretches whom he judged to be not worth killing, and by searching cross-examination of them endeavoured to ascertain whereabouts their king was at that time residing. It seems that a report had reached him that the glorious King Eadmund, who was in the prime of life, and in the fulness of vigour, was a keen soldier. On this account Inguar made it his business to cut off all the men he could find round about, so that the king, deprived of the support of a compact force for the defence of his kingdom, should be unable to offer effective resistance. Eadmund, it happened, was at that time staying at some distance from the city, in a township which in the native language is called Hægelisdun, from which also the neighbouring forest is called by the same name. The monster of impiety calculated, as was indeed the truth, that whatever number of the natives his murderous minions could succeed in destroying, so many the less would there be, if it came to a pitched battle, for the king to lead against his foes. Moreover, Inguar did not venture to leave his fleet without a strong guard; for, just as the wolf is accustomed to steal in the evening down to the plains, and to return with haste by night to his lair in the woods, so it was the practice of the Danish and Manic people, always intent upon a career of theft, never to risk an open and fair fight with their enemies, unless through being entangled in an ambush they had lost all hope of regaining their ships in harbour.

VII. Accordingly, with excessive caution he summoned one of his array, and despatched him to the king, who was devoid of any such harassing anxiety, with orders to ascertain the amount of his possessions, hoping to take him unawares, as in fact happened, and to daunt him by tortures if he should refuse to comply with the murderous demands of the Dane. Inguar, accompanied by a great throng, followed in support with leisurely steps. He had given orders to the agent of this wicked mission, thus relieved of all apprehension of danger, to accost the unsuspecting king as follows: 'My august master, and unconquerable sovereign Inguar, a terror by land and sea, having by force of arms brought divers countries into subjection to himself, has landed with a great fleet on the desirable shores of this territory with the intention of fixing his winter-quarters here, and in pursuance thereof commands you to share with him your ancient treasures, and your hereditary wealth, and to reign in future under him. But if you hold in contempt his power, which is fortified by innumerable battalions, it will be to your own prejudice, as you will be accounted unworthy to live or to reign. And who are you that you should presume to oppose so great a power? The storms and tempests of the deep subserve the purpose of our fleets;

and cannot turn from the accomplishment of their settled intentions men who, by grace and favour of the elements, have never suffered injury from the awful thunders of heaven, or from the oft-repeated lightning flash. Submit therefore with all your people to this greatest of monarchs whom the elements obey, since he is prepared in his great clemency in all that he undertakes, "To spare the meek, while he o'er-whelms the proud."'

VIII. On hearing this, the most saintly king groaned in profound grief of mind, and hailing one of his bishops, who was his confidential adviser, consulted with him as to the answer which was proper to be returned to the demands preferred. The bishop, alarmed for the safety of the king, used a number of arguments in favour of compliance; but the king, staggered by such advice, and fixing his eyes on the ground, was silent for a little while. Then finally he spoke his mind as follows: 'Bishop, I have reached a point in my life of which I never had any apprehension. See! a barbarous stranger with drawn sword menaces the old occupants of my realm, and the once prosperous natives are reduced to sighs and groans and silence. Would that those who now live in dread of perishing by a bloody death might be spared to survive amid the beloved fields of their country, even though I should fall, and that they might in course of time be restored to the brightness of their former prosperity.' Here the bishop interposed: 'How can you speak of survivors in the land, seeing that the enemy's sword has left scarcely one alive in the whole city? Their axes are blunted with the slaughter of your subjects; you are left without a guard, and they will bind you fast with thongs. And therefore, my sovereign, dear to me as my soul, unless you seek safety in flight, or have recourse to the ill-omened alternative of surrender, I fear the tormentors will soon arrive, and you will forfeit your life through the unholy execution of their orders.' 'That,' answered the king, 'is what I desire; that is my dearest wish, not to survive my loyal and dear subjects, who have been bereft of their lives and massacred with their children and their wives as they lay in bed, by a bloodthirsty brigand. And what do you advise? that in life's extremity, bereft of my comrades, I should besmirch my fair fame by taking to flight? I have always avoided the calumnious accusations of the informer; never have I endured the opprobrium of fleeing from the battlefield, realizing how glorious it would be for me to die for my country; and now I will of my own free will surrender myself, for the loss of those dear to me has made light itself hateful. The Almighty disposer of events is present as my witness that, whether I live or die, nothing shall separate me from the love of Christ, the ring of whose faith I took on me in the sacrament of baptism, when I renounced Satan and all his vanities. And by that renunciation it ensued that I gained a triple title to be devoted to the praise and glory of the Eternal Trinity, having been cleansed with a view to the reward of endless life by the anointing of the consecrated chrism. Firstly, to wit, I put on the robes proper for the font of healing; in the second place, I received confirmation with the larger episcopal signet; and thirdly, by general acclaim of yourself and the people at large, I acquired the sovereign power of this realm. And thus bedewed in threefold manner with the ointment of mystic consecration, I have determined to be the benefactor rather than the ruler of the English Commonwealth, in scorning to bow my neck to any yoke but that of the service of God. It is with a mere pretence of goodwill that my cunning foe now spreads the meshes of his machinations, by which he calculates on ensnaring the servant of Christ, above all when he promises that which the divine bounty has already conferred upon me. He allows

me life, for which I no longer care; he promises me a kingdom, that I already possess; he would bestow on me riches, of
which I have no need. Is it for these things that I am now to
begin serving two masters – I who have dedicated myself
before my whole court to live and to rule under Christ alone?'

IX. Then, turning to the messenger whom the impious Inguar
had sent to announce the terms on which his kingdom might
be retained, Eadmund exclaimed: 'Reeking as you are with
the blood of my countrymen, you might justly be doomed to
death; but to speak plainly, I would follow the example of
Christ my Lord, and refrain from staining my pure hands; and
for his name's sake, if the need arise, I am willing and glad to
perish by your weapons. Therefore return as fast as you can at
once to your lord, and take forthwith this message to him:
"Son of the devil, well do you imitate your father, who
through his swelling pride fell from heaven, and striving to
involve mankind in his falseness, rendered multitudes liable
to his punishment. You, his chief follower, are powerless to
terrify me by threats, nor shall you deceive me with the snares
and sophistries that inveigle to destruction, for you will not
find me lacking the armour of Christian principles. As for the
treasures and the wealth, which till now God's favour has
bestowed on me, take and squander them as your insatiable
greed may prompt, since, even though you should break in
pieces this frail and perishable body, like a potter's vessel, my
soul, which is truly free, will never for a moment submit to
you. For it is more honourable to champion the cause of per-
petual freedom, if not with arms, at any rate with life, than
to spend tearful complaints in redemanding it when lost,
since in the one case death is glorious, but in the other the
opposition is but the rebellion of slaves. That is to say, a slave,
whatever terms he may have accepted at the hands of his

master, is bound to observe them as he accepted them; if he repudiates them, iniquitous though they may be, he is guilty of treason, and is liable to the punishment of a slave. But enough; grievous as may be the burden of such a servitude, still more grievous is the rankling sore which misfortune of this kind usually begets, seeing that, as is within the knowledge of those who, as advocates, are practised in the discussion of cases in the law-courts, when a conclusion is deduced from repugnant circumstances, it is certain that, if freedom be aimed at, the tyrant is undoubtedly prejudiced by contempt of himself. Consequently, willingly or unwillingly, let my free spirit wing its way from its prison to heaven, untainted by any appearance of sale or surrender; for be assured, Dane, you shall never see me, a king, survive the loss of freedom to adorn your triumph. You ply me with expectations of a continued reign, after the slaughter of all my people, as if I were possessed by so mad a lust of rule, that I could have the heart to reign over houses emptied of their noble inhabitants: their precious garniture. Let your savage ferocity go on as it has begun: after the subjects let the king be snatched from his throne, dragged away, spat upon, struck and buffeted, and finally butchered. The King of kings sees all that with compassion, and will, I am confident, translate the victim to reign with him in life eternal. Know, therefore, that for the love of this earthly life Eadmund the Christian king will not submit to a heathen chief, unless you first become a convert to our religion; he would rather be a standard-bearer in the camp of the Eternal King.'"

X. The saintly man had but just ended his speech, and the soldier taken his departure from the palace to carry back the answer, when behold, Inguar met him, and bade him waste no words in declaring the final purport of the king's reply. As the

messenger obeyed this behest, the tyrant ordered the crowd of
his attendants to form a ring round the place, and to take the
king alone prisoner, as showing palpable defiance of the conditions laid down. Then the holy King Eadmund was taken in
his palace, as a member of Christ, his weapons thrown aside
and was pinioned and tightly bound with chains, and in his
innocence was made to stand before the impious general, like
Christ before the governor Pilate, and eager to follow in the
footsteps of Him who was sacrificed as a victim for us. And so
in chains he was mocked in many ways, and at length, after
being savagely beaten, he was brought to a tree in the neighbourhood, tied to it, and for a long while tortured with
terrible lashes. But his constancy was unbroken, while without ceasing he called on Christ with broken voice. This roused
the fury of his enemies, who, as if practising at a target, pierced
his whole body with arrow-spikes, augmenting the severity of
his torment by frequent discharges of their weapons, and
inflicting wound upon wound, while one javelin made room
for another. And thus, all haggled over by the sharp points of
their darts, and scarce able to draw breath, he actually bristled
with them, like a prickly hedgehog or a thistle fretted with
spines, resembling in his agony the illustrious martyr
Sebastian. But when it was made apparent to the villainous
Inguar that not even by these means could the king be made
to yield to the agents of his cruelty, but that he continued to
call upon the name of Christ, the Dane commanded the executioner to cut off his head forthwith. The king was by this
time almost lifeless, though the warm life-stream still
throbbed in his breast, and he was scarcely able to stand erect.
In this plight he was hastily wrenched from the blood-stained
stem, his ribs laid bare by numberless gashes, as if he had been
put to the torture of the rack, or had been torn by savage
claws, and was bidden to stretch forth the head which had

ever been adorned by the royal diadem. Then, as he stood in all his meekness, like a ram chosen out of the whole flock, and desirous of hastening by a happy exchange this life for eternity, absorbed as he was in the mercies of God, he was refreshed by the vision of the light within, for the satisfaction of which he earnestly yearned in his hour of agony. Thus, while the words of prayer were still on his lips, the executioner, sword in hand, deprived the king of life, striking off his head with a single blow. And so, on the 20th November, as an offering to God of sweetest savour, Eadmund, after he had been tried in the fire of suffering, rose with the palm of victory and the crown of righteousness, to the court of heaven, to enter as king and martyr the assembly of the court of heaven.

XI. Thus in his departure from life, the king, following the footsteps of Christ his master, consummated that sacrifice of the Cross which he had endured continually in the flesh. Just as Christ, free from all taint of sin, left on the column to which he was bound, not for himself, but for us, the blood which was the mark of his scourging, so Eadmund incurred a like penalty bound to the blood-stained tree, for the sake of gaining a glory that fades not away. Christ, whose life was without stain, suffered in his great benignity the bitter pain of unmerciful nails in his hands and feet in order to cleanse away the foulness of our sins; Eadmund, for the love of the holy Name, with his whole body bristling with grievous arrows, and lacerated to the very marrow by the acutest tortures, steadfastly persisted in the avowal of his faith which in the end he crowned by undergoing the doom of death. The Danes, with their instigator, instruments of the devil, left his body mutilated, as has been described, and transfixed with javelins, while the sacred head which had been anointed not with the oil of sinners, but with the sacramental chrism of mystery, was carried by them as they retired into a wood, the name of which is Haglesdun, and was thrown as far as possible among the dense thickets of brambles and so hidden; the Danes contriving this with the greatest cunning, so that the Christians, but few of whom were left alive, should not be able to commit to such decent burial as their limited means of interment would allow, the sanctified body of the martyr conjoined with the head.

XII. Of this appalling scene there was present as a spectator, though in hiding, one of our religion, who was rescued, as I believe, by God's providence from the swords of the heathen, and so preserved to bring to light the traces of these events, although he was entirely ignorant what had been done with the head, beyond the fact that he had seen the Danes betaking themselves with it into the depths of the wood. Accordingly, when peace of some sort had been restored to the churches, the Christians began to emerge from their hiding-places, and to make diligent and busy search with the intention of joining the head of their king and martyr, when found, to the rest of the body, and laying them to rest with due honour according to their means. And so, on the depar-ture of the heathen, who engaged in the work of devastation elsewhere, the sacred body, still lying above ground, was with no difficulty found in the very field where the king died, when he finished the course of his trial. Thither, spurred by the recollection of former benefits, and of the gentle nature of their king, the populace, coming together from all directions, began with rueful hearts to lament the loss of so important a part of the body. Inspiration came by benign suggestion from above and, after listening to the helpful narrative of the wit-ness who had, as I have said, been a witness of the dreadful scene, they united in great numbers to institute a search in

every part of the wood's recesses, in the hope of reaching by
hazard the spot where the head of their holy hero was lying.
All who were possessed of true insight were confident that the
Danes, as worshippers of strange gods, had out of spite to our
faith abstracted the head of the martyr, which they had probably hidden not very far away in the dense thicket, and had
left concealed by the coarse undergrowth a prey to birds
and beasts, A council was held, and all unanimously agreed
upon a plan; it was decided that each individual should be
accoutred with horn or pipe, so that the searchers, in their
explorations hither and thither, could by calling or by the
noise of their instruments signal one to another, and so avoid
going twice over the same ground, or missing some localities
altogether.

XIII. When they carried out this plan, a thing happened
marvellous to relate, and unheard of in the course of ages.
The head of the holy king, far removed from the body to
which it belonged, broke into utterance without assistance
from the vocal chords, or aid from the arteries proceeding
from the heart. A number of the party, like corpse-searchers,
were gradually examining the out-of-the-way parts of the
wood, and when the moment had arrived at which the sound
of the voice could be heard, the head, in response to the calls
of the search-party mutually encouraging one another, and as
comrade to comrade crying alternately 'Where are you?' indicated the place where it lay by exclaiming in their native
tongue, Here! Here! Here! In Latin the same meaning would
be rendered by Hic! Hic! Hic! And the head never ceased to
repeat this exclamation, till all were drawn to it. The chords
of the dead man's tongue vibrated within the passages of the
jaws, thus displaying the miraculous power of Him who was
born of the Word, and endowed the braying ass with human

speech, so that it rebuked the madness of the prophet. And to this miracle the Creator of the world added another by attaching an unwonted guardian to the heavenly treasure. In fact, a monstrous wolf was by God's mercy found in that place, embracing the holy head between its paws, as it lay at full length on the ground, and thus acting as sentinel to the martyr. Nor did it suffer any animal whatever to injure its charge, but, forgetful of its natural voracity, preserved the head from all harm with the utmost vigilance, lying outstretched on the earth. This was witnessed with astonishment by the crowd which had assembled, and they recognized in the most blessed king and martyr Eadmund a worthy parallel to that enviable man who, unharmed among the gaping jaws of hungry lions, laughed to scorn the threats of those who had plotted his destruction.

XIV. Lifting up, therefore, with concordant devotion the pearl of inestimable price which they had discovered, and shedding floods of tears for joy, they brought back the head to its body, blessing God with hymns and lauds, while the wolf, which was the guardian and bearer of the relic, followed them to the place of entombment, and keeping close behind them, though seemingly grieved for the loss of the pledge it had had in keeping, neither did harm to any one though provoked, nor gave trouble to any one, but again betook itself unharmed to the familiar seclusion of its congenial solitude; and never afterwards was there seen in that neighbourhood any wolf so terrible in appearance. When the wolf had retired, those who were intrusted with the duty, with the utmost care and with all possible zeal and skill provisionally fitted the head to the sacred body, and committed the two joined together to a becoming sepulchre. And there they built over the grave a chapel of rude construction, in which the body rested for many years, until the conflagration of war and the mighty storms of persecution were over, and the religious piety of the faithful began to revive, upon relief from the pressure of tribulation. And so, when a seasonable opportunity was found, they displayed in many ways the devotion which they cherished in regard to the blessed king and martyr Eadmund. They were stirred by the occurrence of marvellous works. For the Saint, from beneath the lowly roof of his consecrated abode, made manifest by frequent miraculous signs the magnitude of his merits in the sight of God. These events aroused great numbers of the inhabitants of that province, high and low alike; and in the royal town which, in the English tongue, is named Bedrices-gueord, but in Latin is called Bedrici-curtis, they erected a church of immense size, with storeys admirably constructed of wood, and to this they translated him with great magnificence, as was due.

XV. But, marvellous to tell, whereas it was supposed that the precious body of the martyr would have mouldered to dust in the long interval of time which had elapsed, it was found to be so sound and whole that it would be out of place to speak of the head having been restored to and united with the body, for there was absolutely no trace apparent of wound or scar. And so the king and martyr Eadmund was with reverence pronounced to be a Saint, and was translated whole and entire, and wearing every semblance of life, to the place above mentioned, where to this day without change of form he awaits the covenanted felicity of a blessed resurrection. One thing only is to be noticed round his neck, as an ensign of his martyrdom, there was seen an extremely thin red crease, like a scarlet thread, as was frequently attested by a certain woman of blessed memory called Oswen, who shortly before these recent times of ours passed many years in succession near his consecrated tomb, absorbed in fastings and prayers. This venerable woman, either from some divine intuition, or from excess of devotion, made it her constant practice to open the sepulchre of the blessed martyr year by year, at the anniversary of the Lord's Supper, and to trim and pare his hair and nails. These relics, one and all, she studiously collected, and stored in a casket; nor did she ever omit, as long as she lived, to cherish them with an affection that was wonderful, having placed them on the altar of the church to which I have referred. And there they are still preserved with due veneration.

From Abbo's Latin *Passio Sancti Eadmundi*, in the translation of Lord Francis Hervey. Lord Hervey's translation is in the high Victorian manner, even though it post-dates Victoria's reign. And in this matter of style it almost perfectly matches the high-flown Latin of the original. The story, nevertheless, is well told and, in its way, entertaining.

TEXT 23
ROGER OF WENDOVER'S VERSION OF THE ST EDMUND LEGEND

As in that persecution the glorious king and martyr Edmund
fell by the swords of the wicked brothers Hinguar and Hubba,
it is worth while in this place to relate the cause of so illustrious a martyrdom and what it was that gave occasion to the
aforesaid leaders to condemn so pious a king to such cruel
sufferings. There was not long ago, in the kingdom of the
Danes, a certain man named Lothbroc, who was sprung from
the royal race of that nation, and had by his wife two sons,
Hinguar and Hubba. One day he took his hawk and went out
unattended in a little boat to catch small birds and wild fowl
on the sea-coast and in the islands. While thus engaged, he
was surprised by a sudden storm which carried him out to sea
where he was tossed about for several days and nights, and at
last, after much distress, he was driven to the English coast,
and landed at Redham, in a province of the East-Angles
called Norfolk by the natives. The people of that country by
chance found him with his hawk and presented him as a sort
of prodigy to Edmund, king of the East-Angles, who for the
sake of his comely person gave him an honourable reception.
Lothbroc abode some time in the court of that monarch; and
as the Danish tongue is very like the English, he began to
relate to the king by what chance he had been driven to the
coast of England. The accomplished manners of King Edmund
pleased Lothbroc, as well as his military discipline and the
courtly manners of his attendants, whom the king had indus-
triously instructed in every grace of speech and behaviour.
Emulous of the like attainments, Lothbroc earnestly asked
permission of the king to remain in his court that he might be
more fully instructed in every kingly accomplishment; and

having obtained his request, he attached himself to the king's huntsman, whose name was Berne, that he might with him exercise the hunter's art in which he was well practised; for such was his skill, both in hawking and hunting, that he was always successful in the pursuit both of birds and beasts. And being deservedly a favourite with the king, the huntsman began to envy him exceedingly because of his superiority in these arts; and giving way to deadly hatred to Lothbroc, he one day, when they went hunting together, attacked him by surprise and wickedly slew him, leaving his body in a thicket. This done, the wicked huntsman called off the dogs with his horn and returned home. Now Lothbroc had reared a certain greyhound in King Edmund's court, which was very fond of him, as is natural, and which, when the huntsman returned with the other dogs, remained alone with his master's body. On the morrow, as the king sat at table and missed Lothbroc from the company, he anxiously asked his attendants what had befallen him; on which Berne the huntsman answered and said, that as they were returning from hunting the day before, the other had tarried behind him in a wood, and he declared that he had not seen him since; but scarcely had he so said, when the greyhound which Lothbroc had reared entered the king's house and began to wag his tail and fawn on all, and especially the king; who on seeing him exclaimed to the attendants, 'Here comes Lothbroc's dog; his master is not far behind'; he then in his joy began to feed the animal hoping quickly to see his master; but he was disappointed, for no sooner had the greyhound appeased his hunger than he returned to keep his accustomed watch by his master's body. After three days he was compelled by hunger to come again to the king's table, who, greatly wondering, gave orders to follow the dog when he returned from the hall, and to watch whither he went. The king's servants fulfilled his commands and followed the dog until he led them to Lothbroc's lifeless body. On being informed thereof, the king was greatly disturbed, and directed that the body should be committed to a more honourable sepulture.

King Edmund then caused diligent inquisition to be made touching the death of Lothbroc; and Berne the huntsman being convicted of the abominable deed, the king commanded the captains of his court and the sages of the law to pass sentence on the homicide. The judges unanimously agreed that the huntsman should be put into the boat in which the said Lothbroc had come to England and should be exposed in the midst of the sea without any instrument of navigation, that it might be proved whether God would deliver him from the danger. The huntsman accordingly was sent out to the open sea, and was carried in a few days to Denmark; and being found by the keepers of the ports, the Danes recognized the boat as that in which their lord Lothbroc was wont to go fowling. Taking him, therefore, to Hinguar and Hubba, the sons of the Dane who had been slain in England, and who were men of great power and cruelty, they straightway put Berne to the torture with a view to make him disclose what had befallen their father, who had been carried from them in that boat. After undergoing severe and varied torments, Berne falsely asserted that their father had chanced to land in England, and being found by Edmund, king of the East-Angles, had by his orders been put to death. On hearing this they burst into the most bitter weeping, and, in the excess of their grief for their father's death, they swore by their omnipotent gods that they would not suffer it to pass unavenged. With a view, therefore, to take vengeance on King Edmund, they made Berne the huntsman, who had arrived in their father's boat, their guide. Then assembling a numerous force, they took to sea and turned their sails towards the country of the East-Angles, with an armament of twenty thousand men, to punish King Edmund for a murder of which he was wholly innocent; but the winds driving their fleet in a contrary direction, they were compelled to land at Berwick-on-Tweed in Scotland, where they commenced their ravages, which they continued on all sides, till at length they reached East-Anglia, where they pitched their camp at a village called Redford, and put to the edge of the sword all they found, whether men or women. At length, when the tyrant Hinguar, who was the most atrocious of the murderers, had somewhat satiated his rage, he called to him some rustics whom he deemed unworthy of his sword, and straitly questioned them as to the place where their king was then living; for the fame had reached him of the might and prowess of the most pious king Edmund, as also of his incomparable bodily size and stature; wherefore he was the more anxious to put to death all he found, that the king might not be able to form an army for the defence of his country. Now the glorious king and future martyr Edmund was abiding at that time in a royal vill called Haeilesdune, which was also the name of a neighbouring wood as the wicked robber had learned from the common people. Calling, therefore, to one of his followers, he despatched him to the king with a deceitful message that if he would divide with him his riches he should retain the kingdom under him; but Hinguar demanded the treasure to conceal his real object, which was rather the head than the money of that most merciful king. The soldier thereupon, proceeding with all despatch to King Edmund, addressed him after this manner: 'My lord Hinguar, ever to be feared, the unconquered king of the Danes, has come to this country to winter. If you despise his power, you shall be accounted unworthy of your life and kingdom.' And so when he had delivered the whole of his message to the king as had been enjoined him, and which we have mentioned above, the most pious King Edmund groaned from the bottom of his heart, and calling to him Humbert, bishop of Helmham, asked counsel of him, saying, 'O Humbert, servant of the living God, and the half of my life, the fierce barbarians are at hand, who have in part devastated my beloved country and destroyed the inhabitants, and are endeavouring to blot out that which remains from the memory of our successors. But oh that I might fall so that my people might thereby escape death; for I will not, through love of a temporal kingdom or the gain of the present life, subject myself to a heathen tyrant, when by dying for my people and country I can become a standard-bearer of the eternal kingdom.'

On which the prelate replied, 'Unless you save yourself by flight, most beloved king, the wicked traitors will presently be here, and will seek to destroy both yourself and your subjects whom you desire to save.' 'What I desire above every thing,' said the most merciful king, 'is not to survive my faithful and beloved friends, whom the fierce pirate has surprised and slain; and truly what you advise would tarnish my glory, who have never hitherto incurred disgrace in war. Moreover the King of heaven is my witness that no fear of the barbarians shall separate me from the love of Christ, whether living or dead.' Turning then to the messenger who had been sent by the impious Hinguar, the most blessed King Edmund addressed him as follows: 'Stained as you are with the blood of my people, you deserve the punishment of death; but following the example of my Christ, I do not shrink from willingly dying for his sake if it shall so befall; hasten, then, back to your master and bear him my reply. Though you may violently rob me of the wealth which divine Providence hath given me, you shall not make me subject to an infidel; for it is an honourable thing to defend our liberties and the purity of our faith; and, if need be, we deem it not in vain even to die for them. Proceed then, as your haughty cruelty has begun, and after slaying the servants, slay also the king, for the King of kings regards me, and will translate me to reign for ever in heaven.'

On the departure, therefore, of the fierce messenger, King Edmund commanded his companions to fly to arms, declaring it to be an honourable thing to fight for one's faith and country, and exhorting them not to betray the same by their cowardice. Encouraged, therefore, by bishop Humbert and his nobles and companions in arms, the most blessed king Edmund advanced boldly against the enemy with all the forces he could raise, and falling in with them as they came to meet him not far from the town of Thetford, he fought a severe battle with them, in which both sides sustained excessive loss, inflicting mutual slaughter from morning until evening, so that the whole field was red with the blood of the slain, insomuch that the most pious king Edmund not only sorrowed for the slaughter of his companions fighting for their country and for the faith of Jesus, and who he knew had attained the crown of martyrdom, but also bitterly bewailed the fate of the infidel barbarians who were precipitated into the gulf of hell. After the pagans had retired from the place of slaughter, King Edmund, the most blessed confessor of Christ, led the residue of his forces to the royal vill of Haeilesdune, steadfastly purposing in his mind never again to fight with the barbarians, and declaring that it was necessary that he alone should die for the people, that the whole nation might not perish.

While Hinguar was inconsolable on account of the slaughter of his followers, his brother Hubba, who had just ravaged the whole of Mercia, joined him at Thetford with ten thousand men. Resolved to take vengeance on the holy king

Edmund, they united their forces, and, moving their camp, quickly reached the village of Haeilesdune, where the most blessed king Edmund then was. The tyrant Hinguar then commanded the king and all his followers to be surrounded, that not one of them might escape alive; whereupon the most holy king Edmund, perceiving himself to be hedged in by his enemies, by the advice of Humbert, bishop of Helmham, fled to the church that he might show himself a member of Christ, and there exchanging his temporal for celestial weapons, he humbly prayed the Father, the Son, and the Holy Ghost to grant him fortitude in suffering. The most merciful king Edmund was then forcibly bound by the ministers of iniquity, and led forth from the church before their wicked chief, as was Christ before the governor Pilate; at whose command he was tied to a neighbouring tree; after which he was scourged for a long time, and insulted with every species of mockery. But the undaunted champion of Christ, by continuing to call on him between every lash, provoked to fury his tormentors, who then in their mockery using his body as a mark, shot at him with their bows till he was entirely covered with arrows so that there was not a place in the martyr's body in which a fresh wound could be inflicted, but it was as completely cov-ered with darts and arrows as is the hedgehog's skin with spines. And so the fierce executioner Hinguar, not being able to make the holy martyr Edmund relinquish his faith in Christ and the confession of the Trinity, so as at all to yield to his wicked persuasions, ordered one of his attendants to cut off the martyr's head with his bloody sword; whereupon the executioner, with one fierce stroke, severed his holy head from its trunk on the 20th day of November, as he was pray-ing and confessing the name of Christ. Being thus made an offering most acceptable to God, and fully tried in the furnace of suffering, he was translated to heaven with the palm of victory and the crown of righteousness. The headless body of the blessed martyr was carried by these servants of the devil to Haeilesdune Wood, where they left it among the thick briars; for these wicked tormentors took great pains that the martyr's body might not be committed to decent interment by the few surviving Christians; for the atrocious robbers, Hinguar and Hubba, had heard that their father Lothbroc had been murdered in that wood. Instigated, therefore, by the lies of Berne the huntsman, and desiring to retaliate on the blessed king and martyr Edmund, they ignominiously threw his head into the same wood, where they left it to be devoured by the birds of heaven and the beasts of the field. The most holy king Edmund had as a partner in suffering his inseparable companion Humbert, bishop of Helmham, who had raised him to the throne, and who, encouraged by the king's undaunted spirit, endured martyrdom and with him attained the kingdom of heaven. The most blessed king being thus translated to heaven, the pagans triumphed beyond measure, and wintered in those parts, having driven out the few inhabitants who survived the aforesaid slaughter. In the same year Ceolnoth, archbishop of Canterbury, ended his days, and was succeeded by Ethelred, a venerable man and of sufficient knowledge in divine things.

After the martyrdom of the most blessed king Edmund, the brothers Hinguar and Hubba, so hateful to God, wintered in the country of the East-Angles, giving themselves up to plunder and rapine, during which season they were joined by Gytro, a very powerful king of the Danes, who came to winter with them; but on the approach of spring all the pagans returned together from East-Anglia. On hearing of their departure the Christians came forth from their hiding-places from all quarters, and did their best endeavours to find the head of the blessed king Edmund, that it might be united to the body; and the whole committed to sepulture in a royal manner. When they had all met together and were diligently searching the woods for the martyr's head there appeared a wonderful and unheard-of prodigy; for while searching among the woods and brambles, and calling out to each other in their native tongue, 'Where are you? Where are you?' the martyr's head made answer in the same tongue, 'Here, here, here,' and did not cease repeating the same till it brought them all to the spot; where they found a huge and horrible looking wolf embracing the head with its paws, and keeping watch over the blessed martyr. Boldly seizing the head and offering praises unto God, they conveyed it to the body, followed by the wolf as far as the place of sepulture; then uniting the head to the body, they deposited both in a suitable tomb, after which the wolf returned to his wonted solitude. A small church of mean workmanship was erected by the faithful on that spot, where the holy body rested during the lapse of many years. Now the most veritable king and martyr Edmund suffered in the year of our Lord 874 in the twenty-ninth year of his age and the sixteenth of his reign, the twelfth day of December, in the third indiction, in the twenty-second moon.

From Roger of Wendover's Latin *Flowers of History* in the translation of J.A. Giles. Roger is obviously using (at least) two completely different sources: one which justifies the savagery of the Danish attacks by the revenge motif, and another, which is Abbo's *Passio Sancti Eadmundi*.

TEXT 24.
LINES FROM THE DREAM OF THE ROOD

He tasted death there, yet the Lord rose again
by his mighty power to aid all people.
He then ascended to the heavens. He, the Lord
    himself,
God almighty, and his angels with him,
105 will come back here to this earth
to seek mankind on the day of judgement,
when he, the one who has the right to judge,
wishes to judge each one according
to what they have earned in this passing life.
110 No one will be able to be without fear there,
because of the word that the Lord will say:
he will ask before the multitude where the man might be
who for the sake of the Lord's name would be willing
to taste bitter death, as he formerly did on the cross.
115 They will then be afraid, and few will have thought
what they will be able to say to Christ.
No one who carries within their breast the best
    of signs
need be over-fearful there,
for by means of the cross each soul
120 who intends to dwell with the Lord
must seek the kingdom in the paths of the earth.
135 ... I look forward
each day to the time when the Lord's cross,
that I saw previously here on earth,
will fetch me from this passing life
and bring me to where there is great bliss,
140 joys in heaven, where the Lord's people
are seated at the banquet, where there is eternal bliss –

and then set me down where I for ever after may be
    allowed
to remain in glory, richly to enjoy with the holy ones
heavenly pleasures. May the Lord be my friend
145 who here on earth formerly suffered
on the gallows tree for the sins of men.
He redeemed us, gave us life
and a heavenly home. Hope was renewed
gloriously and blissfully, for those who endured burning
    there:
150 the Son was victorious on that expedition,
powerful and successful, when he came with a host,
a whole troop of spirits, into God's kingdom,
the almighty sole ruler, to the bliss of angels
and all the holy ones who formerly had dwelt in heaven
155 and remained in glory, when their Lord, almighty God,
came back to where his home was.

Eschatological lines from the Old English poem, *The Dream of the Rood.*

TEXT 25
THE TREATY OF ÆTHELRED
AND THE VIKINGS

These are the peace terms and conditions that King Æthelred and all his council have come to with the Viking army who were with Olaf, Josteinn and Guthmund son of Steita.

First, that a general peace stand between King Æthelred and all his subjects and all the Viking army to whom the king gave money, according to the agreement which Archbishop Sigeric and Ealdorman Æthelweard and Ealdorman Ælfric made when they got permission from the king to buy peace for the areas they controlled under the king.

And that if any fleet should ravage in England, we have the assistance of them all; in that case we must provide them with food as long as they are with us.

And every area that harbours in any way those who ravage England is to be outlawed by us and by the entire Viking army.

And every merchant ship that passes the mouth of the river should have peace, even if the ship is from an area not covered by this truce, that is, if it is not driven ashore.

And if it is driven ashore and it escapes to any of the towns covered by this truce, and the men break out into the town, then the men and whatever they bring with them should have peace.

And each of the men covered by this truce should have peace, whether on water or on land, whether inside the estuary or outside.

If a subject of King Æthelred covered by this truce arrives at an area where the truce does not apply, and the Viking army arrives there, his ship and all his goods are to have peace.

If he has pulled his ship ashore, or built a shed, or pitched a tent, he and all his goods are to have peace there.

If he carries his goods into a house with those of men not covered by this truce, he is to forfeit his goods, but he is to have peace and life if he declares himself.

If a man covered by this truce flees or fights and does not wish to declare himself, if he is killed he is to lie uncompensated for.

If a man is robbed of his goods and he knows which ship did it, the steersman is to return the goods or go with four others, himself the fifth, and deny it, or swear that he took it lawfully, as mentioned earlier.

If an Englishman kills a Dane, a freeman kills a freeman, he is to compensate for him with 25 pounds, or the perpetrator is to be handed over; and similarly a Dane is to do the same if he kills an Englishman.

If an Englishman kills a Danish slave, he is to compensate for him with a pound, and similarly a Dane is to do the same if he kills an Englishman.

If eight men are killed that is a breach of the truce, whether it is inside or outside of a town. Full compensation is to be paid if fewer men than eight are killed.

If this breach of the truce take place inside a town, the citizens themselves are to go and take the killers, alive or dead, or their nearest kinsmen, head for head. If they do not comply, let the ealdorman go there; if he will not, the king is to go. If the king will not, the shire is no longer covered by the truce.

With reference to all the killing and ravaging and injury that was done before the truce was established, it is to be entirely ignored; no one is to avenge it or demand compensation.

And neither we nor they are to harbour the other's slave, or the other's thief, or a party to the other's feud.

And if a man of this country is accused of stealing cattle or killing a man, and the accusation is made by one Viking and one man of this country, then he is not allowed to deny it.

And if their men kill eight of us, then they are to be outlawed on both sides, and they are not entitled to compensation.

Twenty-two thousand pounds of gold and silver were paid from England to the Viking army for this truce.

From the Old English.

SOURCES AND
FURTHER READING

It is almost impossible to give an exhaustive bibliography for such a range of subjects as has been touched on in this book. The works mentioned here are those which I think the general reader will find most helpful, and those which I have used particularly in the course of writing.

GENERAL

The best history of Anglo-Saxon England is Stenton, F.M., *Anglo-Saxon England*, 3rd edn, Oxford, The Oxford History of England vol. 2, Clarendon Press, 1971. See also Hunter Blair, Peter, *An Introduction to Anglo-Saxon England*, 2nd edn, Cambridge, Cambridge University Press, 1977, and Campbell, James, ed., *The Anglo-Saxons*, London, Penguin Books, 1991. For a useful collection of Anglo-Saxon literature translated from Latin and Old English, see Whitelock, D., ed., *English Historical Documents Vol. I, c. 500–1042*, 3rd edn, London, Eyre Methuen, 1979. For a survey of Old English literature and the early progress of Christianity in England, see Cavill, P., *Anglo-Saxon Christianity*, London, Fount, 1999. For studies of topics, many of which are touched on in the text, see Godden, Malcolm, and Lapidge, Michael, ed., *The Cambridge Companion to Old English Literature*, Cambridge, Cambridge University Press, 1991.

In the text and translations, the source of quotations from the *Anglo-Saxon Chronicle* is most often Plummer, Charles, ed., *Two of*

*the Saxon Chronicles Parallel: ... On the Basis of an Edition by John
Earle*, 2 vols, Oxford, Clarendon Press, 1892–99, reissued with a
bibliographical note by Whitelock, D., 1952. I supplement Plummer
with Dumville, D. and Keynes S., ed., *The Anglo-Saxon Chronicle: A
Collaborative Edition*, in a projected series of 22 volumes, Cambridge,
D.S. Brewer, 1985– . This series includes the *Annals of St Neot's*.
Good translations include: Whitelock, D., with Douglas, David C.
and Tucker, Susie I., *The Anglo-Saxon Chronicle: A Revised
Translation*, London, Eyre and Spottiswoode, 1961; and Garmonsway,
G.N., *The Anglo-Saxon Chronicle*, 2nd edn, London, Everyman,
1954. Gransden, Antonia, *Historical Writing in England c. 550 to c.
1307*, London, Routledge and Kegan Paul, 1974, is one of the best
introductions available to the historical literature.

The edition used for the Old English poems quoted is Krapp,
George Philip and Dobbie, Elliott Van Kirk, ed., *The Anglo-Saxon
Poetic Records: A Collective Edition*, 6 vols, New York, Columbia
University Press, 1931–42.

Except where noted, quotations from the Bible are from the New
International Version, London, Hodder and Stoughton, 1979.

BOOKS ON THE VIKINGS

There are many of these, but some of the more relevant and recent
ones are: Loyn, H.R., *The Vikings in Britain*, London, B.T. Batsford,
1977; Page, R.I., *Chronicles of the Vikings*, London, British Museum,
1995; Richards, Julian D., *Viking Age England*, London, B.T.
Batsford, 1991; Roesdahl, Else, trans. Margeson, Susan M. and
Williams, Kirsten, *The Vikings*, London, Allen Lane, 1987; Sawyer,
Peter H., *The Age of the Vikings*, 2nd edn, London, Edward Arnold,
1971, —, *Kings and Vikings*, London, Routledge, 1982, and —, ed.,
The Oxford Illustrated History of the Vikings, Oxford, Oxford
University Press, 1997.

CHAPTER 1

Tacitus's *Germania* is available in Penguin, trans. by Mattingly, H., rev. Handford, S. A., Harmondsworth, Penguin, 1979. *The Chronicle of Æthelweard* is ed. and trans. Campbell, A., London, Nelson's Medieval Texts, Thomas Nelson, 1962, and the translation is from this edition. The edition of *Egils saga* is that of Nordal, Sigurður, ed., Reykjavík, Íslenzk Fornrit 2, Hið Íslenzka Fornritafélag, 1933; the best translation is Fell, C.E., with Lucas, J., *Egils Saga*, London, J.M. Dent, 1975. The standard text of Alcuin's letters is Dümmler, E., *Monumenta Germaniae Historica, Epistolae Tomus IV, Karolini Aevi II*, Germany, Weidmann, 1974; a biography is Duckett, E.S., *Alcuin, Friend of Charlemagne*, New York, Macmillan, 1951; a selection of Alcuin's letters are trans. Allott, S., *Alcuin of York: His Life and Letters*, York, Sessions, 1974. The text of Symeon of Durham's *History of the Kings* is Arnold, Thomas, ed., *Symeonis Monachi Opera Omnia*, London, 2 vols, Rolls Series 75, 1882–5; it is trans., with Symeon's *History of the Church of Durham*, by Stevenson, J., *The Historical Works of Simeon of Durham*, London, The Church Historians of England, vol. 3 part 2, Seeleys, 1855; the text of the latter is ed. and trans. Rollason, David, *Symeon of Durham: Libellus de Exordio atque Procursu istius hoc est Dunhelmensis Ecclesie*, Oxford, Oxford Medieval Texts, Clarendon Press, 2000.

The laws of Ine and the Treaties of Alfred and Guthrum, and Æthelred and the Danes are ed., with many other legal texts, by Liebermann, F., *Die Gesetze der Angelsachsen*, 3 vols, Max Niemeyer, Tübingen, 1898–1903. Skaldic verse is discussed and trans. by Hollander, Lee M., *The Skalds*, Princeton, The American-Scandinavian Foundation, 1945. Olaf Tryggvason's career is traced by Snorri Sturluson, a great Icelandic historian of the 13th century, in *Heimskringla*, a trans. of which is Monsen, Erling, and Smith, A.H., *Heimskringla, or the Lives of the Norse Kings*, Cambridge, Heffer, 1932.

The material relating to the Anglo-Saxon period from William of Malmesbury's *Gesta Regum Anglorum* is ed. and trans. Mynors, R.A.B., Thomson, R.M., and Winterbottom, M., vol. 1, Oxford, Oxford Medieval Texts, Clarendon Press, 1998; *The Chronicle of John of Worcester* for the same period is ed. Darlington, R.R. and

McGurk P., and trans. Bray, Jennifer, and McGurk, P., vol. 2, Oxford, Oxford Medieval Texts, Clarendon Press, 1995; Henry of Huntingdon's *Historia Anglorum* is ed. and trans. Greenway, Diana, Oxford, Oxford Medieval Texts, Clarendon Press, 1996. All three works are trans. Stevenson in The Church Historians of England series mentioned above. The translation of John of Wallingford's *Chronicle* is quoted from Stevenson. Osbern's Life of Ælfheah, *De Sancto Elphego Martyre* is ed. Wharton, H., *Anglia Sacra*, 2 vols, London, 1691.

CHAPTER 2

For the variations in the Chronicle accounts of Kings Alfred and Æthelred, see Davis, R.H.C., 'Alfred the Great: propaganda and truth', History, 56 (1971), pp. 169–82, Keynes, S.D., 'The declining reputation of King Æthelred the Unready' in Hill, D., ed., *Ethelred the Unready: Papers from a Millenary Conference*, Oxford, British Archaeological Reports, British Series 59, 1978, pp. 227–54 and —, 'A tale of two kings: Alfred the Great and Æthelred the Unready', *Transactions of the Royal Historical Society*, 5th series, 36 (1986), pp. 195–217.

Bede's *Historia Ecclesiastica Gentis Anglorum* is ed. and trans. Colgrave, B. and Mynors, R.A.B., *Bede's Ecclesiastical History of the English People*, Oxford, Oxford Medieval Texts, Clarendon Press, 1969. The *De Excidio Britanniae* of Gildas is ed. and trans. Winterbottom, Michael, *Gildas: The Ruin of Britain and Other Documents*, London, Arthurian Period Sources vol. 7, Phillimore, 1978. Place-names are explored by Kenneth Cameron, *English Place Names*, 3rd edn, London, B.T. Batsford, 1996. Wulfstan's *Sermo Lupi* in its various extant forms is ed. Bethurum, Dorothy, *The Homilies of Wulfstan*, Oxford, Clarendon Press, 1957.

The *Life* of Bishop Wilfrid is ed. and trans. Colgrave, Bertram, *The Life of Bishop Wilfrid by Eddius Stephanus*, Cambridge, Cambridge University Press, 1927, and see further Kirby, D.P., ed., *Saint Wilfrid at Hexham*, Newcastle, Oriel Press, 1974. The letters of Boniface are ed. Dümmler, E., *Monumenta Germaniae Historica, Epistolae Tomus III, Bonifatii et Lulli Epistolae*, Berlin, 1892, and are trans. Emerton, Ephraim, *The Letters of Saint Boniface*, New York, Records of Civilization 31, Columbia University Press, 1940; the translation given is Emerton's. The *Encomium Emmae Reginae* is ed. Campbell, Alistair, with a supplementary introduction by Keynes, Simon, Cambridge, Camden Classic Reprints 4, Cambridge University Press, 1998. Swedish runes are treated by Jansson, Sven B.F., *Runes in Sweden*, Stockholm, Gidlunds, 1987, and see also —, 'Swedish Vikings in England: the evidence of the rune stones', Dorothea Coke Memorial Lecture, University College London, 1965.

CHAPTER 3

Just one example of Victorian piety towards King Alfred is the Jubilee Edition, ed. Giles, J.A., of *The Whole Works of King Alfred the Great*, London, Bosworth and Harrison, 1858, dedicated to Queen Victoria. Modern works include: Duckett, Eleanor, *Alfred the Great and his England*, London, Collins, 1957; Frantzen, Allen J., *King Alfred*, Boston MA, Twayne, 1986; Smyth, Alfred P., *King Alfred the Great*, Oxford, Oxford University Press, 1995; and Abels, Richard, *Alfred the Great: War, Kingship and Culture in Anglo-Saxon England*, London, Longman, 1998. Asser is ed. Stevenson, William Henry, *Asser's Life of King Alfred, Together with the Annals of Saint Neot's Erroneously Ascribed to Asser*, Oxford, new impression with article on recent work ... by Whitelock, Dorothy, Clarendon Press, 1959, and trans. Keynes, Simon and Lapidge, Michael, *Alfred the Great: Asser's* Life of King Alfred *and Other Contemporary Sources*, Harmondsworth, Penguin, 1983. The story of Alfred and the cakes is first found in the *Life* of St Neot, ed. Whitaker, John, *the Life of Saint Neot, the Oldest of All the Brothers of King Alfred*, London, 1809. The *Historia de Sancto Cuthberto* is ed. by Arnold, Thomas, *Symeonis Monachi Opera Omnia*, London, 2 vols, Rolls Series 75, 1882–5. The 13th-century poem attributing proverbs to King Alfred is Stanley, Eric Gerald, ed., *The Owl and the Nightingale*, London, Nelson, 1960, and *The Proverbs of Alfred* are ed. Skeat, Walter W., Oxford, Clarendon Press, 1907. Bede's *Life* and the Anonymous *Life* of St Cuthbert are both ed. and trans. Colgrave, Bertram, *Two Lives of Saint Cuthbert*, Cambridge, Cambridge University Press, 1940.

King Alfred's works, and the prose works of his court, are available as follows: Sweet, H., ed. and trans., *King Alfred's West-Saxon Version of Gregory's Pastoral Care*, 2 vols, London, Early English Text Society Original Series 45 and 50, Oxford University Press, 1871–2; Sedgefield, Walter John, ed., *King Alfred's Old English Version of Boethius, De Consolatione Philosophiae*, Oxford, Clarendon Press, 1899, and trans. Fox, Samuel, *King Alfred's Anglo-Saxon Version of Boethius De Consolatione Philosophiae*, London, Bohn's Antiquarian Library, 1864; Hecht, Hans, ed., *Bischofs Wærferth von Worcester Übersetzung der Dialoge Gregors des Grossen*, Bibliothek der angelsächsischen Prosa 5, Leipzig, Wigand, 1900; Miller, Thomas, ed., *The Old English Version of Bede's Ecclesiastical History of the English People*, 4 vols, London, Early English Text Society Original Series 95, 96, 110 and 111, Oxford University Press, 1890–8, and see also Whitelock, D., 'The Old English Bede', *Proceedings of the British Academy*, 48 (1962), pp. 57–90; Bately, Janet, ed., *The Old English Orosius*, London, Early English Text Society Supplementary Series 6, Oxford University Press, 1980; Endter, Wilhelm, ed., *König Alfreds des Grossen Bearbeitung der Soliloquien des Augustinus*, Darmstadt, Bibliothek der angelsächsischen Prosa 11, Wissenschaftliche Buchgesellschaft, repr. 1964; Alfred's laws are printed by Liebermann (above); *Genesis B* is ed. Timmer, B.J., *The Later Genesis: Edited from MS. Junius 11*, Oxford, The Scrivener Press, 1948.

The sailors' accounts are ed. and trans. Lund, Niels and Fell, Christine E., *Two Voyagers at the Court of King Alfred*, York, Sessions, 1984. The story of Cynewulf and Cyneheard has attracted a lot of discussion, most recently from Scragg, Donald, '*Wifcyþþe* and the morality of the Cynewulf and Cyneheard episode in the Anglo-Saxon Chronicle', pp. 179–86, in a most useful collection of essays, ed. Roberts, Jane, Nelson, Janet L. and Godden, Malcolm, *Alfred the Wise*, Cambridge, D.S. Brewer, 1997. For genealogies, see Sisam, K., 'Anglo-Saxon royal genealogies', *Proceedings of the British Academy*, 39 (1953), pp. 287–348. For Nennius's *Historia Brittonum* and the Welsh annals, see Morris, John, ed. and trans., *Nennius: British History and The Welsh Annals*, London, Arthurian Period Sources vol. 8, Phillimore, 1980. The Finnsburh material from *Beowulf* and *The Finnsburh Fragment* are ed. Fry, D.K., *Finnsburh*

Fragment and Episode, London, Methuen, 1974. For a lengthier treatment of wisdom literature see Cavill, Paul, *Maxims in Old English Poetry*, Cambridge, D.S. Brewer, 1999.

CHAPTER 4

The Battle of Brunanburh is ed. Campbell, A., *The Battle of Brunanburh*, London, Heinemann, 1938. The following are articles on the poem: Addison, J.C., 'Aural interlace in *The Battle of Brunanburh*', *Language and Style*, 15 (1982), pp. 267–76; Anderson, E.R., 'The sun in *The Battle of Brunanburh*, 12b–17a', *Notes and Queries*, 20 (1973), pp. 362–3; Campbell, A., 'The Old English epic style' in Davis, N. and Wrenn, C.L., ed., *English and Medieval Studies Presented to J.R.R. Tolkien*, London, Allen and Unwin, 1962, pp. 13–26; Conquergood, D., 'Boasting in Anglo-Saxon England: performance and the heroic ethos', *Literature in Performance*, 1 (1981), pp. 24–35; Dodgson, J.McN., 'The background of *Brunanburh*', *Saga Book of the Viking Society*, 14 (1953–7), pp. 303–16; Higham, N.J., 'The context of *Brunanburh*' in A.R. Rumble and A.D. Mills, ed., *Names, Place and People: An Onomastic Miscellany in Memory of John McNeal Dodgson*, Stamford, Paul Watkins, 1997, pp. 144–56; Isaacs, N.D., 'Battlefield tour: Brunanburg', *Neuphilologische Mitteilungen*, 63 (1962), pp. 236–44; —, 'The Battle of Brunanburh, 13b–17a', *Notes and Queries*, 208 (1963), pp. 247–8; Johnson, A.S., 'The rhetoric of *Brunanburh*', *Philological Quarterly*, 47 (1968), pp. 487–93; Lipp, F.R., 'Contrast and point of view in *The Battle of Brunanburh*', *Philological Quarterly*, 48 (1969), pp. 166–77; Niles, J.D., 'Skaldic technique in *Brunanburh*', *Scandinavian Studies*, 59 (1987), pp. 356–66; Swanton, M., 'Heroes, heroism and heroic literature', *Essays and Studies*, 30 (1977), pp. 1–21; Walker, S., 'A context for *Brunanburh*?' in Reuter, T., ed., *Warriors and Churchmen in the High Middle Ages*, London, Hambledon, 1992, pp. 21–39; Wood, M., '*Brunanburh* revisited', *Saga Book of the Viking Society*, 20 (1980) pp. 200–17. For a more detailed study of place-names on the Wirral, see Cavill, Paul, Harding, Stephen E. and Jesch, Judith, *Wirral and its Viking Heritage*, Nottingham, English Place-Name Society Popular Series 2, English Place-Name Society, 2000.

The best books on *The Battle of Maldon* are: Scragg, D.G., ed., *The Battle of Maldon AD 991*, Oxford and Cambridge, MA, Blackwell, 1991 (this includes an edition and translation); and Cooper, J., ed., *The Battle of Maldon: Fiction and Fact*, London, Hambledon, 1993. The following are articles on the poem: Blake, N.F., 'The Battle of Maldon', *Neophilologus*, 49 (1965), pp. 332–45; —, 'The flyting in *The Battle of Maldon*', *English Language Notes*, 13 (1976), pp. 242–5; —, 'The genesis of *The Battle of Maldon*', *Anglo-Saxon England*, 7 (1978), pp. 119–29; Britton, G.C., 'The characterization of the Vikings in *The Battle of Maldon*', *Notes & Queries*, 210 (1965), pp. 85–7; Busse, W.G. and Holtei, R., 'The Battle of Maldon: a historical, heroic and political poem', *Neophilologus*, 65 (1981), pp. 614–21; Cavill, P., 'Interpretation of *The Battle of Maldon*, lines 84–90: a review and reassessment', *Studia Neophilologica*, 67 (1995), pp. 149–64; —, 'Maxims in *The Battle of Maldon*', *Neophilologus*, 82 (1998), pp. 631–44 (a slightly different version of this article is in Cavill, P., *Maxims in Old English Poetry*, Cambridge, D.S. Brewer, 1999, chap. 6); Clark, Cecily, 'Byrhtnoth and Roland: a contrast', *Neophilologus*, 51 (1967), pp. 288–93; —, 'On dating *The Battle of Maldon*: certain evidence reviewed', *Nottingham Medieval Studies*, 27 (1983), pp. 1–22; Clark, George, 'The Battle of Maldon: a heroic poem', *Speculum*, 43 (1968), pp. 52–71; —, 'The hero of Maldon: *vir pius et strenuus*', *Speculum*, 54 (1979), pp. 257–82; Cross, J.E., 'Oswald and Byrhtnoth: a Christian saint and a hero who is Christian', *English Studies*, 46 (1965), pp. 93–109; Doane, A.N., 'Legend, history and artifice in *The Battle of Maldon*', *Viator*, 9 (1978), pp. 39–66; Fletcher, A.J., 'Cald wæter, scir wæter: a note on lines 91 and 98 of *The Battle of Maldon*', *Neuphilologische Mitteilungen*, 85 (1984), pp. 435–7; Frank, R., 'The ideal of men dying with their lord in *The Battle of Maldon*: anachronism or *nouvelle vague*', in Wood, Ian and Lund, Niels, ed., *People and Places in Northern Europe 500–1600: Essays in Honour of Peter Hayes Sawyer*, Woodbridge, Boydell, 1991, pp. 95–106; Gneuss, H., 'The Battle of Maldon 89: Byrhtnoð's *ofermod* once again', *Studies in Philology*, 73 (1976), pp. 117–37; Griffith, M.S., 'Convention and originality in the "beasts of battle" typescene', *Anglo-Saxon England*, 22 (1993), pp. 179–199; —, 'Alliterative licence and proper names in *Maldon*', in Toswell, M.J., ed., *Prosody and Poetics in the Early Middle Ages:*

Essays in Honour of C.B. Hieatt, Toronto, 1995, pp. 60–79; Hill, T.D., 'History and heroic ethic in *Maldon*', *Neophilologus*, 54 (1970), pp. 291–6; Hillman, R., 'Defeat and victory in *The Battle of Maldon*: the Christian resonances reconsidered', *English Studies in Canada*, 11 (1985), pp. 385–95; Irving, E.B., Jr, 'The heroic style in *The Battle of Maldon*', *Studies in Philology*, 58 (1961), pp. 457–67; Macrae-Gibson, O.D., 'How historical is *The Battle of Maldon?*', *Medium Ævum*, 39 (1970), pp. 89–107; McKinnell, J., 'On the date of *The Battle of Maldon*', *Medium Ævum*, 44 (1975), pp. 121–36; Mills, A.D., 'Byrhtnoð's mistake in generalship', *Neuphilologische Mitteilungen*, 67 (1966), pp. 14–27; North, R., 'Getting to know the general in *The Battle of Maldon*', *Medium Ævum*, 60 (1991), pp. 1–15; Robinson, F.C., 'Some aspects of the *Maldon* poet's artistry', *Journal of English and Germanic Philology*, 75 (1976), pp. 25–40; Samouce, W.A., 'General Byrhtnoth', *Journal of English and Germanic Philology*, 62 (1963), pp. 129–35; Tolkien, J.R.R., 'The homecoming of Beorhtnoth, Beorhthelm's son', *Essays and Studies*, new series 6 (1953), pp. 1–18; Woolf, R., 'The ideal of men dying with their lord in the *Germania* and in *The Battle of Maldon*', *Anglo-Saxon England*, 5 (1976), pp. 63–81.

The *Book of Ely* is ed. Blake, E.O., *Liber Eliensis*, London, Camden Third Series 92, 1962. Byrhtferth's *Life of St Oswald* is ed. Raine, J., *Historians of the Church of York*, 3 vols, London, Rolls Series, 1879–94. The *Ramsey Chronicle* is ed. Macray, W. Dunn, *Chronicon Abbatiæ Rameseiensis*, London, Rolls Series, 1886. *Wyrdwriteras* is from a sermon by Ælfric, ed. Pope, John C., *Homilies of Ælfric: A Supplementary Collection*, 2 vols, London, Early English Text Society Original Series 259 and 260, Oxford University Press, 1968, vol 2, pp. 725–33.

CHAPTER 5

Work on the leaders of the Benedictine reform can be followed up in three excellent collections of essays: Ramsay, Nigel, Sparks, Margaret and Tatton-Brown, Tim, ed., *St Dunstan: His Life, Times and Cult*, Woodbridge, Boydell, 1992; Yorke, Barbara, ed., *Bishop Æthelwold: His Career and Influence*, Woodbridge, Boydell, 1988;

and Brooks, Nicholas and Cubitt, Catherine, ed., *St Oswald of Worcester: Life and Influence*, London, Studies in the Early History of Britain, Leicester University Press, 1996. See also Robinson, J. Armitage, *The Times of St Dunstan*, Oxford, Clarendon Press, 1923; Duckett, Eleanor Shipley, *Saint Dunstan of Canterbury*, London, Collins, 1955; Dales, Douglas, *Dunstan: Saint and Statesman*, Cambridge, Lutterworth Press, 1988; and Lapidge, Michael and Winterbottom, Michael, ed. and trans., *Wulfstan of Winchester: The Life of St Æthelwold*, Oxford, Clarendon Press, 1991. Collected articles on the work of the reform movement are: Lapidge, Michael, *Anglo-Latin Literature 900–1066*, London, Hambledon, 1993; Dumville, David N., *Liturgy and the Ecclesiastical History of Late Anglo-Saxon England: Four Studies*, Woodbridge, Studies in Anglo-Saxon History 5, Boydell, 1992, and —, *English Caroline Script and Monastic History: Studies in Benedictinism, AD 950–1030*, Woodbridge, Studies in Anglo-Saxon History 6, Boydell, 1993.

For the 'three orders', see Powell, Timothy E., 'The "Three Orders" of society in Anglo-Saxon England', *Anglo-Saxon England*, 23 (1994), pp. 103–32. The 'Monastic Agreement' is ed. Symons, Thomas, *Regularis Concordia*, London, Nelson's Medieval Texts, Nelson, 1953. *Ælfric's Colloquy* is ed. Garmonsway, G.N., rev. edn Swanton, M.J., Exeter, Exeter University Press, 1991. *The Blacksmiths* is ed. Sisam, K., *Fourteenth Century Verse and Prose*, Oxford, Clarendon Press, repr. 1973. Bede's letter to Ecgberht is ed. Plummer, Charles, *Venerabilis Baedae Opera Historica*, 2 vols, Oxford, Clarendon Press, 1896, vol. 1, pp. 405–23. B's *Life of Dunstan*, and various letters between popes and church dignitaries referred to in the chapter, can be found in Whitelock, trans., *English Historical Documents* (above).

The Lindisfarne Gospels are discussed and illustrated by Janet Backhouse, *The Lindisfarne Gospels*, Oxford, Phaidon, 1981, and a full facsimile is available, ed. Kendrick, T.D., Brown, T.J., and Bruce-Mitford, R.L.S., *Euangeliorum quattuor Codex Lindisfarnensis*, 2 vols, Lausanne, 1960. *The Benedictional of Æthelwold* is studied by Deshman, Robert, Princeton, Studies in Manuscript Illumination 9, Princeton University Press, 1995. The Stowe 944 picture of the Judgement is printed by Dodwell, C.R., *Anglo-Saxon Art: A New Perspective*, Manchester, Manchester University Press, 1982, pp.

104–5. Alcuin's poem is ed. and trans. Godman, Peter, *Alcuin: The Bishops, Kings, and Saints of York*, Oxford, Oxford Medieval Texts, Clarendon Press, 1982. The gospels are ed. Liuzza, R.M., *The Old English Version of the Gospels*, London, Early English Text Society Original Series 304, Oxford University Press, 1994. The poetic version of *The Benedictine Office* is ed. Ure, James, Edinburgh, Edinburgh University Press, 1957. The prayer of confession is ed. Muir, Bernard James, *A Pre-Conquest English Prayer-Book (BL MSS Cotton Galba A.xiv and Nero A.ii)*, Woodbridge, Henry Bradshaw Society vol. 103, Boydell, 1988, pp. 136–7.

CHAPTER 6

One of the best introductions to hagiography remains Delehaye, Hippolyte, trans. Attwater, Donald, *The Legends of the Saints*, London, Chapman, 1962. More recent and modern in outlook is Brown, Peter, *The Cult of the Saints*, London, SCM Press, 1981. Farmer, David Hugh, *The Oxford Dictionary of Saints*, 3rd edn, Oxford, Oxford University Press, 1992, is a useful reference guide. There is an excellent short essay, Woolf, Rosemary, 'Saints' lives', in Stanley, E.G., ed., *Continuations and Beginnings: Studies in Old English Literature*, London, Nelson, 1966. The essay by Peter Clemoes on Ælfric in the same volume is also valuable. Michael Lapidge's essay, 'The saintly life in Anglo-Saxon England', in Godden, Malcolm and Lapidge, Michael, ed., *The Cambridge Companion to Old English Literature*, Cambridge, Cambridge University Press, 1991, is a good survey.

An Old English Martyrology is ed. Herzfeld, George, London, Early English Text Society Original Series 116, Oxford University Press, 1900. Bede's *Lives of the Abbots* is ed. Plummer, Charles, *Venerabilis Baedae Opera Historica*, 2 vols, Oxford, Clarendon Press, 1896; Bede's *Life of Cuthbert* is ed. Colgrave (above). A collection of essays on *St Cuthbert: His Cult and His Community to AD 1200* is ed. Bonner, Gerald, Stancliffe, Clare and Rollason, David, Woodbridge, Boydell, 1989. *The Life of St Anselm, Archbishop of Canterbury by Eadmer*, where the discussion about whether Ælfheah should be regarded as a martyr or not is recorded, is ed. and trans. Southern,

R.W., Oxford, Oxford Medieval Texts, Clarendon Press, 1962. Thietmar of Merseburg is trans. by Whitelock, *English Historical Documents* (above). Hrolf Kraki's Saga is trans. as 'King Hrolf and his champions' in Jones, Gwyn, *Eirik the Red and Other Icelandic Sagas*, Oxford, The World's Classics, Oxford University Press, 1980.

The various texts relating to St Edmund are gathered by Hervey, Lord Francis, ed., *Corolla Sancti Eadmundi: The Garland of Saint Edmund King and Martyr*, London, John Murray, 1907. The most recent edition of the *Passio sancti Eadmundi Regis et Martyris* by Abbo of Fleury, is Winterbottom, M., *Three Lives of English Saints*, Toronto, Toronto Medieval Latin Texts, 1972. A full historical and textual study of the material is Ridyard, Susan J., *The Royal Saints of Anglo-Saxon England: A Study of West Saxon and East Anglian Cults*, Cambridge, Cambridge Studies in Medieval Life and Thought, Cambridge University Press, 1988. Ælfric's homily on St Edmund is translated in full by Swanton, M.J., *Anglo-Saxon Prose*, London, Dent, 1975. Dorothy Whitelock's study, 'Fact and fiction in the legend of St Edmund', *Proceedings of the Suffolk Institute of Archaeology*, 31 (1967–9), pp. 217–33, remains seminal. Ari Thorgilsson is ed. Benediktsson, Jakob, *Íslendingabók, Landnámabók*, Reykjavík, Íslenzk Fornrit 1, Hið Íslenzka Fornritafélag, 1886. The St Edmund memorial coinage and the Cuerdale hoard are illustrated in Philpott, Fiona A., ed. Graham-Campbell, James, *A Silver Saga: Viking Treasure from the North West*, National Museums and Galleries of Merseyside, 1990. A full study of the stories of Ragnar's sons is McTurk, Rory, *Studies in Ragnars Saga Loðbrókar and its Major Scandinavian Analogues*, Oxford, Medium Ævum Monographs New Series 15, Society for the Study of Mediæval Languages and Literature, 1991. Gransden, Antonia, 'The legends and traditions concerning the origins of the Abbey of Bury St Edmunds', *English Historical Review*, 394 (1985), pp. 1–24, expresses doubts about the St Edmund story. Roger of Wendover is ed. Luard, Henry Richards, *Flores Historiarum*, 3 vols, London, Rolls Series, 1890, and trans. Giles, J.A., *Roger of Wendover's Flowers of History*, London, Bohn's Antiquarian Library, 1849.

Ælfric's sermons on the saints are ed. Skeat, Walter W., *Ælfric's Lives of Saints: Being a Set of Sermons on Saints' Days Formerly Observed by the English Church*, 2 vols, London, Early English Text

Society Original Series 76, 82, 94 and 114, Oxford University Press, 1881–1900, repr. 1966. A general study with bibliography to 1974 is White, Caroline R., with bibliography by Godden, Malcolm R., *Ælfric: A New Study of his Life and Writings*, Connecticut, Archon Books, 1974. The information about the veneration of English saints in Scandinavia is from Toy, John, 'The commemorations of British saints in the medieval liturgical manuscripts of Scandinavia', *Kyrkohistorisk Årsskrift*, (1983), pp. 91–103.

CHAPTER 7

All the poetic texts are taken from Krapp and Dobbie, *The Anglo-Saxon Poetic Records* (above). For a brief essay on the Anglo-Saxon conversion, see Cavill, P., 'A dangerous, wearisome and uncertain journey' in Chadwick, Henry, ed., *Not Angels, But Anglicans: A History of Christianity in the British Isles*, Norwich, Canterbury Press, 2000, pp. 17–24. For a fuller treatment of the *Beowulf wa-wel* maxims, see Cavill, P., *Maxims in Old English Poetry* (above).

Bede's chronological works are ed. Jones, C.W., *Bedae Opera de Temporibus*, Cambridge MA, The Mediaeval Academy of America, 1943, and trans. Wallis, Faith, *Bede: The Reckoning of Time*, Liverpool, Translated Texts for Historians 29, Liverpool University Press, 1999. Ælfric's sermons (other than the *Lives of the Saints*) are ed. and trans. Thorpe, Benjamin, *The Homilies of the Anglo-Saxon Church: The First Part, Containing the Sermones Catholici or Homilies of Ælfric*, 2 vols, London, Ælfric Society, 1844–6, and ed. more recently Godden, Malcolm, *Ælfric's Catholic Homilies: The Second Series Text*, London, Early English Text Society Supplementary Series 5, Oxford University Press, 1979, and Clemoes, Peter, *Ælfric's Catholic Homilies: The First Series Text*, Oxford, Early English Text Society Supplementary Series 17, Oxford University Press, 1997. Ælfric's concern with millennial things is examined by Godden, Malcolm, 'Apocalypse and invasion in late Anglo-Saxon England' in Godden, Malcolm, Gray, Douglas and Hoad, Terry, ed., *From Anglo-Saxon to Middle English: Studies Presented to E.G. Stanley*, Oxford, Clarendon Press, 1994, pp. 130–62, and the general issues are discussed in Gatch, Milton McC., *Preaching and Theology in*

Anglo-Saxon England: Ælfric and Wulfstan, Toronto, University of Toronto Press, 1977. The anonymous collections of Old English homilies are ed. and trans. Morris, R., *The Blickling Homilies*, London, Early English Text Society Original Series 58, 63 and 73, Oxford University Press, 1873–80, and ed. Scragg, D.G., *The Vercelli Homilies and Related Texts*, London, Early English Text Society Original Series 300, Oxford University Press, 1992.

Snorri Sturluson is ed. Faulkes, Anthony, *Snorri Sturluson Edda: Prologue and Gylfaginning*, Oxford, Clarendon Press, 1982, and trans. —, *Snorri Sturluson Edda*, London, Everyman, Dent, 1987. The poem *Völuspá* is ed. and trans. Dronke, Ursula, *The Poetic Edda: Volume II Mythological Poems*, Oxford, Clarendon Press, 1997. *Byrhtferth's Enchiridion* is ed. and trans. Baker, Peter and Lapidge, Michael, Oxford, Early English Text Society Supplementary Series 15, Oxford University Press, 1995. The stonework is discussed in Bailey, Richard N., *Viking Age Sculpture in Northern England*, London, Collins Archaeology, 1980, and the Aldbrough sundial is discussed in Lang, James, *Corpus of Anglo-Saxon Stone Sculpture: Volume III, York and Eastern Yorkshire*, Oxford, The British Academy, Oxford University Press, 1991, pp. 123–4.

CHAPTER 8

For a general survey of the conversion, see Whitelock, Dorothy, 'The conversion of the eastern Danelaw', *Saga Book of the Viking Society*, 12 (1941), pp. 159–76. The names and place-names are treated by Fellows-Jensen, Gillian, 'The Vikings and their victims: the verdict of the names', Dorothea Coke Memorial Lecture, University College London, 1994, and Cameron, Kenneth, 'Viking settlement in the east Midlands: the place-name evidence' in Schützeichel, Rudolf, ed., *Gießener Flurnamen-Kolloquium*, Heidelberg, Carl Winter, 1985, pp. 129–53. See also Gover, J.E.B., Mawer, Allen and Stenton, F.M., ed., *The Place-Names of Nottinghamshire*, Nottingham, English Place-Name Society vol. XVII, 1940, repr. 1999.

The excavations in York have been extensively covered in a series of publications by the York Archaeological Trust. Scandinavian borrowings in English are treated by Björkman, E.,

Scandinavian Loan-Words in Middle English, Halle, Niemeyer, 1900–02. The survival of English and Scandinavian personal names is studied by Clark, Cecily, 'Women's names in post-Conquest England: observations and speculations', *Speculum*, 53 (1978), pp. 223–51. The names with 'church' are discussed by Gelling, M., 'The word "church" in English place-names', *Bulletin of the Council for British Archaeology Churches Committee*, 15 (1981), pp. 4–9. Wirral place-names are treated in Cavill, Paul *et al.*, *Wirral and its Viking Heritage* (above). Stones from Scandinavia and their imagery are treated in McKinnell, John, *Both One and Many: Essays on Change and Variety in Late Norse Heathenism*, Rome, Il Calamo, 1994. English stones are discussed by Lang, James, *Corpus of Anglo-Saxon Stone Sculpture: Volume III, York and Eastern Yorkshire*, and Bailey, Richard N., *Viking Age Sculpture in Northern England* (above).

INDEX

Also available from HarperCollins*Publishers:*

ANGLO-SAXON CHRISTIANITY

PAUL CAVILL

Celtic spirituality was not the only form of early Christianity in the British Isles. In fact, a larger number of original texts from the Anglo-Saxons remain today. This rich vein of simple, but moving, prose and poetry is explored in *Anglo-Saxon Christianity*. The key figures of Bede, Cuthbert and others are introduced alongside new translations of classic texts taken from Beowulf and Old English poetry.

For all who appreciate Celtic spirituality, here is a fresh and alternative source of nourishment and inspiration. For those looking for an authentic Christian faith *Anglo-Saxon Christianity* reaches back into the very birth of the English people.

Dr Paul Cavill is a former UCCF staff worker and now lectures in Old English at the University of Nottingham, England.